The Left and rights

The International Library of Welfare and Philosophy

General Editors

Professor Noel Timms
School of Applied Social Studies,
University of Bradford

David Watson
Department of Moral Philosophy,
University of Glasgow

The Left and rights

A conceptual analysis of the idea of socialist rights

Tom Campbell

Professor of Jurisprudence
University of Glasgow

Routledge & Kegan Paul
London, Boston, Melbourne and Henley

First published in 1983
by Routledge & Kegan Paul plc
39 Store Street, London WC1E 7DD,
9 Park Street, Boston, Mass. 02108, USA,
296 Beaconsfield Parade, Middle Park,
Melbourne, 3206, Australia, and
Broadway House, Newtown Road,
Henley-on-Thames, Oxon RG9 1EN
Printed in Great Britain by
Redwood Burn Ltd, Trowbridge, Wiltshire
© Tom Campbell 1983

Library of Congress Cataloging in Publication Data

Campbell, Tom

The Left and rights.
(International library of welfare and
philosophy)
Includes bibliographical references and
index.
1. Civil rights and socialism. I. Title.
II. Series.
K3240.4.C36   323.4'01   82–7636
ISBN 0–7100–9085–4

To Magnus and Flora

Contents

Preface

The dogmatic type of linguistic philosopher who insists upon a particular set of meanings and concepts as the correct or only proper explication of a given area of discourse is less common than a decade or two ago, but the intellectual constraints imposed by inherited conceptual outlooks still present major hindrances to progressive social theorising. This is particularly evident in those central contested concepts of practical philosophy which are used to express competing ideological viewpoints. In this book an extended analysis of the idea of rights is undertaken in order to undermine some common prejudices against the concept of socialist rights in the hope that this will promote linguistic tolerance and perhaps help to establish a shared conceptual base for fruitful dialogue between theorists of the political Left and Right.

My thanks are due to numerous colleagues and friends at the Universities of Glasgow, Stirling, British Columbia and Vanderbilt, but especially to Antony Duff for his friendly scepticism, to Gerry Maher for his scholarly reassurances, to Mrs Helen MacDonald for her patient typing and retyping of the text, and to Mr Richard Susskind for his meticulous proof-reading.

Glasgow

1   Reformists and revolutionaries

If we value and defend our rights is this an expression of
human dignity or an indication of our selfish and alienated condition? Is the notion of individual rights tied to
the competitive individualism of liberal capitalism or
would rights have a central place even in a socialist
utopia? Is socialism the fulfilment or the negation of
human rights? These abstract and largely conceptual questions seem unrelated to immediate political concerns, and
yet the answers to them overflow with fundamental practical implications that can alter our whole approach to the
central ideological disputes of the twentieth century. A
clear grasp of the nature of rights is vital to our understanding of the disagreements which recur between the
Soviet bloc and the Western powers over human rights and
can radically affect the way in which we think about
social policy issues in the modern democratic welfare
state.

If the ideals of socialism can be expressed in terms of
individual rights then, however different socialist rights
may be from those most highly prized by the classical
liberals, there is at least a continuity and similarity of
thought forms and basic concepts in which major political
disagreements can be clarified and debated. But if the
ideological basis of socialism is so far removed from that
of liberal democracy that it has no use for the language
of rights, then there can be little room either for compromise or for significant dialogue between socialists and
liberal democrats. In so far as the peaceful solution of
political disputes depends on sustaining communication
between those in serious disagreements, the conceptual compatibility of 'rights' and 'socialism' has a bearing on
the prospects of reducing the political uses of violence
both within and between nations.

The compatibility of socialism and rights can be

approached either as a factual and empirical matter,
requiring study of the actual practices of socialist
societies (assuming that there are some at least partially
socialist societies in existence), or as a doctrinal or
philosophical question involving the careful analysis of
the meanings and background assumptions of our ideas of
'rights' and 'socialism'. In this book I adopt the second
approach and investigate whether or not there is a philosophically acceptable theory of rights which holds for
socialist as well as non-socialist systems of thought.
But the two approaches - empirical and conceptual - are
not altogether unrelated. The failures of many so-called
socialist societies to respect what, in the West, are
regarded as fundamental rights naturally gives rise to
the presumption that, despite the references to individual
rights in the constitutions of many of these countries,(1)
there is something inherently antithetical between socialist theory and respect for individual rights. It may be
no accident that governments espousing 'collectivist' doctrines appear to place less weight on freedom of speech,
freedom of movement and the right to take part in the
selection of political authorities than those nations
which regard themselves as liberal democracies. (2) And
the explanation for the alleged failures of ostensibly
socialist societies to match standards of protection for
the individual normally attained in Western democracies
could be due in part to fundamental incompatibilities between socialist doctrine and the concept of rights as well
as to wider and less intellectual determinants of political and legal practice.

THE DISPUTE WITHIN SOCIALISM

To ask whether socialism is a friend or foe of individual
rights may seem to draw the lines of conceptual battle between the allies and enemies of socialism, the former taking the position that socialism is the only effective pro-
tector of the essential rights of the individual, and the
latter responding with the view that the corporate goals
and methods of socialism grant no significance to and offer
no protection for the most basic rights of free men. But
this is far too simple a picture of this particular conceptual war. The dispute about rights and socialism is
as much a debate within socialism as about it. True,
there is a great deal of literature from what might be
called a 'right-wing' liberal stance to the effect that
the introduction of new social and economic rights, such
as the right to free health-care, education and employment,

are in effect an undercover attack on the traditional
civil liberties, and behind this there lies the more
general charge that under socialism the individual counts
for little against the requirements of society as a whole,
or, more specifically, the working-class section of it.
But a fiercer and in many ways more interesting and significant battle goes on within socialism itself between
those who wish to reform and those who seek to jettison
the liberal idea of individual rights. It is primarily to
this family quarrel that I direct my attention.

Those socialists who reject the incorporation of the
language of rights within socialism draw heavily upon certain non-socialist theories of rights, particularly those
which propound an analytical connection between rights and
law, and between law and coercion. This means that, in
defending the view that socialism need not and indeed
should not dispense with the idea of rights, I shall become deeply immersed in the criticism of those liberal
theories of rights which are taken up into socialist critiques of rights. Thus, although my overall objective is
to investigate a dispute within socialism, a great deal of
the path to this objective will pass through the terrain
of the central theories of rights in contemporary philosophical discussions.

The contending parties within socialism may be divided
into revolutionaries and reformists. Those socialists who
are revolutionaries on the issue of the place of rights
within socialism argue that the whole notion of rights is
incurably bougeois. They concede that right-claims may
have played an important role in the emergence of capitalism from the constraints of feudalism and have a minor
role in the transition from capitalism to socialism, but
argue that they will have no place in a socialist society.
In a community of genuinely social beings, it is argued,
people will be united by bonds deeper than those of individual rights and sanctioned obligations. Under socialism
all will work together spontaneously in a willing spirit
of co-operation unencumbered by restrictive regulations
and the self-interested competitivism in which the language of rights is rooted.

Reformists, on the other hand, while admitting the
relative and inadequate nature of bourgeois rights, seek
to salvage something of lasting value from the traditional
concept of rights. By making a judicious selection from
the list of liberal rights, dropping some, such as the
right to own the means of production, introducing the economic and social rights associated with a full-employment,
welfare-orientated society, and relating the idea of rights
to human needs rather than to a priori conceptions of

individual liberty, they hope to develop a distinctively socialist scheme of rights. Such rights do not serve to regulate the 'free' competition of self-centred individuals in the pursuit of scarce resources, but govern the communal arrangements of socially motivated persons committed to the co-operative satisfaction of human needs. On the reformist view, therefore, rights will not wither away along with the antagonisms of class-dominated societies, rather they will be transformed to serve the true interests of humanity. In some cases this will involve the actual satisfaction of interests to which bourgeois societies have paid only lip-service, in other cases old rights will be superseded by new ones, and in general the whole approach to rights will change from a situation in which rights mark the boundaries of legitimate, self-regarding behaviour to one in which they are part of the rule-governed framework within which the individual can fulfil his potential as a social being. (3)

The split between revolutionaries and reformists may be seen in the different positions they take up regarding human rights, in particular in the debate over the updating of the traditional concept of natural rights into the modern idea of human rights. (4) This issue has tended to divert attention from the more general question of whether rights of any sort are compatible with socialism, and the particular difficulties which some socialists see in the alleged universality and inalienability of human rights has helped to bias them against the whole notion of rights. Nearly all socialists agree with John Lewis that 'the conception of absolute, inherent and imprescriptible rights based on man's origin and nature antecedent to society' is a myth and that the alleged natural right to property, for instance, is an historically conditioned expression of bourgeois interests. (5) Some, like Lewis himself, have contended that by excising those liberal rights which are used by sectional interests to block government action for the common good, by ceasing to regard any rights as literally absolute or indefeasible, and by drawing up a new list of 'human' rights 'based upon human needs and possibilities and the recognition by members of a society of the conditions necessary in order that they may fulfil their common ends', it is possible to establish a set of socialist human rights, including the right to various forms of economic and welfare benefits as well as the traditional rights to free speech, freedom of the person, freedom of association and political activity. These rights, in a socialist society, could only be 'set aside temporarily ... in the gravest emergency and after the most critical scrutiny of the reasons'. (6) But others - like, most recently, Ruth Anna

Putnam - deny that the goals of socialism can be captured by the conceptual apparatus of rights. Putnam insists that all rights are 'context-dependent' in that the interpretation of what counts, for instance, as 'liberty' will vary with circumstances, and the relevance of any list of rights will depend on the particular forms of oppression in a given society. She argues that 'recognition of this double context-dependency involves a denial of an essential element of the original doctrine ... independence of social context', (7) hence the inherent theoretical weakness of the idea of the rights of persons. Putnam goes on to assert, in a manner reminiscent of liberal critics of the new social and economic rights, that elaborations of the sort suggested by Lewis have serious limitations since multiplying rights reduces liberty and therefore inevitably dilutes the force of existing rights. She would presumably agree with Maurice Cranston (8) that to add the new economic rights to the old civil liberties results in a weakening of the effectiveness of the latter. Thus there appears to be something like an unholy alliance between Left and Right on the practical and conceptual difficulties inherent in the reformist position.

Without denying that much of interest and importance has emerged from the debate about the incorporation of social and economic rights into the conception of human rights, it is unfortunate from some points of view that so much of the theoretical discussion about socialism and rights has centred on the notion of human rights, for there are logically more fundamental issues at stake concerning socialism and rights in general. Tangled up in the objections laid by socialists against the universality of human rights are reservations about rights as such. Many of Putnam's points are not directed solely at the fallacies of the natural rights tradition but are relevant to all attempts to express the socialist ideal in terms of rights of any sort. Appeals to rights, she notes, involve the demand that these rights be embedded in legal codes, but laws involve a state and 'the socialist regards the state as an instrument of class oppression'. In a socialist society there would be no state, hence no laws and no role for the language of rights. A socialist society is a co-operative society and where there are no conflicts of self-interest between competitively minded beings there is no need for the regulation provided by a system of rights and duties. 'Rights' we are told 'are the prized possessions of alienated persons'. (9)

LIBERAL CONCEPTS AND SOCIALIST IDEALS

The revolutionary's view that there is a conceptual tie
between the notion of rights and the model of a society
composed of self-interested competitive individuals of the
sort who are said to exist in a capitalist society, but
not in a communist one, finds some support in a recent
attempt by Richard Flathman to provide a systematic analysis of the concept or - in the author's terminology -
'practice' of rights, which has, on the surface, no ideological axe to grind. Flathman argues that: (10)

> a right provides the agent who holds it with a warrant
> for taking or refusing to take an action or range of
> actions that he conceives to be in his interest or
> otherwise to advantage him.... The actions or warrants
> are commonly viewed by other persons as contrary to
> their interests, or limiting their freedom, or as in
> other ways disadvantaging them personally or as members
> of the society in which the right is held.

Flathman goes on to argue that there cannot be a right to
an X unless having or doing X is in general, and in A's
(the right-holder's) judgment, advantageous for A and in
some way disadvantageous for B (the person with the correlative obligation), so that B will typically wish to
avoid fulfilling his obligation to A, for to say that X
is a right is to say that some A is warranted in doing X
despite the fact that doing it will be thought to have
adverse effects on the interests of some B. (11) Thus
Flathman sees it as an analytic truth that the practice of
rights involves a conflict between the interests of the
right-holder and the interests of other members of the
society, particularly those who may have obligations to
act or refrain from acting in certain ways which are to
their disadvantage but for the benefit of the right-
holder.

Flathman's analysis of rights as warrants for the assertion of the legitimate self-interest of the right-holder
against and in conflict with the interests of others is
typical of those liberal theories on which socialists draw
to point to the alleged unsocialist nature of all rights.
As Flathman himself admits, his analysis, presupposing as
it does a conflict of individual interests, is at variance
with the ideal of community, for 'rights involve a certain
holding back, a reserve ... a competitive as well as a co-
operative attitude ... limits to sharing', and he notes
that there is 'a whole range of concepts at odds with the
practice: gratitude, generosity, charitableness'. Hence
'asserting and respecting rights against one another is
surely not, as such, a feature of relationships among or

between friends', (12) and thus, it may be inferred,
between members of a completely socialist society. If
there is anything at all in the image of a socialist
society as a society of abundance in which individuals
will willingly contribute what they can to the productive
processes and everyone will be provided with what they
require to fulfil their human potentialities, all without
the intervention of laws backed by sanctions, then the
conflict of interests which Flathman argues is presupposed in the practice of rights could not arise and
socialism, in the end, must involve not the revision but
the abandonment of the notion of rights, along with the
institution of the state and its laws. Thus a patently
old-style liberal analysis of rights fits neatly into the
socialist critique.

Although there is this degree of theoretical accord between some liberal and some socialist interpretations of
rights, the actual inspiration for the revolutionary
socialist's rejection of rights can be traced to Marx and
Engels, and in particular to their attacks on the inef-
fectualness of 'Utopian' socialists such as Proudhon,
Saint-Simon, Fourier, Owen and Lassalle, who criticised
capitalism for not giving the workers their full rights
to what they produce and called for the establishment of
a new society based on an ideal of social justice. (13)
Marx himself is said not to have condemned capitalism as
unjust. (14) Following this line, many Marxian socialists
reject the language of rights, except perhaps for short-
term tactical purposes in the organisation of political
parties around legislative programmes, on the grounds that
such moral stances are basically futile since social
change does not come about through exhortation and moralising, but by timely political action in line with changes
taking place in the economic base of society. They therefore reject appeals to rights as an irrelevant and ineffective strategy which exhibits a misunderstanding of
political realities, a characteristic failure of Utopian
socialists.

We shall have frequent recourse to the writings of Marx
and Engels in the course of this book, for although they
are but two amongst thousands of contributors to socialist
ideas, their influence has been of such magnitude as to
set them above all the rest as authoritative socialist
writers. But part, at least, of the explanation for the
absence of a socialist orthodoxy on the matter of rights
lies in the paucity of material on this topic to be found
in the writings of Marx and Engels and the difficulty of
interpreting such as there is. An important passage in
the 'Critique of the Gotha Programme' appears to disown in

their entirety the ideas of justice, rights and law (15)
and there are many other passages of which the obvious,
but perhaps superficial, reading counts against the
reformist position. (16) But the primary and overriding
concern of Marx and Engels was the exposure of the ideological, and hence deceiving, nature of bourgeois ideas
and institutions. This, coupled with their general reluctance to enter into speculation about the nature of the
future socialist or communist society, renders almost
everything they say on these issues radically ambiguous,
much depending on essentially terminological points such
as whether we may use the term 'law' for non-imposed and
non-coercive right-conferring rules, and whether there is
a valid sense of 'state' in which it is not identified as
an instrument for the exploitation of one class by another,
but refers to those general administrative arrangements of
a society which Engels, and almost certainly Marx, assumed
would in communist society replace the use of physical coercion. (17) Marx and Engels can be viewed as being so
involved in the criticism of capitalism that they were
simply not concerned with developing a conceptual scheme
to describe socialism. In this case to raise the prospect
of socialist rights is to go beyond rather than to repudiate their work. (18) Thus although Marx and Engels do
provide - particularly in their rejection of the juridical
concepts of capitalist legal systems - most of the ammunition for those who would abandon rather than reform the
concept of rights, their views, even if they can be definitively ascertained, cannot be regarded as conclusive on
this issue, even for socialists. And it is to be regret-
ted that their no doubt tactically justified refusal to
anatomise the form of the socialism that was to come has
done so much to inhibit open-minded discussion amongst
socialists over what it is, or could be, to have a right.
    To cast doubts on the usefulness of Marx and Engels as
final authorities in this internal socialist debate is
philosophically liberating, but presents us with the
immediate problem of saying what is to count as socialist
for the purpose of our argument. The prospect of becoming
involved in the misconceived enterprise of determining
what is 'genuine' socialism is a daunting one and yet it
is necessary to have some working definition of socialism
if we are to make progress with the conceptual tasks before us, for to say whether rights are compatible with
socialism depends in large part on what counts as socialism. (19) Fortunately, this problem can be circumvented
to some extent by adopting the permissive line of granting
the socialist critics of rights almost all that they desire
by accepting, for the sake of argument, their particular

versions of what a socialist society would be like. This means, in the main, accepting a relatively extreme and idealistic form of socialism according to which it involves the belief in the possibility and desirability of the successful pursuit of a society characterised by the self-conscious deployment of all human and natural resources, including the communally owned means of production, to satisfy the needs of 'social' man, whose behaviour will be marked by unsullied sociability, developed social responsibility, willing co-operation and the virtual absence of aggression, hostility, competitiveness and the desire to dominate others. If it can be established that even in such an ideal society there would still be occasion to maintain and protect individual rights, then the revolutionary critique of the significance of rights will have been adequately answered. We can then work out the conceptual implications of any retreat we may feel it necessary to make from this ideal type of socialism, and it is clear that massive retreat will be in order if the conceptual relations worked out for the ideal model of socialism are to be applied to existing societies.

There must, however, be some limits to the indulgence offered to socialist visionaries and I shall endeavour to keep in touch with reality by confining my attention to those models of socialism which are based on extrapolations of behavioural phenomena with which we are already familiar in less than fully socialist societies. We may be prepared to grant the possibility of extensive altruism because we have experience of limited altruism and we might accept the idea of non-competitiveness in all spheres because we have come across it at least to a degree in some. But it is another matter to grant the prospect of men's intellectual and physical capacities, as distinct from those of the machines they might invent, becoming of a different order from their highest existing manifestations and I shall reject as lacking in all plausibility projections which incorporate wholly new elements into human behaviour, and in particular the possibility that in some future society precise instinctual patterns of behaviour adapted to a complex variety of situations would emerge, thus rendering entirely unnecessary the processes of socialisation, education and organisation which are in some shape or form part of all known human societies. For some socialists this may vitiate the entire enterprise for they believe that we can put no restrictions on our expectations concerning the unknown future in which total socialism will emerge. But clearly such an agnostic attitude to the content of the socialist goal renders it totally irrelevant to the questions of constructive political theorising to which it is hoped to contribute and makes all conceptions of how we might progress to socialism, either before or after the revolutionary overthrow of capitalism, vacuous. As it is, we will have problems enough in attempting to envisage a society lacking in many of the characteristic features of all known societies and we will have accomplished enough if we show that the more plausible of the radical socialist visions can be analysed in terms of a notion of rights which is continuous with at least some existing theories of rights.

SUMMARY

In this study I shall first examine the grounds on which some socialists have rejected the whole idea of individual rights as irrelevant to socialist or communist societies, pointing out how their arguments often fit neatly into many ostensibly ideologically neutral analyses of the language of rights developed by philosophers and jurists in non-socialist societies, in particular the thesis that rights are analytically tied to conflict, coercion and self-interest. I shall reject some of the easier ways round this critique of rights which involve diluting the language of rights so that it becomes little more than an expression of general moral and political ideals, and then go on to criticise many of the standard assumptions about rights made in analytical jurisprudence and political philosophy on the grounds that, by incorporating contingent features of existing social and political systems into the very concept of rights, they put artificial conceptual barriers in the way of developing a notion of rights which is adapted to clarifying current ideological disagreements. Much of this discussion will involve demonstrating the weaknesses of some of these theories of rights even within their own terms, that is in relation to non-socialist societies. In part the method of argument will be to show that many rights theories are inadequate even as attempts to capture the full range of rights within existing societies. This part of the book (chapters 1-5) is of relevance to the general understanding of what it is to have a right quite apart from its significance for the discussion of socialist rights. Indeed, the conceptual issues discussed throughout have intellectual and practical import even for those who share the author's doubts as to the feasibility of the emergence of a socialist society of the ideal type assumed for our purpose of conceptual clarification.

Those whose special interest is in the content and justification of specific socialist rights may find that the discussions in chapters 6 to 9 help to give content to the general conceptual theses developed earlier in the book. In chapter 9 I focus on the idea of the right to work as a characteristic socialist right, the analysis of which will cast light on socialist rights in general; in chapter 8 I examine the extent of and rationale for the retention under socialism of certain of the rights which are particularly associated with liberal democracy, such as the right to free speech. These discussions feed upon and back into the analysis of chapter 7 on the general justificatory principles of socialist philosophy and the attempt to free the discussion of socialist rights from the often unilluminating but nevertheless important controversies over what is and what is not a 'human' right, which is the subject of chapter 6. Finally, in chapter 10, I discuss the nature of welfare rights in connection with issues of social policy arising in non-socialist welfare state societies. This chapter illustrates the relevance of the conceptual issues raised in the rest of the book to the formulation of political disagreements in existing states.

The fundamental conclusion to which the argument of the book moves is that the reformist is correct when he maintains that there is no inherent contradiction in speaking of 'socialist rights', but that the differences between socialist and existing liberal systems of rights are not simply a matter of differences in the content of rights or even of differences in the justifications given for the rights which feature in both systems, but involve some shift in standard theoretical assumptions about what it is to have a right. In other words, speaking of socialist rights involves some change of form as well as of content. To this extent, there is substance to the revolutionary's critique of rights as such. But the changes in our understanding of what it is to have a right which are required to give credence to the idea of socialist rights do not represent a radical departure from a version of one theory of rights which has many non-socialist advocates, namely the 'interest' theory, according to which the essential function of rights is to defend the interests of the right-holders. It is one of the subordinate aims of this book to make certain developments in the interest theory of rights which render it more acceptable in itself, as well as more suited to the analysis of the concept of socialist rights. Overall it is hoped that the specific solution offered to this unresolved problem within socialism will contribute to the formation of a set of common

concepts and vocabulary which will help to clarify and
even partially to resolve ideological conflicts concerning
social and economic policy. (20)

2 The moralism of rights

The main objections lodged against the idea of socialist rights by the conceptual revolutionaries amongst socialist theorists are directed at the juridical and coercive associations of rights discourse, the political and intellectual ineffectiveness of the moral rhetoric of rights, and their association with bourgeois individualism. For these theorists, rights have to do with law and law is a coercive institution, destructive of community relations and personal autonomy, which is required only in those societies marked by economic competition between self-interested individuals with vested property interests. Once the causes of economic, and hence social, antagonisms have been eliminated and the classless society has emerged – things which will not come about by moral exhortation – the state and its laws will cease to exist, making way for a co-operative and harmonious form of society in which there will be no room for clashes of individual wills that have to be settled by recourse to legal adjudication. Meanwhile appeals to individual rights can do nothing to resolve social conflict in pre-socialist societies. These theorists are revolutionaries with respect to rights because for them socialism is not just the replacement of one type of government by another or the abolition of one set of rights in favour of a new, more socialist, set; rather it involves the creation of a wholly novel form of social order which dispenses altogether with such legalistic institutions, an order which cannot be presented or recommended in the moralising terminology of the system which is to be superseded by socialism.

This sweeping critique of rights can be broken down into four distinct elements concerning, in turn, the legalism, the coerciveness, the individualism and the moralism of rights.

The revolutionary holds, first, that rights are analytically tied to rule-governed human relationships in
which the propriety of interactions is determined by the
conformity or lack of it between actual behaviour and
authoritative norms of conduct. He sees no value in rule-
conformity as such, believing it to be an unnecessary and
destructive intrusion into the spontaneous, uncalculating
and unreserved mutual service and care between self-
directed human beings which is attained in a genuine community. Hence rights are to be rejected as a manifestation of the inhuman and stultifying constraints of 'legalism', that is the process of subjecting human behaviour to
the governance of rules. The revolutionary goes beyond
the more common position that rule-conformity is an inadequate social ideal because it is compatible with social
inequality to the stronger thesis that rule-conformity is
in itself objectionable. (1) In a community there is no
right to be loved, no duty to love, no rules directing the
members to care for each other. Love has no need of law
and law destroys wholesome relationships between autonomous human beings. This thesis is taken over from those
liberal theorists who seek to exclude law from the domes-
tic spheres of family and friendship (2) and extrapolated
to apply to society as a whole.
   Second, as a juridical concept, rights are a matter of
law and law is the modus operandi of the state which is at
best a transient means for establishing socialism and at
worst an instrument of class oppression in which 'rights'
serve only to mask the fact that the law is a coercive
device for protecting the interests of economically powerful minorities. (3) Hence rights are to be rejected because they are tainted by the stain of coerciveness and
are incompatible with the liberty to be enjoyed only by
those who have emerged from the constraints of capitalism
into the genuine freedom which comes when the means of
production are taken into the control of the proletariat.
   Third, the idea of rights focuses attention on the individual as the possessor of rights, rights being a type of
possession which give the owner certain powers over the
actions of others, thus protecting his self-interests and
enabling him to ignore the moral claims of the common good
in the pursuit of his own self-centred objectives. Rights
are said to go with an 'atomistic' model of society in
which the constant clash of individual interests necessi-
tates measures to protect one individual against the predations of his fellows by using the force of the community
to establish the priority of some of these interests over
others. Interests so protected are called rights and
rights are regarded as the intrinsic possessions of

individuals in abstraction from their social relationships: men bring rights with them into society and
society is designed to protect them in that to which they
have a pre-social right, hence the theory of social contract which is totally at variance with the socialist concept of man as originally and essentially a social being
who brings nothing distinctively human into society and
whose nature is inseparable from his social relationships. The idea of rights is part and parcel of this
asocial and 'selfish' view of man. (4) This is the nub
of the objection to rights as an expression of individualism.

Fourth, in the revolutionary's view, when so-called
socialists resort to appeals to 'rights' in order to condemn existing societies and urge action to create new
post-capitalist systems, they are adopting intellectually
muddled moral rhetoric which has no objective basis and
which can have no significant impact on the course of
events. In Marxian terms, rights are a part of the super-
structure of a society, that is they are the products not
the causes of those economic changes on which all else in a
a society depends. Rights are therefore of no strategic
importance in the struggle for socialism, and those
socialists who concentrate their attention on demanding
rights for the workers ignore the real issues and the real
determinants of social change and indulge in empty, because groundless and ineffective, moralising. 'Rights'
are thus said to have essentially moral connotations, and
the use of the language of rights either to describe or
to bring about socialism is seen as a manifestation of un-
real and futile Utopian moralising. (5) Thus the fourth
type of objection is directed against the moralism of
rights.

In this chapter I examine the alleged moralism of
rights and introduce the core of the legalism objection,
commenting on the lack of coherence between these two
elements in the socialist critique, and introducing some
of the analytic issues concerning the nature of rights to
which these criticisms give rise. In the next chapter I
explore further the functions of law and its connection
with rights. Subsequent chapters deal with the alleged
coerciveness and individualism of rights.

THE 'MORALISM' OBJECTION

Although the revolutionary critique of rights is to some
extent cumulative, there is one respect in which it is not
internally coherent, for the objection to rights as a form

of coercive legalism depends on a rather different view of rights from that presupposed in the moralism objection. The legalism and coerciveness charges look at rights as part of a legal or quasi-legal structure, that is, in a positivistic manner, a person's rights being those of his interests which are protected and furthered by those actual laws or rules of his society which permit him to act or refrain from acting in certain ways or require others to do so with respect to him. Thus if it is argued that rights are bound to fade away as the state and its laws become redundant and are gradually dispensed with, then the notion of rights is clearly being given a purely juridical interpretation in terms of that to which a person is entitled or able to do or receive or have in law; and rule-following in general presupposes a set of existing rules. Legalism thus assumes a positivistic account of rights, that is, one which ties them to the actual laws or rules operative in a society, and on this basis it is often argued that where there is no positive law (e.g. in a socialist society) there cannot (logically) be any rights.

However, the fourth element in the revolutionary's onslaught, which arises from his rejection of morality and moralising, requires us to regard rights primarily as a moral concept, one which is used in the moral criticism of existing social relationships in terms of extra-legal values. Thus a legally constituted government may be said to be tyrannical because it denies its subjects certain rights, perhaps to freedom of movement or freedom of speech. Such uses of the language of rights feature in strong moral criticisms of existing practices, criticisms which do not depend on the prior existence of any positive laws but require only the recognition of certain moral standards or objectives to which positive laws ought to, but, in the cases criticised, do not conform. It would seem, if we are to defend the concept of rights against these objections, that we must first get clear what it is that we are seeking to rebut; more specifically, we have to know whether we are to take rights as legal or moral phenomena, as part of positive law or expressing some sort of normative moral standards which may be used in the evaluation of positive law.

It is tempting, if we wish to defend the reformist position, to take the moral option and say that in speaking of rights we are referring to a set of human interests and needs which have high moral priority and which any good society must be able to satisfy in an adequate manner. In this case a person's right to life would be a pre-legal moral possession or moral fact about him, in the light of which we can evaluate actions and societies as morally good or bad according to how far they protect and enhance people's lives. To speak of a person's rights in this moral or ideal sense involves no immediate reference to laws or societal rules and points only to those morally significant aspects of his existence that laws and rules, as well as actions and inactions which fall under no laws or rules, ought to protect and promote. These rights may be to something as precise as life or as nebulous as happiness, but they represent the various respects in which individual existence is valuable and the ends to which individual and social action should be directed, or at the very least should not obstruct. On this view, legal rights are secondary phenomena in the hierarchy of rights discourse for they are simply one amongst many ways in which societies may seek to further the moral or ideal rights of their members. (6)

This approach to rights is tempting because it appears to be easier to see how we can use moral terminology in our description of a socialist society than it is to find a place for legalism within socialism. The moral use of rights language can and has frequently been used to denounce the evils of capitalism and fits in with standard analyses of rights in terms of demands (7) and claims. (8) Even the socialist who believes in economic determinism and accepts that moralising is an ineffectual method of bringing about reform can still retain a use for the conception of moral rights to express an evaluation of socialism as in some way superior to other systems without committing himself to the view that a socialist society could ever be the product of moral persuasion or demands. Capitalist 'democracies' may be graded low in the scale of desirable economic and political forms because they do little that is effective to protect the individual's moral rights, whereas socialism may be regarded as a system in which these aspects of human interests can flourish and be fulfilled. (9)

All this could be said without implying that the law is the instrument whereby socialism protects moral rights. Legal regulations might be phased out as the danger of rights-violations diminishes, and the desired socialist objectives may be approached directly without the intermediacy of rules. Thus there would be no need for a legal right to life once no one was motivated to kill another or failed to aid those needing help to preserve their lives. Removing the causes of violations of moral rights could thus have the effect of rendering legal rights redundant, but socialist societies could still be highly valued because they effectively protect the moral rights of their members.

Even allowing that socialism can be presented at least
in part as a set of moral ends does not, of course, demonstrate that these ends are felicitously expressed in the
language of rights. Objections may be raised to setting
out socialist objectives in this guise and these will be
discussed when we come to the third source of socialist
hostility to rights, namely their individualistic nature.
But to adopt the moral analysis of rights does enable us
to side-step, rather neatly, what is perhaps the most
dominant and devastatingly rigorous ground for the socialist rejection of rights, namely their essentially juridical or legal nature. And yet to adopt this view of rights
is to concede much too much far too quickly. Thinking of
rights as merely a set of important socially relevant
moral goals is to deprive ourselves of what is distinctive
about rights as a concept and to submerge it in the mass
of undifferentiated general terms of moral approval, such
as 'right', 'good' and 'desirable', whereas in fact it has
an important function of its own to fulfil in moral and
political discourse, namely to identify those ingredients
of human life which are protected and furthered in a particular way, that is by the acceptance within a community
that certain acts are or are not permitted or required.
It is in relation to such permissions and mandatory
requirements that the distinctive use of the language of
rights has application. At this point we must therefore
break off our analysis of the socialist critique of rights
to elaborate briefly on the reasons for rejecting a
'moral' in favour of a positivistic interpretation of
rights.

THE CRITIQUE OF 'MORAL RIGHTS'

There are strong practical arguments - if we look at the
matter from the point of view of developing a precise and
comprehensive set of concepts for the discussion of moral
and legal issues - for resisting the dilution of the concept of rights which occurs when it is applied to any
desirable social goal which can be stated in terms of
individual benefits and claimed with special moral force.
And there are also substantial, although perhaps not overwhelming, conceptual reasons for adopting the legal use
of 'rights' as at least logically prior to the moral use,
for it is not only possible but illuminating and clarifi-
catory at the level of normative political and legal
philosophy, to define rights in a positivistic manner as
those interests which are protected and furthered by laws
(or, as I shall argue, by societal rules), and to treat as

a separate, because normative, question the issue of what
rights persons ought to have. To talk of moral rights is
on this (Benthamite) view simply to make assertions about
the moral ground for having certain positive rights,
either legal or societal. (10)

Moreover, it takes little reflection to see that the
moral reasons that are relevant to the determination of
normative questions about the content of rights are of as
many different types as there are ultimate moral principles and theories, so that utility is, for instance, at
least one reason - and for the utilitarian the only reason
- for establishing and maintaining rights. This means
that it would be misleading to give the impression that
all normative recommendations regarding the proper content of positive rights must be couched in terms of so-
called 'moral rights' as if this was a distinct category
of moral reason of special and inclusive application to
the determination of legal rights. Unless, therefore, it
is being argued that there is a 'moral law' analogous to
positive law to which we must make reference to find out
the proper content of positive law (the natural law tradition) it is better to drop the misleading terminology of
'moral rights' or to use it only to refer to those rights
which the speaker believes ought to exist, and thus make
it easier to bring into the open the fact that actual
positive rights may be justified by the whole range of
moral values.

Maintaining a clear distinction between what it is for
a right to exist and what rights ought to exist and so
separating analysis from justification has obvious attrac-
tions for the tidy-minded philosopher, but to those who
take ordinary language as definitive of conceptual propriety it will seem cavalier to dismiss a use of the term
'rights' which is not only common but pervasive in political
discourse; there are few political programmes, particularly in the social policy area, which are not justified
by their supporters in terms of the 'rights' of citizens,
irrespective of whether or not such rights are part of the
law of that society.

This 'manifesto' use of rights language seems too well
established to be declared inadmissible since it is all
but universal to argue that policies ought to be adopted
because human beings have certain rights in a non-
positivistic sense. (11) Moreover, this is clearly an intrinsic part of the tradition of natural rights and hence
of its modern version, human rights: the rights that all
human beings are said to have whether or not they are
protected by actual laws and customs of particular countries. Surely it would be sacrificing too much on the

altar of clarity if we were to declare inadmissible the
whole idea of human rights?

However, the political philosopher is of all philosophers the least likely to be totally subservient to the
discourse he seeks to analyse, for politics is notori-
ously an arena for rhetorical debate designed to gain
assent rather than give clear expression to policies and
their purported justification. Because of the strong
persuasive and emotive associations of so many key moral
and political terms, a whole range of political terminology – such as justice, democracy and liberty – has become
so extended and weakened as to be all but useless for precise theorising until these terms are given back more specific and distinguishable conceptual limitations. Of none
is this more true than 'rights' which has become – outside
of a minority of thinkers on both the Left and Right – one
of the emotively favourable words of current political
rhetoric and hence particularly vulnerable to the danger
of being rendered vacuous by persuasive definition. Moreover, it cannot be assumed that the uninterpreted contents
of ordinary political language is unambiguous or consistent. Thus it is equally common in justifying political
policies to say that citizens ought to have certain rights
as it is to insist that they do have these rights:
putting the two ways of speaking together, it often
appears that we are being told that citizens ought to have
certain rights because these do have these rights.

Of course, it is possible to make this coherent by
saying that what is meant is that citizens ought to have
certain positive rights because they have certain moral
rights and this is no doubt the standard interpretation
of such opaque arguments, but it is not the only interpretation; it is possible to take the statements about
the 'moral' rights that citizens are alleged to have as
being misleading in a way common in all moral discourse
in that they make normative or imperative assertions in
the indicative mood, a linguistic fact which no longer
deters philosophers from doubting whether such moral
statements as 'X is good' are purely descriptive. (12)
And just as philosophers have resolved the ambiguity and
inconsistencies in moral language in general by offering
alternative non-propositional analyses of pseudo-
statements such as 'X is morally right', we can properly
think of 'statements' about so-called moral rights as
being disguised moral recommendations or evaluations.
This then directs our attention to positive law and custom for an answer to the question – what then are our
rights? This has the advantage of taking us to a body
of institutional practices which presents a corpus of

relatively objective and manageable evidence with which to
give precision and clarity to the idea of rights. Moreover, it should be noted that to take up this philosophical position is not to insist that people cease talking as
if there were 'moral rights', but only that such pseudo-
statements be interpreted as normative judgments about
actual rights for the purpose of the systematic examination of how positive rights are to be justified.

Arguing against my interpretation of moral rights,
Peter Jones contends that its effect is to 'remove rights
from the armoury of critical morality'. (13) By this he
means that we would no longer be correct to say, for
instance, 'that they [rights] must be recognised and respected and that they ought not to be violated'. But
while it is correct to say that it is, strictly speaking,
improper to use the language of rights to make such moral
points, this does not mean that we cannot morally condemn
the violation of rights. The assertion 'A ought to have a
right to X' need not be translated into 'A has a right to
have a right to X'. Indeed, it is wildly implausible to
confine moral discourse within rights discourse in this
way. Rights may, therefore, be removed from the 'armoury
of critical morality' without this entailing that we must
abandon moral comment and exhortation concerning the
rights that ought to exist and be protected. Moreover, it
is the contention of those who wish to do without the idea
of moral rights that the appeal to moral rights gives a
spurious impression of objectivity and precision which is
unwarranted by the complex moral considerations which have
bearing upon the justification of genuine or positive
rights. R.G. Frey is surely correct when he argues that
the appeal to moral rights is simply a roundabout way of
referring to the principles which are used to justify
rights. Pointing to the radical disagreements which
exists about the content of moral rights, Frey concludes:
'either moral rights are superfluous or we are not yet in
a position to affirm that there are any; whichever it is,
I cannot see that anything is lost by giving up claims or
moral rights altogether'. (14)

The analysis of moral rights is tied up with an ambiguity in the thesis that rights are a species of demands or
claims. It is often argued that to say that A has a right
to X is to make an assertion to the effect that A has a
strong, perhaps overriding, claim to X which either justifies or can be expressed in a demand that A be permitted
or enabled to have or receive X. Since such demands or
claims arise in both moral and legal contexts, it seems
reasonable to speak of and distinguish moral and legal
rights. (15)

However, while it is clear that the existence of a right can make a claim or demand appropriate when this would not otherwise be the case, this does not mean that rights are to be equated with claims or demands. Rights can serve to justify certain claims or demands, hence their close association, particularly where rights are being violated. It is easy, therefore, to think of rights as species of claims. But this too confuses the claim with its possible justification. (16) A right is not a justified claim, but it may justify a claim. This confusion is compounded by the failure to distinguish between demanding that a right be created and demanding that an existing right be acted upon or enforced. But the assertion that certain rights be recognised, in the sense of accepted as binding, is different from the demand that recognised rights be implemented in specific instances within a community which already accepts that right as binding. Claims may thus arise in connection with either the creation or the specific implementation of rights. The former type of claim can plausibly be equated with 'moral rights', the latter type having to do with the enforcement of legal rights. But in line with the analysis adopted here, the former type of claim are misleadingly expressed in terms of moral rights (they are, in fact, demands that certain rights be created), and the latter type of claim is to be interpreted as a claim that a right independently identified and validated should be actually implemented. In neither case are rights to be equated with claims of either sort.

The common notion that to assert a right is to make a particularly strong claim is explicable by the fact that to claim a right is to allege the existence of a rule which gives the holder title to some benefit without the need for further argument. If such a claim is successfully made it has indeed important normative consequences, but this is not because of the force or strength of the act of claiming but because of the nature of what is being claimed (a right). The special normative force of a right is distinct from the existence, force or further justification of any claims which may invoke it. Thus in moral discourse it is often false to say that a claim of right is the strongest sort of claim there is, for it is often immoral to insist on one's rights when this would entail harm to others. Once we have prised apart rights and claims in this manner it is less plausible to adopt the thesis that rights are essentially instruments for making moral demands on others.

If it is insisted that statements of moral and, in particular, human rights are meant literally in that they

are rights laid down in actual moral law, so that to say
that A has a moral right to X is to say that there is a
moral law giving A this right, rather than expressions of
the moral judgments of the speaker, then this is to assume
the existence of an objective or 'natural' law in the
sense of a law which exists prior to and independently of
any human decisions and enactments. If we presuppose some
such notion, then there is indeed a clear descriptive
meaning for assertions about moral rights which are not
positivistic in the sense that they are necessarily part
of the law or mores of any society but nevertheless have
an existence just as real in ontological terms as positive
law. However, this is in a way to grant the positivist
his point that the language of rights is tied to the
reality of actually existing laws; in the case of 'natural' laws this actuality is metaphysical rather than empirical, but the two are to this extent analogous in that
we 'discover' what rights a person has by finding out
about the content of a code of laws which exists independently of the moral beliefs and assertions of the persons
involved. Natural law, so interpreted, can be regarded
as a form of positive - in the sense of actual - law.

It can readily be acknowledged that, if there is such a
natural or moral law, then there can be natural or moral
rights. Indeed it is one further reason for rejecting
the concept of moral rights that, literally interpreted,
they presuppose just such a theory and it is best used,
therefore, only by those who accept the theory of natural
law. I cannot here argue the plausibility of natural law
theory, (17) but must simply assert that, outside a theo-
logical context, any version which is literal enough to
provide a basis for talking of moral rights as existing
analogously to the positive rights of actual societies,
lacks the necessary philosophical support. Moreover, it
is not a promising basis on which to seek to establish
common conceptual ground between socialists and liberals.
Few socialists could accept the notion of moral rights if
this saddles them with a theory of natural law for
although, as we shall see, the socialist emphasis on the
permanent importance of the essentially creative nature of
man has something of the flavour of natural law theory,
the idea of a detailed substantive body of 'laws' manifest
to human reason, either intuitively or by deduction from
self-evident facts about human nature, is incompatible
with characteristic socialist accounts of the emergence
and function of moral rules in pre-socialist societies.

If we reject the literal analysis of the idea of moral
rights as pre-existing entities on which positive laws
can be based, this enables us to deal with Paul Hirst's

contention that the notion of rights is politically unhelpful and intellectually confused. Hirst argues that
'attempting to solve questions of divergent interests in
terms of "rights" can only lead to impossible contradictions'. (18) He adopts this position because he assumes
that to speak of rights is to espouse the ontological doctrine according to which 'institutions or laws are conceived as the expressions or recognition of certain prior
or privileged attributes of subjects ... deriving from
their nature or essence'. (19) On this view, to attempt
to settle rival claims based on conflicting interests,
for instance as between a pregnant woman and her potential
child over a putative abortion, is to generate useless
ontological arguments about the 'rights' of the two claimants. R.M. Hare expresses the same point in connection
with the abortion issue. Hare's contention is that the
appeal to (moral) rights is effectively an appeal to intuition and therefore contributes nothing to the solution
of real conflicts of interest. (20)

Such objections are apposite to moral rights whose
ontological status as non-observable possessions or
attributes of individuals is indeed problematic, as is
reflected in the insoluble conflicts which arise over
what moral rights people actually have. But the same
objection does not apply to positive rights which, as we
shall see, are determinable social phenomena whose existence can be ascertained with some objectivity. We can
therefore grant Hirst's philosophical points without
accepting his conclusion that the language of rights
should have no place in the socialist vocabulary. (21)

There is, however, one further interpretation of 'moral
rights' that does not ensnare us in natural law theory,
namely its use to refer to those rights which are established in the non-legal customs and conventions of societies. It is indisputable that there are such non-legal
mores in all societies and that we do speak of rights in
relation to these customs and established practices.
However, positivistic theories of rights can readily
accommodate this usage by accepting an extension of the
narrow legal theory of rights to cover the rights which
we have under customary social rules. These rules are
social phenomena to be observed and described by the same
sort of empirical methods as we use to establish the content and operation of laws. If a parent has, in custom, a
right that his adult children respect and care for him,
something which involves keeping in touch with the parent
and offering such assistance as he can when the parent is
in need, then this is a fact about a society which can be
established by observing the behaviour of adult children,

the use of praise and blame in relation to the fulfilment
and non-fulfilment of these activities and the general
operation of public opinion on such matters.

Any analysis of rights must be able to incorporate such
phenomena, but to do so it need not step outside an essentially positivistic theory, for such rights can be understood in terms of the positive morality of a society, what
are often called mores, but which I shall talk of as
social rules. (22) Indeed, we shall see that this idea of
non-legal or social rights can be very important in
developing a positivistic socialist analysis of rights.
However, it is not necessary to regard such rights as
'moral' rights and it is often misleading to do so since
it suggests that morality is to be identified with mores
whereas it is no more or less relevant to the critique of
social than of legal rules, and I shall therefore call
them social rights to minimise the confusion and ambiguities inherent in the idea of moral rights. (23) (The
term 'societal rule' can usefully be deployed to cover
both legal and non-legal or social rules.)

Assuming, then, that we adopt a positivistic definition
of rights, where does this leave the socialist's 'moralising' objection to rights? Rejecting the moral interpretation of rights certainly enables us to speak of
rights in a purely descriptive manner and hence to ask
what it is to have a right and whether there would be
rights in socialist society, without immediately entering
the realm of moral debate. Thus if a socialist is committed to a self-denying ordinance with respect to making
moral evaluations, this does not mean he cannot employ
the terminology of rights in a purely descriptive manner
as part of his analysis of social and political relations.
For instance a positivistic analysis makes it intelligible how Marx could be said to have discussed the place
of rights in capitalist society without indulging in moral
denunciation. It then remains an open question for the
anti-moralising socialist whether or not there will be
rights in a socialist society.

But, as we noted, the socialist withdrawal from moralising may not go to the length of rejecting all moral discourse, but may stop with the contention that social and
political change cannot be brought about by moral exhortation. Some socialists may therefore want to make comparative moral judgments about different social and political systems and this, on the positivistic analysis of
rights, they are permitted to do, provided, of course,
that they do not assume that there are in some literal
sense existing 'moral rights' by reference to which such
evaluations can be made. This is not likely to cause

such socialists any difficulties since the rhetoric of
moral rights has been developed in the process of making
moral exhortations of the sort that they reject and
ridicule. In so far as they do enter into moral evaluations of social and political systems socialists are less
likely than other theorists to wish to appeal to pre-
political moral rights as their standards of judgment,
for this terminology is associated with intuitionistic
and ahistorical traditions of thought which, perhaps because of their deployment by liberal-capitalist theorists, socialists have tended to reject.

It can be argued that this is the position adopted by
Marx himself, for although he utterly rejected the idea
of 'eternal and immutable right' this could have been on
account of his hostility to the anti-historical nature of
appeals to unchanging moral standards and his criticism
of 'rights' and 'justice' as juristic concepts which are
at home only in a certain type of commercial society.
This does not rule out the possibility that he has his
own moral position - perhaps a utilitarian one- and he
does appear to have used utilitarian standards in his
scarcely concealed preference.for communism over capitalism as forms of society. (24) And, of course, those
socialists who do not reject entirely the use of moral
language to further political and social change may still,
without violating positivism, recommend, for instance,
that capitalism ought to be overthrown because it tramples
on the 'moral rights' of workers provided this is seen as
a form of strong moral exhortation about the rights which
ought to be enacted and operated (rather than as an appeal
to some metaphysical natural law), for this is a form of
discourse which can be reduced, without loss of meaning,
to more general moral terminology.

By rejecting the notion of moral rights, except as a
shorthand way of making moral assertions about what rights
persons ought to have, and settling on a positivistic
analysis of rights I have undercut the 'moralising' element in the socialist critique of rights, for 'rights' becomes essentially a descriptive rather than an evaluative
term, albeit descriptive of social norms. We may therefore by-pass the complex question of the alleged unreality
and inefficacy of moral language. But this still leaves
undetermined whether or not socialist societies would have
a use for rights and how, if at all, such rights would be
justified. The socialist's rejection of positive rights
is based on the other elements in the critique and in particular the objection to the legalism of rights to which
we must now turn.

RIGHTS AND RULES

To side-step the 'moralism' objection is only, it appears,
to fall foul of that based on the alleged legalism of
rights. If rights are a matter of positive law and the
socialist view is that law is essentially a device of the
state and the state is by definition an instrument of
class oppression, then rights must be analytically tied to
an institution to whose abolition or withering-away revolutionary socialists are committed both in theory and in
practice. This would seem to establish an irreconcilable
conflict between socialism and rights. However, two
related ingredients of this apparent conflict are amenable
to revision in a way which opens up the prospect of a re-
conciliation. Marx, it seems clear, excluded law from
communism, but he and others who think along the same
lines are not necessarily thereby committed to the exclusion of all rules, but only those which are in some way
coercive and oppressive. Add to this that the positivist
is not mortgaged to an analytic connection between rights
and law, but only an essential relationship between rights
and rules of one sort or another, and we can contemplate
the idea of socialist rights based on societal rules or,
if the analysis of law outlined in chapter 4 is acceptable, uncoercive laws.

The prospect of arriving at a conception of positive
rights in terms of uncoercive societal norms or laws makes
it worth while exploring the nature of the rules which
pertain to rights and asking whether a socialist society
might require such rules. In the remainder of this chapter I will analyse and comment on some connections between
rights and rules in preparation for taking up the wider
issue of the social (and possibly, the socialist) functions of rules, which is the main topic of the next
chapter.

The version of a juristic concept of rights which I
shall defend and develop in the course of setting up a
more precise target for socialist criticisms of rights is
one in which a right is defined as a legally (or, as we
shall see, quasi-legally) protected or furthered interest.
I shall examine in some detail, in chapter 5, the meaning
and role of 'interest' in this definition, but for the
moment it is the idea of legal protection and furtherance
of interests that calls for comment. My definition of a
right presupposes that law is a system of behavioural
norms associated with institutional procedures for the
administration and application of the behavioural norms to
which recourse may be had to settle disagreements about
how social interactions are to be ordered. These societal

norms or rules may permit (explicitly or by default), prescribe, proscribe or enable action or inaction. When they
do so in a manner directed towards defending or furthering
the interests of certain individuals or groups, then these
individuals or groups may be said to have the right to do,
have or receive that which the rules proscribe, permit,
prescribe, or enable. This means that for there to be a
right it is necessary for there to be a rule which warrants, entitles or enables certain actions or inactions of
right-bearers or requires others to act or refrain from
acting in ways which are favourably directed to the interests of right-bearers. Rights connect in a rule-governed
fashion individual actions and individual interests
(either directly or through the mediation of collective
actions and collective interests).

   The varied connections between rights and rules can be
illustrated by a classification of rights based on Wesley
Hohfeld's well-known scheme of jural relations. (25) In a
not wholly successful attempt to capture all legal relationships in an interrelated pattern of connected rights
and duties, Hohfeld distinguished between liberties (or,
as he called them, privileges), claim-rights (or rights in
the narrow sense), powers and immunities, all of which are
classified as 'rights' in a broad sense. These distinctions demonstrate the different ways in which rights presuppose rules, and an appreciation of them will help us to
deal in a more precise way with the social functions of
rules and related questions about the rights which would
be characteristic of a socialist society.

   A person is said to have a liberty-right (or privilege)
to X if, and only if, there is no law or rule prohibiting
him from doing X, and he has a liberty-right not to X if,
and only if, there is no rule requiring him to X. Liberties correlate with what Hohfeld calls 'no-rights' of
others. This is best interpreted by saying that if A has
a right to X, others do not have a right that he not do X,
and if A has a right not to X, then others do not have a
right that he do X. We thus have a liberty to do anything
which is not forbidden and not to do anything which is not
required.

   Hobbes uses the concept of liberty-rights when he
argues that in the state of nature, in which there are no
laws and hence no obligations, men have what he called a
'natural right' to everything. (26) Such natural rights
are Hohfeldian liberties because they are defined in terms
of the absence of rules. Thus I have a liberty-right to
harm another if there is no rule prohibiting such action.
As rules feature only negatively in the analysis of
liberty-rights it can be argued that they are not strictly

rights at all, a point which is underlined by Hohfeld's rather odd notion of a correlative 'no-right' which refers to no more than the absence of a right. Certainly, liberties may be of little use in protecting the interests of the right-bearer unless they are accompanied by rules preventing others from interfering with the actions which the liberty-right-bearer is 'free' to do. Pure liberty-rights, unsupported by at least the general assumption of the illegitimacy of interference with the freedom of others, are not likely to be of great value to the bearers. They may be of some significance in competitive situations by signifying who is entitled to compete, but such rights do nothing to prevent the powerful, the strong and the rich from destroying any advantages the absence of legal constraints might confer on others. The fact that a man is not forbidden to defend himself or to compete for scarce resources is of little significance to him if he is unable to achieve these objectives. Hence the disagreeableness of Hobbes's state of nature and the scorn poured by socialists on the economic 'liberties' of capitalist systems. However, there are circumstances in which the absence of a rule proscribing certain behaviour may be an advantage to persons and this is sufficient for us to count liberties as a species of rights, leaving open for the moment whether such rights would feature in a socialist society.

It is doubtful if pure liberty-rights could have an important function in a situation where there are no rules at all (such as Hobbes's state of nature). Warrants provided by liberties normally serve to indicate those acts which are not proscribed or prescribed in a context in which there are many prohibitions and prescriptions. In such a context it serves a real purpose to point out, in the justification of an action, that there is or is not, contrary to what might be expected or claimed, any rule against the action or inaction in question. Where this is accompanied by a societal or constitutional rule explicitly forbidding the enactment of rules limiting the individual's freedom in the relevant respect then a purely formal liberty is transformed into a more important type of right, which I shall call a protected or fundamental liberty.

Claim-rights, or rights in the narrow sense, in contrast to liberties, do correlate with the obligations of others towards the right-holder, so that a person (A) has a claim-right to X if, and only if, there is a rule stating that others have obligations either to permit A to do X (in which case I will speak of a substantive liberty or a negative right) or to give positive or actual assistance

to A (which may be called a positive or affirmative
right). An example of a substantive liberty is the
negative right to life where this implies a rule obliging
others not to kill the right-holder; a positive or affirmative right to life would be one which correlated with
the obligation of others to take active measures to keep
the right-holder alive. In both cases appeal may be made
to obligation-imposing rules in order to provide a warrant
for requiring the action or inaction of others to preserve
A's life. These are the standard and central types of
rights to which we shall devote most attention.

Many socialists are almost as sceptical of the significance of substantive liberties (or negative rights) as
they are of formal or Hohfeldian liberties since they
offer no guarantee that the right-bearer is actually able
to do that which he or she has the (negative) right to do.
Such a right, if enforced, means that others will not
interfere with the right-bearer's actions or inactions,
but this may be of little importance if, for reasons other
than the immediate behaviour of other people, such as
poverty or physical incapacity, the right-bearer is unable
to make use of his substantive liberty or negative right.
But given that socialists often denounce or regret the
oppressive nature of some laws, it seems reasonable to
hold that substantive liberties could be of importance in
certain social (but not necessary socialist) situations.
It seems likely, however, that in a society marked by genuine care of each for other people, positive or affirmative
rights would feature more prominently than merely negative
rights. It may be, therefore, that the shift from negative to positive rights is a measure of social progress in
a socialist direction. (27)

Third, rights in the sense of powers exist where A has
the legal capacity to make decisions which are binding on
or affect the legal standing of himself or others. Power-
rights are said to correlate with the liabilities of those
affected, although the effects may not, in fact, be detrimental to those concerned. Thus I have a power right if,
as a parent, I can disinherit my children or, as a chairman of a company, I can declare an increased dividend or,
as a citizen, I can vote in an election. (28) These are
things that I could not do unless there were rules stating
the legal consequences of certain of my actions and in
general they presuppose whole systems of rules relating to
such institutions as property, the family, schools and
other organisations. The term 'power-right', with its
connotations of the domination of one person by another
and its close association with various legal capacities
which are dependent on the institution of property, makes

this third type of right a prime target for socialist
denunciators. But it cannot be assumed at this stage
that the powers in question are coercive in the sense that
correlative liabilities are rejected or resented by those
on whom they fall. There is nothing in the notion of a
power-right to imply that the use of such rights must be
solely for the benefit of their holders or that the allocation of such rule-governed (and sometimes rule-
originating) capacities must be based on non-socialist
principles.

Last, there are immunity-rights, a term used to denote
those cases where B has no power to affect or alter the
legal standing or position of A. Thus when a class of
persons, such as diplomats, are explicitly excluded from
the normal application of a rule, they may be said to have
immunity-rights. Like pure liberty-rights, their existence depends on the absence of rules, in this case power-
conferring rules. Again, similarly to liberty-rights,
while we can make sense of such immunity-rights without
assuming that the immunities are exceptions to generally
applicable liabilities, it is normally in the context of
such exemptions that immunities are established and have
significance. Moreover, they, like liberty-rights, become more significant if they are turned into substantive
rights, in this case by the existence of rules forbidding
the creation of the correlative powers.

I shall return to these distinctions later and pursue
the question of whether some types of rights are more
acceptable than others within a socialist system, but for
the moment we may simply note that in every case it is
part of what it means to say that A has a right to X that
the relevant actions or claims are justified within the
legal system by reference to the existence or absence of
some obligation or power-conferring rules. Thus to establish that A has a right in any of the above senses it is
necessary to demonstrate that there is or is not a rule
which warrants, entitles or enables A to have or do the
thing or act in question, this warrant having specific
legal consequences depending on the type of right involved.

It would be as well to pause and reiterate this fundamental point as it is crucial for the understanding of
what it is that distinguishes saying that A has a right to
X from saying that A is right or not wrong to X, and thus
for preserving the distinctive meaning of rights discourse.
The distinction between right in general and rights in particular is traceable to some way of spelling out a special
sort of reason why or sense in which A would be right and
not wrong to do X, that way being, I suggest, the appeal to
existing rules, conventions or understandings to establish

legal or quasi-legal warrant, entitlement or capacity.
Rights discourse points to a specific type of argument
about the propriety of behaviour, argument which gives as
a reason 'because A has a right to X' in which the fact
that there is a rule or law is presented as sufficient
reason for permitting A to have or do X, or as giving A a
warrant or capacity to have or do X. At its strongest,
where there is such a rule or law, A (or others on A's
behalf) is not required to give any other reasons for
being permitted to do or have X. Once it is established
that A has a right to do X, there is no need to justify
any further his doing X. It excuses him or his representatives from further justificatory arguments, at least in
a legal or quasi-legal context. Strictly speaking, however, this covers only what are called absolute rights,
that is rights, such as, perhaps, the right to a fair
trial, which there is never any legal justification for
overriding, so that, as it stands, this claim is too
sweeping. Further questions can always be raised (in
addition to issues of moral justification) concerning the
rights of others which may be endangered by actions warranted by the initial right: most rights are, for this
reason, prima facie rather than absolute, in that they
are but one legal consideration amongst others in a complex rule-constituted situation in which rights conflict
and overriding principles may apply. However, to have a
right is at least to have a warrant to have or do X which
gives a prima facie case for having or doing X without
reference to further justificatory support. It blocks,
for instance, the argument that a right-holder cannot
exercise a right because another finds it objectionable,
or not in his interests, or because others do not consent
to his actions. And it blocks also objections based on
general policy considerations which are not embodied in
any rule-established limitations on this right. This is
why rights may readily be presented as opposed to utility,
for it is inappropriate to deny a person his rights on
the grounds of the utility of doing so, although this does
not mean, of course, that utility is irrelevant to the
determination of what rights ought to exist or that it can
never override constituted rights.

This 'exclusionary' aspect of rights is inseparable
from the notion of what it is to have a right. (29) To
have a right is to be in a position to override or render
irrelevant at least some possible objections to my action
or inaction, including objections that exercising my right
may detrimentally affect others, and maybe to rule out
altogether, or at least to a degree, arguments being
effectively deployed against my action which rest on an

appeal to utility in the sense of the good society as a
whole. For this to be possible it must be the case that
there is a system of rules which is regarded as authoritative in determining how individuals are to act, so that
behaviour is thus governed to some extent by rules which
are accepted or enforced within the social group in question and what ought to be done is determined neither by
the unregulated choice of individuals nor directly and in
each case by any individual or collective decisions about
what it would be right or productive of good consequences
to do in that particular circumstance. This is why it is
the primary function of courts of law to determine the
rights and obligations of the parties to a dispute, or of
accused persons, rather than make their judgments according to a view of what would be the best outcome in the
light of the facts of the situation and their own or some
authorised set of moral or political values, although
these factors clearly do, and probably ought to, affect
their interpretation of the relevant rules.

We do not have to go any further into the different
ways in which legal rights confer warrants or powers on
their holders in order to formulate a central socialistic
objection to the legalism of rights. This objection is
frequently expressed by those who believe that socialism
is a movement towards social justice. It rests on the
feeling that decisions concerning the distribution of
benefits and burdens in a society should not be taken in
accordance with a book of rules, but in the light of
the objectives of social policy. For, it is pointed out,
not only may particular decisions made according to rules
result in material injustice, but a rule may systematic-
ally discriminate against the poor and the oppressed. In
such circumstances, to be committed to applying the rules,
however fairly or impartially administered, come what may,
is to ignore the more obvious and direct demands of justice and human welfare which socialism is intended to
serve. More generally and more radically, mutual loving
care is directed not by a set of rules with their inevitably limited obligations, but by an application of an
open-ended concern for the welfare of particular persons.

Such criticisms are not made only by socialists. In so
far as legalism has pejorative connotations it is because
it betokens a misplaced concern for doing things in
accordance with rules so that rule-following becomes an
end in itself and hence an instrument of inhumanity, in
that rule-abidingness is given priority over meeting the
needs of individuals. Legalism may therefore be seen as
an enemy of justice in a morally more fundamental sense of
justice than the impartial administration of rules. But,

although he is not alone in his criticisms of legalism, the socialist's awareness of the co-existence of a fair degree of such legal impartiality with gross oppression and injustice in certain stages of capitalism leads him to make it with particular force.

Is, then, the upholder of rights committed to the sort of legalism which gives priority to rule-following over policy objectives in the treatment of individuals? The simple answer is: by and large, in the short term he is. This follows from the definition of rights in terms of rules which entails that to respect rights is to respect rules. Rights could not be what they are and fulfil the function which they do if the right-conferring rules were in practice subordinate to other non-legalistic considerations. On the other hand, rules can be changed and their application to specific cases leaves room for interpreting the rules in ways which take into account the assumed or known purposes which those rules serve. And the strictest conformity to rules need not be rule-worship if we mean by this the belief that conformity to rules is justified without reference to the consequences of so doing. In fact, most arguments in favour of legalism are along the lines that rule-following has beneficial long-term consequences even if, in particular cases, it seems to be counter-productive in relation to the ends which the law is meant to serve. We must therefore examine the general arguments in favour of legalistic regulation of social behaviour before we can assess the nature and implications of the socialist objection to legalism.

3 The legalism of rights

Rights in the literal sense (that is, positive as opposed
to 'moral' rights) involve an essential reference to the
presence or absence of societal rules, that is, rules
concerning human interactions which are accepted as
authoritative within a social group. Not every societal
rule has to do with rights. Some social obligations (such
as the duty to vote) can be analysed without reference to
anyone's correlative rights, and there are many liberties
and immunities which, because of their lack of relevance
to the interests of those who possess them, we would not
normally think of as rights. Chapter 5 takes up the question of what sort of rules generate or constitute rights.
The prior question, dealt with in this chapter, is whether
any sort of rule-following would be part of a socialist
way of life. This requires a survey of the variety of
purposes served by societal rules. Once we are satisfied
that these purposes feature amongst socialist objectives
and that rules are necessary for their successful pursuit,
then we can turn to the relationship between socialist
societal rules and the concept of rights.

FORMAL JUSTICE

Before examining utilitarian or instrumental reasons for
having societal rules we must first take up the legalistic
criticism of rights in its strongest form which is directed
against pure legalism, a doctrine which can be designated
pejoratively as 'rule-worship' or 'legal-fetishism'. Pure
legalism is the belief that conformity to societal rules
is intrinsically desirable, an end in itself, which has
sufficient import to justify the creation of rules, and
gives rule-conformity a significance which conflicts with
and perhaps overrides other desirable social objectives.(1)

Pure legalism in its most sweeping form is the view that all aspects of social life ought to be governed by rules and that actions are to be judged good or bad, desirable or undesirable, according as they do or do not conform to pre-existing rules. Thus morality is a matter of following rules embodying community standards and the purpose of law is to ensure general adherence to whatever rules are recognised as binding within a society. (2) The prime values of legalism are adherence to, and the impartial application of, existing authoritative societal rules. Legalism is opposed to the exercise of discretion in the following and applying of rules, actions based on the calculation of consequences, ad hoc adaptations of rules to suit the peculiarities of individuals in situations not covered by the rules, and the creation of new rules to judge the propriety of past behaviour. (3) Its nature is exemplified in those aspects of bureaucratic organisation which require strict adherence to a book of rules rather than assigning an area of discretion to a hierarchy of officials, deontological moralities which emphasise conformity to a set of shared social norms, and in the formal or deductive theory of judicial reasoning according to which the purpose of the courts is the rigid application of general rules to particular circumstances. Legalism appears, therefore, to be the antithesis of the freedom, spontaneity and purposive outlook which many theorists see as hallmarks of socialism. The legalists' devotion to rules rather than to the solution of problems and the furtherance of human welfare seems inhuman and misplaced, hence the designation 'legal-fetishism'.(4)

It is not easy to see why pure legalism should be accepted as a serious doctrine. To anyone - liberal or socialist - with a regard for human freedom it must seem that the subordination of human choice to societal rules always requires further justification. Such plausibility as pure legalism has may derive from the mistaken belief that it is entailed by one or other of two more fundamental and more attractive propositions: first, that rational beings ought to act consistently, and second, that morality requires the moral agent to universalise his or her moral judgments. The idea that rational beings must be consistent, however, does not mean that a rational being must always act in an identical manner in identical situations, as if to throw one stone in the sea commits the rational agent to throwing all similar stones into the sea. (5) Rather, the consistency required of rational beings, in so far as it goes beyond refraining from self-contradiction, is that where there is a reason for acting in a particular manner then that reason must be accepted

as applying to all similar situations. Such requirements,
however, apply solely to the thoughts and behaviour of
the individual and imply no commitment to setting up and
following shared or societal rules for all rational
beings. It may be that, if there are rules which all
rational beings must follow, then they will in practice
conform to the same rules, but they will not do so
because these rules are shared but because they, as
rational beings, hold them to be justified.

Similarly, it is a truism of moral philosophy that if a
person makes the moral judgment that 'X is right' then he
is committed to believing that all Xs are right, and to
doing X whenever the opportunity arises unless there are
other moral reasons which take precedence. This requirement of universalisability is one which all moral beliefs
must satisfy. (6) Universalisability can be expressed by
saying that the moral agent must guide his action by moral
rules or maxims, but it is not the following of rules that
makes his actions right. If it is right for the agent to
keep a particular promise, then it must be right for him
to keep such promises in all similar circumstances; but
this is not because in so doing he will be rule-abiding,
but rather because if it is correct in the first situation to keep his promise then it is a logical consequence
that it is correct to do so in all similar circumstances.
The rule merely expresses the requirement of universalisability. There is no suggestion that the requirement of
universalisability entails a commitment to follow any
rules other than the agent lays down for himself. Indeed,
to follow societal rules simply because they are societal
rules is, in effect, for the moral agent to abdicate his
duty to make up his own mind on moral issues.

There are two less radical forms of pure legalism to
which the socialist must give more detailed attention.
The first is the concept of the rule of law and the second
the idea of formal justice. The doctrine of the rule of
law, which derives from Aristotle, is that government
ought to be through general rules and not by the arbitrary
decision of individuals: the rule of law not the rule of
men. (7) This doctrine takes it for granted that every
society will have a government, but recognises that the
powers of government are often abused. These abuses are
to be limited by restricting governmental power to the
promulgation of general rules which are applied by an
authority independent of both the legislative and executive branches of government and ensuring that the actions
of the executive officers of governments remain within the
parameters laid down by the legislative authority. It is
generally agreed amongst liberal theorists that the rule

of law prevents some abuses and does have the advantage
of treating the citizen as an intelligent person who is
able to conduct his affairs in the light of known rules.
It has even been argued that the rule of law guarantees a
certain minimum moral content to the law. (8) But given
the stress on the control of the abuse of power by political authorities, presupposing as it does both the existence of political power and the tendency of those holding
power to use it for their own ends, the socialist may feel
that the safeguards of the rule of law will be unnecessary
in a socialist society in which there would be either no
government or, if there were a government, one which is in
the hands of genuinely altruistic and trustworthy people
to whom it would be reasonable to give discretionary
powers which they could exercise for the common good in
overriding or ignoring any societal rules that there happen to be. (9) We cannot, therefore, take a view on the
importance which the socialist would attach to the rule of
law until we have determined whether a socialist society
would require binding rules and political authority.

It is possible to give more immediate attention to the
view that pure legalism is a prerequisite of the attainment of formal justice. Analyses of justice often distinguish between material or substantive justice, which
refers to the content of societal rules, and pure or
formal justice, which refers to the impartial and hence
fair application of rules whatever their content. (10)
It is a characteristic argument of legal positivists that
only the latter has any genuine and objective meaningfulness since there can be agreement on what constitutes the
accurate application of a rule but not about the so-
called 'justice' or otherwise of their content. (11) It
is a corollary of this position that the significance of
legal systems is primarily a matter of formal, rather than
material, justice and that the attainment of formal justice in the impartial administration of rules is in itself
a laudable objective.

Such a legalistic idea gets some support from the common assumption that it is just - in Aristotle's terms -
to treat equals equally and unequals unequally. (12) On
this view, where there are rules applied in any degree to
a social group, it is unfair to those who suffer the burdens or do not enjoy the benefits which application of
these rules will produce, if the actual administration of
the rules does not place similar burdens or benefits on
all those who should suffer or enjoy these things according to that rule. Thus, irrespective of the material
justice of a tax regulation, it is said to be unfair if
one person to whom the regulation applies is required to

pay, while another, to whom the regulation also applies, is not required to do so. Or, when one group of employees gain a large increase in wages or salaries it is often assumed that, irrespective of the rights or wrongs of this increase, other similar groups are unfairly treated if they do not receive an equivalent award. The argument is not that if it is right to treat A in a certain manner logically it must be right to treat all other As in a similar manner (universalisability), but that, because one group has been treated in a particular way other similar groups must be treated in the same way. Comparability of this type is grounded in a sense of formal justice.

Pure legalism, interpreted in terms of formal justice, represents an end-point for the positivist's efforts to expunge value judgments from legal analysis whilst retaining the supposition that there is some basis for the belief that justice is the objective of law. It has the advantage of expressing the neutrality of law, and of societal rules in general, as between different policy objectives, the law being a form or mechanism which can be used for an endless variety of social ends. Courts can then be limited to the pursuit of formal rather than material justice. Hence the lawyer's conception of 'natural justice' as the procedural rules which must be followed in the interests of producing a fair in the sense of an accurate and consistent application of legal rules. Thus no one should be a judge in his own case or show partiality to either party in a dispute by taking into account anything other than the relevant rules and the appropriate factual evidence. Accused persons should have notice of any charges and the opportunity to answer them and cross-examine witnesses. (13) These rules of natural justice are sometimes said to be important because they generate support for the decisions made on the part of those involved, particularly of accused persons, (14) but they can also be seen as ways of attempting to make sure that like cases are treated alike and that people receive only what they are entitled to according to the relevant rules. Similar arguments can be used against granting extensive discretionary powers to officials in the distribution of benefits and burdens or at the stages of investigation, prosecution and disposal in criminal law. Although there are many arguments given in favour of the exercise of discretion in these fields - such as the cost involved in subordinating all official actions to the requirement of rules and the lack of flexibility this gives to government administration and the treatment of offenders - it is a recurring theme of liberal commentators that such discretion is contrary to the ideal of

justice - by which they mean formal justice - and should
be kept to a minimum. (15)
   It is perhaps a fine point of moral intuition whether
or not formal justice is significant in itself, but there
are several reasons why a socialist is likely to be less
sympathetic to this ideal than a liberal theorist, and
the emphasis given to formal justice in positivist legal
theory has done much to explain the hostility of socialists to law and rule-governance in general. Formal
justice is an inherently conservative notion and the fact
that it is compatible with extensive real inequalities
and material injustices means that it seems of little
value to those with radical social objectives. A socialist is therefore inclined to regard formal justice as the
quintessence of misplaced social priorities and dehuman-
ised social relationships.
   Certainly, formal justice is in itself a conservative
ideal. (16) This is because rule-change is bound to give
rise to formal injustice as between those who are treated
under the first rule and those who are treated under the
reformed rule. For instance, the murderer executed for
his crime before the abolition of capital punishment
could - if he were around to do so - regard it as unfair
that he should suffer this fate while those guilty of the
same offence at a later date received a lesser penalty.
And the same sort of injustice occurs when rules are made
more burdensome, since those treated under the new rules
suffer more than those who chanced to be in the same
situation at an earlier time. Nor is there any doubt
that formal justice is compatible with great material injustice, such as extreme inequalities of wealth and life
opportunities. Thus the ideal of liberal capitalism that
all men are equal before the law, since it was combined
with laws which were designed to make all equally able to
enter into contracts and to use their resources as they
wished, meant that those with superior wealth and superior
talents were able to achieve positions far above those
whose resources were more limited and whose capacities
were less. If formal justice has any importance to the
socialist it is likely, therefore, to be relatively superficial in contrast to his evaluation of the outcome of the
fair application of the rules in question. If the distributive rules of an authority are substantively unjust,
then it seems to him a matter of trivial importance that
these rules are not consistently applied.
   Nevertheless, there is some evidence that Marx approxi-
mates to the legal positivist's view of justice in refusing to regard the relationships of capitalist society as
unjust. (17) It has been argued that Marx considers that

the concept of justice is relative to the system of production operative in a society at a particular time. This
would mean that there is feudal justice and capitalist
justice and, perhaps, socialist justice. Along with the
positivist, therefore, he considers it absurd to regard
capitalist distribution as in itself unjust. Thus, in
'Capital', when Marx is discussing the idea that the payment of interest on borrowed money is a 'self-evident
principle of natural justice', he argues that an exchange
'is just whenever it corresponds to the mode of production ... unjust whenever it contradicts that mode'. (18)
This passage is certainly in line with his scepticism
about the ideals of justice and in particular the assumption that there are natural principles of justice which
transcend historical epochs. But it is possible to regard
these remarks on the so-called justice of capitalism as in
fact ironic, (19) and it can certainly be argued that they
do not exclude the possibility that where the rules of
distribution are materially just, perhaps in a socialist
society, then formal justice has an important role to play.
We cannot say, therefore, that Marx is definitively
opposed to formal justice as a means for attaining material
justice, but this is, of course, different from the view
that formal justice has an importance independent of the
content of the rules in question.

If legalism is equated with the view that formal justice
is of fundamental social and political value then socialists are not alone in their condemnation of legalism.
Even those most committed to the moral significance of
pure or formal justice never hold it to be an overriding
consideration which renders unacceptable, for instance,
all rule-change, or makes irrelevant any criticism of the
content of rules. A revolutionary socialist critic of
the legalism of rights cannot, therefore, direct his
attacks simply at the ideal of pure formal justice. If he
thinks that this is the core of the liberal notion of justice then in this, and in other matters, he is being mis-
led by the limited horizons of certain legal positivists.
Moreover, the rejection of formal justice as an independent value does not mean that the rigorous adherence to
rules has no instrumental or utilitarian significance. It
may be that there are advantages in general conformity to
societal rules which override the importance of giving to
the individual the ultimate authority to decide how he is
to act in every circumstance. If legalism is taken to encompass adherence to rules for such ulterior purposes
then, even if the socialist denies any intrinsic benefits
to rule-following, he must be able to counter the instrumental arguments before he can dismiss rights because of

their association with legalism. We must therefore turn
to the alleged benefits which are said to flow from the
creation and application of societal rules.

SOCIAL CONTROL

The benefits and drawbacks of formal justice, and hence of
a legalistic approach to rights, are part of the general
assessment of the function of rules in society. In the
remainder of this chapter I shall outline just some of
these functions and relate them to images of a socialist
society. (20)
     If we take the law to be a body of rules prescribing,
prohibiting and licensing certain types of behaviour which
is, by and large, conformed to in the society to which it
applies, then it is clear that a major element in the
evaluation of particular legal systems, and the very idea
of having a legal system at all, must be based on our
evaluation of the types of conduct prescribed, prohibited
or licensed. For instance, if it is the case that acts of
a certain type (say homicide) are in themselves and prior
to the existence of law considered harmful or immoral, then
it is, prima facie, a desirable objective that all such
acts be prohibited. The importance of having a law against
homicide being that this is one way of reducing the number
of such inherently undesirable acts. Looking at the law
in this way is to regard it as a means of social control
designed to maximise the incidence of beneficial acts and
minimise the incidence of harmful ones, or, if this
sounds too question-begging in its utilitarian flavour,
for encouraging desirable acts and discouraging undesirable ones. Rights are particularly germane to this way
of regarding the law because they can be used to define
what it is that is prescribed, prohibited or licensed by
reference to the good or bad effects which actions and
inactions may have on the welfare of others, for the
language of rights serves to select out those interests
which the law is designed to protect and further by its
control of behaviour. Thus all the multiple obligations
which correlate with A's right to the ownership of his
material possessions can be seen as various ways of ensuring that others act or refrain from acting so as to
promote A's retention and enjoyment of these things; A's
right to his possessions may thus be regarded as generat-
ing the correlative obligations in that these obligations
are designed to protect A in the use of his possessions.
Indeed, it is reasonable to argue that, if it is accepted
that the purpose of law is to prevent harm and promote

welfare, there should be no laws which do not protect or
further human interests, thus giving the notion of rights
a position logically prior to that of obligation. (21)

In so far as rules actually do protect interests, this
accounts for the fact that rights, legalistically interpreted, may be valuable possessions of the individual in
that they provide one means whereby his interests may be
furthered. How valuable they are will depend, of course,
on which of his interests are so furthered and this in
turn depends on the content of the rules or laws. But
leaving aside for the moment the content of the law, the
general point is that rules can be seen as an instrument
for reducing the incidence of intrinsically harmful acts
and encouraging the performance of beneficial ones, a
function they fulfil in proportion to the degree of conformity that there is to the requirement of the rule.
(How this conformity is achieved by the law I will consider in the next chapter.) On this view there need be no
virtue in legalism or rule-abidingness per se, although it
is a necessary instrument for maximising behavioural patterns which are in themselves acceptable without reference to further objectives. The utility of legalism on
this view, is its instrumentality in encouraging and discouraging acts which have beneficial or harmful consequences prior to the existence of behaviour-directing
rules.

This justification of rule-governance is vulnerable to
the socialist argument that such forms of control are unnecessary for achieving these objectives since, in the
right social and economic conditions, no rules or laws
will be required to encourage and prevent the types of
behaviour in question. Thus it is often argued by Marxian
socialists that once the causes of human conflict and hostility have been removed by the socialist revolution and
the development of communist society, there will be no
need for laws to direct human behaviour since men's total
endeavours will be directed towards the betterment of
others through co-operative means, at which time men will
be able to dispense with the dehumanising and impersonal
legal ways of regarding and organising human conduct. (22)
This will avoid the unfortunate side-effects of rigid
adherence to rules in cases where the standard consequences do not pertain.

The Marxist view is that the phenomenon of man harming
man is not a product of fixed human nature, but the consequence of economic and hence social circumstances which
will be done away with in the advance to communist society,
in which there will be no need for rules to restrict or
encourage harmful and beneficial activities; the former

will not occur and the latter will be done spontaneously, and for that reason more effectively.

In assessing this argument, we come right up against the problem of projecting ourselves imaginatively into a radically different form of society, a society in which economic scarcity is unknown and intentionally harmful behaviour unheard of, a society in which there is no property, no fear of the other, no desire to impose one's will. We can readily agree that where there is no 'mine' and 'thine' there can be no such thing as theft and where there is no motive to do acts which are manifestly harmful to others there might seem to be no need to have rules forbidding such acts. But we have to consider whether there would be a residue of potentially harmful actions that would require to be kept in check by some regulatory means, and we also have to ask ourselves about the social mechanisms which would feature in the creation and maintenance of this fraternal type of society.

Even assuming that we may discount intentionally harmful acts within the main areas covered by criminal law, it is not within the bounds of reasonable probability to postulate that human beings could have unlearned or instinctive knowledge of the manifold ways in which such complex and developing creatures as men may be harmed and benefited. Moreover, the notion of 'harm' is evaluative as well as descriptive in that what counts as harm depends in part on the view taken of human wholeness or perfection. Even if we simply equate harm with pain then at the very least a socialist society would have to arrange for the study and communication of knowledge about the ways in which pain can be caused in order to teach its members how to avoid harming others. And if 'harm' is broadened to take in all the ways in which men can fall short of an ideal human nature, such as the socialist norm of a fully developed creative and productive self-directed being, then we can readily see how the principle that harm should be minimised must generate a complex set of directives of a technical nature indicating how we should act in order to avoid harming others. These would become even more extensive if we take in ways of benefiting others, as seems appropriate in a community where the mere abstention from harming others seems an overly-limited objective. It is therefore possible to imagine rules against overfeeding children, or doing so much for others that they lose or never gain the capacity to direct their own lives; rules requiring men to meet the special needs of those with psychological and mental deficiencies not evident to the untutored eye; rules indicating methods whereby we can show an interest in the affairs of others without

intruding on their need for solitude. Such rules would
not be there to restrain malicious selfishness, but to
ensure that human good is protected in ways which are not
self-evident to the ordinary benevolent individual.

Moreover, it cannot be assumed that in a socialist
society there would be no mine or thine, no property whatsoever. Once it is allowed that there are some circumstances in which an individual or group has the use of
particular objects, even if this is limited to specified
occasions or purposes, then there must be some rules
which indicate to others that this use is proper and
hence that they should not seek to prevent it and, where
appropriate, should facilitate such uses. Thus if houses
or even beds are allocated to persons for their temporary
use, this requires that these objects 'belong' to certain
individuals for certain periods of time. This may not
involve the extensive property rights which include the
right to buy and sell or to alter the objects possessed
at will, but it does establish a line between 'mine' and
'thine' which must be drawn by rules indicating usage
rights, otherwise there would be no way in which others,
unintentionally or otherwise, could infringe such entitlements to the use of specific objects, and no amount of
good will could prevent interference with entitlements of
which men had no knowledge, even if we could make sense of
such a notion. (23)

Such rules might not, of course, be regarded as instituting rights and would be educative and informative
rather than coercive, but it is not the coerciveness of
rules that is at present under discussion but simply
whether there would be any role for rules within socialism.
We have looked at some specific examples of rules for
which there would be a need even in a benevolent community, but more generally, it is hard to see how the
successful accomplishment of an harmonious socialist
order, in which none harmed the other and all acted in a
maximally beneficial way, could become a reality without
an educational system to develop the potential goodness
in children and bring them up to play a useful part in
community life, and it is difficult to think of such a
system dispensing altogether with behavioural rules. It
is true that children would not be taught to follow rules
for their own sake, but we have seen that the idea of
rule-following as an end in itself is at most a small part
of the justification for having rules and abiding by them,
and the particular function of rule-following which we are
at present discussing (the minimisation of harmful acts
and the maximisation of beneficial ones) would seem to be
of continuing relevance in any society in which men are

not as naturally and instinctively knowledgeable as they
may be assumed to be spontaneously unselfish; although,
again, it is hard to imagine that satisfactory motivation
will not always require more than a nudge from an at
least partly rule-based process of socialisation.

Inevitable limitations in human knowledge, the requirements for educating the young into the way of life of
socialist societies and the need to establish normative
standards of what counts as harm and benefit, plus the
high standards set by socialists for mutual assistance,
would generate in a socialist society rules whose content
might differ from - but whose function would be the same
as - those rules which are at present used to control
human behaviour in order to minimise harm and maximise
benefit. It may be that such rules would not require
rigid adherence in that individuals could be trusted to
interpret them in the light of particular circumstances,
since they would not be liable to use this discretion for
their own benefit. But it would still be the case that
reasons would be required for not following societal rules
and that persons would be subject to criticism where such
deviations resulted in actions detrimental to the goals of
socialism.   Only such very general rules as 'do not
gratuitously harm others' would require universal conformity. More specific directives would tend to be regarded
as rules of thumb rather than absolute requirements. But
as long as the scope of discretion in the application of
rules is limited by the requirement that departures from
them be justified by the ends which the rules in general
are clearly intended to serve, we can say that in a socialist society something like the social control function of
rules would exist. As long as there is the possibility of
acting otherwise than in the best interests of those
affected, then there will be a need for rules by which to
guide these actions. Rules against homicide and the
deliberate infliction of injury might not be required,
except perhaps for educational purposes, but prohibitions
against spreading disease by insanitary habits, unpunctu-
ality, types of carelessness which can result in injury
and prescriptions requiring positive action in seeking out
those who are in trouble and need help in specified circumstances, all these and many more are likely to feature
in a conflict-free society of unselfish but otherwise
human creatures liable to lapse through ignorance, tired-
ness, forgetfulness and inattention. On account of these
same weaknesses, we can assume that conformity to these
guiding rules could not be total so that there would be a
need for an appeal to the rules as a means to correct and
compensate for the harm or absence of benefit caused by

the deviations and to bring about greater conformity in
the future. Uncoercive mutual monitoring and control of
inter-personal behaviour would feature even in a community
of 'brothers' and could not be achieved without a corpus
of societal rules.

ORGANISATIONAL RULES

Regarding the law as a means of minimising or maximising
types of acts which are individually harmful or beneficial
is only one way of approaching the possible benefits of
legalism. Indeed, this is probably not the type of consideration that is most frequently associated with the
justification of legalism. For instance, the benefits of
law can be seen as organisational in that they provide
opportunities for co-operative social behaviour either of
a private or a public nature. It is not just that ensuring a certain uniformity and hence predictability in
behaviour allows the individual to make rational decisions
about how to pursue his own interests, for sharing systems
of rules makes possible new types of joint activities,
either by ensuring that numbers of people act in unison to
achieve objectives which they could not acquire alone
(such as paying taxes to support medical services) or by
developing rules which relate to separate roles within a
complex social activity as in, for instance, the family,
or economic division of labour. Here the point of rule-
following is that it enables the individual to play a part
in a corporate system which could not operate prior to the
existence of rules and whose benefits cannot be described
simply by the incidence of certain individually harmful
or beneficial acts.
    Such a view of the function of law tends to give rise
to an emphasis on duties or obligations, particularly
positive or affirmative obligations, for these indicate
what the individual is to contribute to the co-operative
enterprise. Because the benefits of the system may be
remote from the fulfilment of the individual obligations
on which it depends, they may not obviously correlate with
anyone's rights. This function also explains the importance of the societal and legal powers by means of which
people are able to enter into binding arrangements with
others. The capacities to make gifts, to enter into contracts or to utilise the institution of promising can all
have the effect of facilitating co-operative social
relationships. All these processes involve rights in the
sense of powers, and so the rules which determine how and
when such capacities or powers are being exercised. It is

only on the basis of such rules that actions of different
role-occupants in complex social situations can be
integrated in a purposeful manner and individuals occupy-
ing the same roles can make ad hoc, but not merely transitory, arrangements with each other.

In such situations the benefits of rule-following are
seldom the sum of each individual act of rule-conformity,
rather they depend on a variable but relatively high
degree of adherence to rules since, in systems of any
complexity, non-performance by a small number of those
involved in the whole institutional organisation can
vitiate the entire enterprise, and performance of the
individual's obligations may in itself, in isolation from
the contribution of others, be of no value at all. This
truism of modern factory production applies to relatively
simple systems in all spheres of social co-operation in
which the contributions of a variety of operations carried
out by different individuals are necessary for the functioning of the whole. Football teams as well as armies,
social clubs as well as large-scale educational and political institutions, all require the input of very different forms of human activity which must form part of an
integrated whole if the units are to function well, and
sometimes if they are to function at all. These forms of
human activity are definable in terms of the rules to
which those performing them must adhere, rules which make
it possible for us to assess their activities as done
well or ill, and hence as conforming or not conforming to
that which is expected of them, their obligations.

While not denying that rules are necessary to provide
for co-operation between self-interested individuals, the
socialist may argue that in his society, co-operation will
not be imposed and regulated but will be spontaneous or
natural and hence more intense and intimate. A group
united by strong ties of love and affection will, it is
said, work together without recourse to regulations and
rule-books which generate nothing but conflict, guarantee
only minimal co-operation and are required only when a
spontaneously affectionate relationship has broken down.
In particular, there will be no need for those power-
conferring rules which give some persons authority over
others.

This argument has some force in small groups where the
objectives and methods of co-operation are immediately
obvious and everyone can, without prior principles of
organisation, readily turn to the next job that requires
to be done and call upon the assistance of others when
necessary. (24) But even here it may save much time spent
in discussion and ad hoc arrangements if some general

co-operative principles and rules are adopted. For
instance, it might prove helpful to have a rule that the
person who is first to start a task draws up the plan of
action for accomplishing it, or a rule that a technical
disagreement about what needs to be done next be settled
by a vote of those present or liable to be involved in
the task. The contrary possibility of each deferring to
the views of others gives no way of determining what is to
be done. Moreover, such a willingly co-operative group is
likely to find that it can best further its corporate
ventures and ease the life of each of its members by
adopting the standard conventions of civilised communal
life; in particular, they would surely find it helpful to
have some acknowledged way of coming to agreements either
by way of contract or promising not because they could not
trust each other to do what each thought best for the
group, but because a contract or promise would enable them
to count on the performance of certain actions which might
not otherwise have been done - since they would not necessarily appear to the person concerned to be beneficial -
without some such formal agreement. Even a society of
altruists would need to distinguish between a statement of
intention and the making of a promise. (25) Making a
promise would exclude the promisor from exercising his
own judgment on whether to do the act in question, thus
the promisee would be able to count on the performance of
the act in a way which would not be possible if the matter
was left to the discretion of the other, and this guarantee might enable him to pursue a line of action which is
beneficial to the group but which would not be so if the
act in question was not performed. The benefits of such
institutions as promising are not always reducible to the
self-interest of either party, and they have an application in the joint activities of small as well as large
groups.
   These considerations apply with greater force if we are
thinking, as most socialists do, of large-scale industrialised societies with complex productive and social
mechanisms in which the basis of co-operation must include
established expectations which cannot arise simply from
long experience of each other's ways and characteristics,
particularly where the actions of one person are meant to
harmonise or supplement those of another. Here it is even
less plausible to think of untutored, unguided individuals
being able to contribute to the community's inter-personal
activities, the very sort of activities which are particularly valued by socialists. The vast range of possible
forms of human organisation makes it impossible for there
to be any large-scale co-operative behaviour, either on

the roads, in factories, in group leisure or educational activities, which does not base itself on the common acceptance of shared rules whose content is to some extent arbitrary and could not, therefore, be arrived at by each individual separately, except by chance, and which does not require to be established de novo in each co-operative situation. Socialist ideals which look to some form of social organisation cannot avoid the incorporation of some such notion of rule-following.

At this point the socialist might interject that such mutually acceptable organisational rules would not be imposed from without or forced on an unwilling population. Using the example of conducting an orchestra, Marx accepts that all harmonious co-operation requires a directing authority. (26) But it is possible for such necessary regulation to flow from the nature of the activity itself and as it is not imposed from without, it cannot be compared to the organisation of capitalist society in which the rules are not internal to the process, as is the case when socialists work together to produce the means of subsistence, but are an external imposition based on the private ownership of the means of production. The idea that some rules are imposed from outside a form of activity while others are part-and-parcel of particular activities, as the rules of good composition are to the writing of music or the drawing of a picture, is an interesting and helpful one, especially if it emerges that it is only the former type of rules that are under the cloud of socialist suspicion. If socialism allows for rules which are intrinsic to a process in that they are designed purely to facilitate the operation of that process in accordance with its own norms, for instance good music or efficient farming, and if such rules arise in co-operative ventures, as it would seem they must, and might even legitimate authority-conferring rules, then it becomes clear that the apparent objection to rules in general is not in fact to rules as such, but to irrelevant, oppressive or imposed rules. And if it is established that those involved in harmonious communal enterprises are consciously following rules internal to the enterprise, then the fact that these rules are designed to assist the corporate project and are adhered to willingly by the participants in that venture does nothing to make their behaviour any less rule-governed, or, if we prefer it, rule-guided.

In speaking of rules designed to maximise and minimise acceptable and unacceptable forms of behaviour, I allowed that, in a socialist society, some discretion could be allowed to those following the rules since particular circumstances may make following the rule less conducive to

the welfare of those affected by it than not doing so, a
process which is not fraught with the dangers of self-
serving inconsistency as it would be in a society of
selfish men. But co-operative rules do not allow such
extensive discretion since it is of their essence that
others should be able to count on the rules being followed
in order to make their own contribution to the total process. No doubt there may be occasions when promises may
be broken because the situation has changed to such an
extent that the intended benefit for which the promise
was made could no longer be realised and no harm could
come of ignoring it, but normally the whole point of
obtaining a promise is to ensure that certain acts are
done or not done and this is not achieved by leaving their
performance to the judgment of the individual who has
made the promise. The rules of promising would therefore,
apart from exceptional circumstances, allow only the promisee to nullify the promisor's obligation. More generally,
exceptions to co-operative rule-following would only be by
mutual agreement. Thus the appeal to these rules would be
rather stricter in its force since the use of individual
discretion is by and large excluded. Hence any rights
there may be under such rules (and I will consider later
whether it is appropriate to think of such rules granting
rights) are more firmly established in the sense that they
are less open to modification according to the judgment of
those with the correlative obligations.

We should also note that in the case of co-operative
rules it is often detrimental to the united purposes of
those involved in a joint activity that a participant
should, perhaps through a desire to do more than his share
and thus go beyond merely doing his duty, use his own
initiative to exceed that which the rules require of him,
for this is to introduce an element of unpredictability,
and perhaps of waste, into a situation that requires
accurate foreknowledge of what the other will do. Thus if
I produce more nails for the communal workshop than can be
used by others, or decline to take my right of way when
driving a car, then, however, laudable my motivation, the
results are likely to be detrimental to those whom I seek
to serve. This follows from the fact that such rules are
not essentially designed to obtain a minimum contribution
from antisocial beings, but rather to co-ordinate in the
most productive way the willing contributions of a variety
of different people. In the case of these rules, at any
rate, we may be thinking of devices for enabling altruism
to express itself rather than ways of minimising the harmful effects of selfish actions.

DISTRIBUTIVE PATTERNS

A third and quite distinct justificatory basis for legalism and hence for legalistic rights, is that rules are a
necessary precondition for the attainment of material or
substantive justice or for any patterned distribution of
benefits or burdens. This is an argument used by those
who equate law and justice, both in the formal sense in
which it is said to be just to treat people in accordance
with rules rather than as particular named individuals,
and in the material sense in which what matters is that
these rules be in accordance with some substantive standard
of justice such as merit, contribution, or desert. The
legal pursuit of formal justice, treating like persons
alike irrespective of the nature of the likeness, is,
arguably, as we have seen, an end in itself, and it can
also be justified in a negative way if the alternative is
considered to be unregulated decisions made on each specific occasion which are liable to be random or to reflect
the personal bias of prejudice of the distributor of benefits and burdens. But leaving aside these aspects of formal justice, the impartial application of general rules is,
failing unexplained coincidence or divine intervention,
necessary for substantive justice according to which all
receive that to which they are entitled under a correct
distribution based on criteria such as merit or desert, or
indeed for any patterned distribution. This function of
rules incorporates many of the central areas of social
policy concerning welfare, employment, housing and health
services.
    Logically, such patterned distribution could occur
naturally, that is, without human contrivance. But even
the most laissez-faire theories of society incorporate
some rules whose enforcement is necessary for the outcome
which is desired. (27) And it is safe to conclude that a
tolerably exact patterned distribution can only be
obtained by the use of rules incorporating some reference
to the relevant criteria for describing the pattern in
question; thus the allocation of punishment according to
the degree of moral guilt needs the application of rules
requiring the infliction of punishment in proportion to
types and degrees of guilt. Here formal justice is not of
significance for its own sake, but features because only
strict adherence to such rules can produce the desired
distribution of punishment. Similar considerations apply
in the distribution of rewards according to status, need
or any other quality or property of human beings according
to which an allocation of benefits and burdens may be made.
It therefore appears that, if a society seeks to achieve
a certain distribution of desired goods, legalism may be

justified as a means to achieve this distribution.

The argument from the desirability of achieving certain patterned distributions is not in itself unequivocal in its implications for the significance of strict adherence to the distributive rules. If what matters is the relative distribution, so that, for instance, the more deserving get a greater share than the less deserving, the less deserving a greater share than the undeserving, and so forth, then the rules would have to be applied in every case in order to achieve the desired rank-ordering in the distribution of available benefits; this would be the normal interpretation of the nature of distributive criteria. But it is also possible to think of there being a correct proportion of a given benefit for a person with a certain quantity of a particular characteristic which can be achieved in individual cases without placing all those with varying degrees of the characteristic in a particular rank-ordering. In this less usual interpretation, each application of the distributive rule is of value as an independent contribution towards the total objective of everyone receiving that to which they are entitled, so that there is always a certain advantage in applying the rule to a particular case, as is the case when using rules for the purpose of social control. But in the more normal, relativistic, idea of the appropriate quantity of any desired benefit to which particular types of individuals are entitled, it becomes much more important to apply the rules across the board since a particular application is unlikely in itself to make a positive difference to the desired distributive goal. In this case, the use of rules to achieve patterned distributions is nearer to the all-or-nothing effect we noted in the case of those organisational rules in which the effectiveness of any specific rule-application depends on the general, if not universal, application of the rules of the system.

The third end served by adherence to rules or laws is, then, the achievement of patterned distributions of benefits and burdens. It might be thought that, in a socialist society, there would be no burdens (and hence no need to distribute them), and such abundance that no question would arise as to how desirable goods should be allocated. (28) But this is an extreme view, and one which is particularly implausible since important material goods, such as land and energy, are limited in fact, and certain social goods, like high esteem and decision-making functions, are limited in principle. It can be acknowledged that as burdens and scarcities diminish, distributive rules become less important: where everyone has enough, no one need care about the distribution of the surplus; where the

chores are slight, there is little need to concern oneself
over their allocation. To this extent the prophecy of abundance does undercut this basis of the need for rules. This
is noted by those who claim that socialism is not so much
about distribution as about liberty and the organisation of
production. In this case, we would expect co-operative
rules to feature more than distributive ones in a socialist society.

Many socialists, however, see themselves as involved in
a movement to obtain a better or more just distribution of
attainable goods and unavoidable evils. To this end
socialists sometimes oppose legalism on the grounds that
it interferes with such distributions. Certainly, the
socialist drive for social and economic equality can be
hampered rather than aided by rule-following; thus the
rule-guaranteed liberties of the individual and the rights
of property-owners can inhibit the redistribution of
wealth.

The same sort of point is made from the opposite end of
the political spectrum by those who see the engineering of
social justice as in conflict with the rights of the individual. (29) The argument here is that the attempt to
establish a certain distribution (to each according to his
x or y, where x and y refer to characteristics of the
individual), constant intervention is required in the normal processes of social and economic interactions. This
means that the application of rules to human behaviour,
and hence the guarantee of rights to the individual, is
vitiated by the constant nullification of the outcome of
everyday rule-governed activities by the intervention of
officials who re-allocate legitimately acquired goods in
order to establish some preconceived pattern of distribution. Thus if people are given certain property rights,
including the right to buy and sell, to set up in business, employ others and agree wages with them, this will
inevitably produce a distribution of goods which fits no
pattern because it is the outcome of the exercise of the
rule-governed rights of the participants. To achieve a
patterned distribution it is necessary to take from some
that which they have legitimately gained and to give it
to others who are not entitled to it according to the
rules of the processes in which all freely participated.
Thus the pursuit of patterned distributions is inimical to
legalism for it involves constantly overturning the
results and hence the legitimate expectations of those who
have conducted themselves in accordance with the rules
that apply to their normal activities.

It seems paradoxical when presenting a justification of
societal rules on the grounds that they are necessary for

achieving desired distributions of benefits and burdens
to be faced with the criticism that the pursuit of such
distributions runs up against rule-imposed limitations.
The glib response to this paradox is to say that it is
merely a conflict between rules with differing contents
and not between having and not having rules. Thus property rules allowing individuals to use their possessions
to produce commodities may lead to inequality, and if
rules requiring redistribution simply return the situation
to its original equality (assuming all start out with
equal amounts of property) then the process seems pointless. But it can be argued that any conflict there may
be between property rules and distributive rules can
readily be solved in a socialist way by rescinding the
property rules and reorganising productive and distributive processes on lines which do not give rise to
inequality.

However, the paradox goes deeper than this. It is a
manifestation of a more pervasive tension between two ways
of looking at rules, one which sees them as essentially
telling the individual what he may or may not do in the
pursuit of his own objectives and the other as directing
him as to how to contribute to a certain outcome or end-
state. On the former model, the idea of rules (and
hence also of rights) is to safeguard certain interests of
the individual and then leave him free to direct his
actions as he pleases. On the latter model, rules are
designed to direct the individual to goals that are at
once personal and social in that they enable him to make
his distinctive contribution to the general welfare. If
the socialist has to choose between these models he will
opt for the latter, and is likely to incorporate an
acceptable distributive pattern as part of his conception
of the general welfare. This will involve giving end-
state distributive rules priority where they conflict with
the outcome of ordinary behavioural rules. But since most
ordinary behavioural rules will be designed to facilitate
the achievement of end-states embodying the application
of distributive rules, such conflicts would not have the
persistent and intractable nature of clashes between individual rights and social welfare in capitalist systems.
Those socialists who share the laissez-faire liberal's
distrust of distributive rules are unable to present us
with a convincing picture of how a desirable ordering of
benefits and burdens will occur. The metaphysically minded
liberal can appeal to the concept of the natural harmony of
interests or the workings of the 'invisible hand' of God or
social evolution, but no such recourse is readily available
to a socialist theorist.

CONCLUSION

I have not, in this chapter, covered all of the many different functions of societal rules. For instance, I have
largely omitted the use of power-conferring rules to grant
authority to assigned individuals to play leading roles in
social organisation, particularly in the creation of rules
through legislation. This will be touched on in chapter 8.
I have also put to one side the utility of rules in the
resolution of disagreements arising in the course of
social interactions. A primary requirement of social life
when confronted by such disagreements is for procedural
rules laying down how disputes are to be brought to the
point where they can be treated as settled, allowing normal interaction to continue. Even where the decision procedure adopted is dependent on the outcome of physical
combat or on some form of lottery, there is a need for
rules to set the format of the battle or indicate the
winner in a determination by chance. Only in the most
extreme state of nature could literal physical submission
be the standard means for settling disputes. Where the
authority for adjudicating in matters which seriously
divide members of a social group is vested in individuals
or officers, then some rule-governed mode of selection
and signification of authoritative decisions will be
required, even if no elaborate rules are necessary to
guide the decisions of such persons or officers.
    This function of societal rules might well be con-
sidered a candidate for extinction, assuming a socialist
system in which there would be no serious disputes requiring to be settled by outside intervention. Compromise
and mutual accommodation should be adequate to deal with
any disagreements that might arise once class antagonisms
no longer sour human relationships. This is, however, to
assume that all disagreements are disputes about conflicts
arising from the interactions of self-interested individuals. But, given the other functions of rules outlined
above, it is inevitable that even where there are no
fiercely contended conflicts of opinion or clashes of incompatible interests between which arbitrary choices have
to be made, there is still room for differences of view on
the creation, interpretation and application of societal
rules. If only for reasons of efficiency, there is a need
for standard ways of resolving such divergencies of opinion. Moreover, the seriousness of a dispute need not be
measured in terms of the private interest involved. Citizens of a socialist society might be expected to treat with
gravity and care any differences they might have as to the
ends and methods of their co-operative activities. The

disputes might be different in content from those arising
in non-socialist societies, but the significance attached
to their resolution would still be sufficient to call into
play agreed methods of coping with them. The resolution
of disputes could therefore be added to the list of types
of societal rule which would survive, albeit in a transformed fashion, within socialism.

Having considered, then, the independent claims of
formal justice and some instrumental reasons for creating
and sustaining societal rules, I will now take it as
established that altruists in a conflict-free society
require societal rules for social control, for organisational purposes, for long-term co-operative agreements,
for bringing about the patterned distribution of benefits
and burdens, probably also for the settlement of disagreements and, perhaps, as we shall see, for the allocation and operation of political authority. At least some
of these objectives (particularly in the sphere of social
co-operation) would require withholding from the individual the discretion to decide whether or not to follow
established societal rules. The implications for the idea
of socialist rights of the existence of such rules in a
socialist society will be explored in chapter 5. First,
it is necessary to tackle directly the allegation of the
intrinsic coerciveness of societal rules which is at the
heart of the radical socialist's rejection of rights.

4   The coerciveness of rights

However much the socialist critic of rights may soften towards the idea that some types of rule might serve a useful function in a socialist community, he still has to
overcome what is perhaps his most fundamental difficulty
with right-conferring rules, namely their coercive back-
ing. (1) Rules which establish rights also, typically,
impose obligations and obligations, where these arise
from positive rules, rest ultimately, it is argued, on
force or coercion. This may in itself be sufficient to
harden a socialist theorist towards rule-based social
relationships and set him implacably against any form of
society involving the right-obligation nexus, leaving room
only for the rights of formal liberty which require only
the absence of rules and which are not the sort of rights
for which there is any compelling justification in a non-
competitive harmonious society.

The connection between rights and coercion is most
evident in the case of legal rights for which the correlative obligations are underwritten by the physical
strength of coercive state agencies such as the police and
the armed forces, but it can also be said to hold for non-
legal rights which rest on the lesser sanctions in which
societal obligations terminate: the pressures of neighbourhood attitudes and public opinion generally, authoritative or manipulative educational methods and even the
unthinking inertia of unexamined habits. Add to this the
'sanctions' of the individual's conscience and it is possible to see all rights as part of forced or at least
pressured social relationships which radical socialists
assume will cease to exist once capitalism is gone and
the private ownership of the means of production no longer
spawns the conflicts which require to be held in check by
physical and psychological pressures. Whatever, therefore, may be said in principle in favour of rule-governed

institutions or practices, it is, for such socialists, a
regressive step to envisage right-conferring rules as
operating within the freedom of socialism since, it is
argued, these must inevitably bring with them that element
of coercion which is the major dehumanising factor in non-
socialist systems.

The most obvious and direct response to the rejection
of rights on the grounds that they are at base coercive
would be to cast doubt on the socialist belief in the
eventual disappearance of conflict and uncompromisable
disagreements between men, but we are not engaged in a
general overview of socialism and its evaluation but in
studying the theoretical compatability of rights and
socialism. For this purpose I have posited a society in
which there are no radical or insurmountable differences
and clashes of interest. Having seen that in these circumstance there would still be good reasons for having
rules of behaviour, I can now address the question of
whether rules must bring coercion with them as the sting
in the tail of an otherwise welcome animal. This takes us
again into the realm of analytical jurisprudence, for it
is there that we find argued the existence of a conceptual
connection between obligation and coercion. This sanction
theory of obligation was the standard view of positivists
at the time when Marx wrote and still remains in a variety
of guises to make a theoretical bedfellow for this particular socialist criticism of rights. My objective in this
chapter is to cast doubt on the logical tightness of the
alleged tie between rights and coercive sanctions as the
next step in undermining the assumption that rights would
not survive the demise of social conflict.

OBLIGATIONS AND SANCTIONS

Coercive theories of legal obligations and, along with
them, coercive theories of obligation in general arose
within positivistic analyses in which the existence of
law is sharply distinguished from its possible moral justification. They are therefore part of that sort of analytical jurisprudence which attempts to state the fundamental internal conceptual relations of the basic ideas
which enable us to speak of law and legal systems in
essentially empirical terms. Stemming from Hobbes, (2)
this approach to the study of law was conducted in terms
of the imperative theory according to which a law is a
command of a sovereign, the person whose commands are
obeyed by the vast bulk of the population in a given
geographical area. It is then assumed that such

obedience would not be forthcoming without the use and the threat of the use of force against those who fail or are tempted to fail to comply with the sovereign's commands. Hence the connection betweem law and coercion: a law is a general command enforced, ultimately by physical means, within a given territory.

The clearest statement of this view is to be found in the work of Bentham, who holds that a legal obligation is 'a command, express or virtual, together with punishment appointed for breach of it'. (3) More generally, Bentham regards a duty as an act the non-performance of which is likely (or, sometimes, liable) to lead to the infliction of a sanction on the non-performer. The best-known exposition of the sanction theory is that of John Austin, whose theory of law is summarised in the dictum that 'laws are orders backed by threats'. (4) Thus a law is said to be 'a rule laid down for the guidance of an intelligent being by an intelligent being having power over him', (5) power being the capacity to inflict evil on another. Both of these founders of modern analytical jurisprudence place this conception of legal obligation within a wider theory of obligation according to which all obligations are analytically linked to the application of sanctions for non-performance, the various types of obligation - such as religious, political (or legal) and moral obligation - being distinguished from each other by the type of sanction used. For instance, in Bentham's scheme, divine punishments are the basis of religious laws and religious obligation, while public opinion is the sanction for moral obligations. (6) He also has the unusual idea of natural obligations as those arising from the unpleasant consequences which occur without any human intervention from acts which are in themselves dangerous. (7) To this J.S. Mill added the idea that moral obligations are grounded in what he called the internal sanction of duty, or conscience, which he described as 'a feeling in our own mind; a pain, more or less intense, attendant on violation of duty', (8) thus giving us a way in which to distinguish between customary or societal morality, which is based on public opinion, and the individual's own morality, which is founded in the feelings of his conscience, without stepping outside the bounds of a sanctions theory. According to Mill: (9)

> We do not call anything wrong, unless we mean to imply
> that a person ought to be punished in some way or other
> for doing it; if not by law, by the opinion of his
> fellow-creatures; if not by opinion, by the reproaches
> of his own conscience.... It is part of the notion of
> Duty in all its forms, that a person may rightfully be
> compelled to fulfil it.

The attraction for positivists of this approach to the notion of obligation is that they are able to appeal to observable or at least experiential phenomena to account for a concept which seemed to emanate from the realm of a priori reason, intuition or revelation, and therefore to lie outside the scope of empiricist methodology and the bounds of empiricist ontology, and at the same time, accord with the canons of good scientific theory by using a single concept (that of a sanction) to explain all the different types of obligation. Its defect is that it appears to confuse obligation with the sanctions which may or may not be used to bring about compliance with obligations or express disapproval of their violation. This is most obvious in the case of moral obligation, for a person's judgment that he (morally) ought to do X (if it is his own autonomous judgment and not just his observation that according to the mores of his society he ought to do X) may run counter to any feelings of guilt or shame that he may have about not doing X. This is not to say that men do not have such feelings, but that it is possible to distinguish them from that person's judgment that he ought to do X and so, in terms of critical or autonomous morality, the judgment that he has an obligation to do X. If it is true that A has a moral obligation to do X, then it is appropriate that he feel guilty if he does not do X, but this does not reduce the concept of moral obligation to the actual or hypothetical occurrence of guilt feelings, for to make sense of the claim that A ought to feel guilty if and only if he is guilty, we have to establish a meaning for 'A is guilty' in a manner which does not incorporate a reference to whether or not A has any guilty feelings, otherwise we simply have the rather odd, and certainly functionless, semi-tautology that A ought to feel guilty if A does feel guilty.

In fact, it is clear that Mill does not use the occurrence of guilt feelings as a criterion of moral obligation, for his thesis is that we do not call anything a violation of a moral obligation unless we believe that it ought to be punished - if only by the pangs of conscience. He has, in fact, another way of determining whether an act is morally obligatory by appealing to the principle of utility: 'actions are right in proportion as they tend to promote happiness, wrong as they tend to produce the reverse of happiness'. (10) Distinguishing criteria of rightness and wrongness from the meaning of right and wrong, we may say that utility provides the criterion of moral rightness but that what we mean when we call an act wrong is that it ought to be punished. But something has gone badly askew here, for we must be able to ask why an act ought to be punished, and if this is a moral question, we should be able to answer that it ought to be punished because it is a violation of a moral obligation. And yet in Mill's terms, this could only be a tautology.

Moreover, to state that A, if guilty, ought to feel the pangs of conscience, is plausible primarily as a statement about the logical appropriateness of such feelings. This is apparent if we think of similar arguments that are put forward to the effect that a person's guilt feelings are misplaced if he is not, in fact, guilty. This is because we think of conscience in its psychological aspects as a support or motivational force which helps the individual to follow his moral judgments in practice and need not serve as the ultimate criterion for the correctness of those judgments. We may, of course, think it right and proper that immoral acts be punished by feelings of remorse and guilt and that morally good actions ought to be rewarded by the internal satisfactions of the clear conscience. But this is to go beyond the claim that such feelings are appropriate, in that it is irrational to have such feelings unless one is guilty, to a substantive moral judgment concerning the proper type and degree of punishment (or reward) that ought to follow upon immoral (or moral) actions. In the latter case, the distinction between the obligation and feelings of conscience is even clearer because conscience is being viewed not as a criterion of whether or not a person has an obligation, but simply as a source of pains and pleasure which may or may not be annexed to the non-fulfilment or fulfilment of moral obligations. And so, while it is hard to deny that feelings of guilt are appropriate if and only if the person concerned is in fact guilty, it is an open moral question whether or not it is desirable that people be punished and rewarded by the occurrence of such feelings. It is therefore implausible as a claim about the meaning of moral obligation to say that A has a moral obligation if, and only if, it is right that he be punished by the pangs of conscience if he acts or does not act in a certain manner. (11)

It is easier to show in the case of morality that sanctions and obligations are conceptually distinct than it is to show that societal and legal sanctions can be separated from societal and legal obligations, but essentially the same form of argument holds. In the case of the mores of a society, it is true that a criterion for the existence of societal rules is that certain types of action or inaction are subjected to criticism from others; if that criticism involves the claim that a generally recognised rule has been broken, then we can say that an individual has broken a societal obligation; if there is no such

criticism, or the criticism involves no implicit or explicit reference to a societal rule, then it is descriptively
incorrect to say that a societal obligation has been violated. But this is not to say that the criticism
expressed is to be regarded as a sanction. Criticism may
be voiced as a form of punishment, since it is known that
people do not like to be criticised, but it need not be.
It is a meaningful act to criticise someone's behaviour
because one believes it to be a violation of a rule without intending, or while explicitly denying, that that criticism is a punishment. And in those cases where criticism is intended as a punishment, it is coherent and
indeed plausible to argue that such punishment (or some
other punishment) is justified by the fact that a societal
obligation has been broken. And it is not incoherent to
argue that violation of societal obligations should not be
met by any punishment. It is mistaken to argue that since
criticism is always painful it is always a punishment,
since this would mean counting as punishment every humanly
mediated unpleasant consequence of wrongdoing.

The alternative view to regarding social criticism as
punishment is to say that social critics are expressing
their view that the actions in questions are wrong either
because they violate a societal rule or because they violate the personal moral rules of the critic. It is not a
particularly mysterious business that people should express such criticism for its own sake or because they believe that societal rules ought to be kept, or because
they approve of the particular societal rule. They may,
of course, express criticism in order to alter behaviour,
in which case such criticism can be regarded as a utilitarian form of punishment, but they must, logically, be
able to justify such punishment by saying that the offender is an offender, that is that he has broken a societal
obligation, and this statement is not itself a punishment.

The same is true of legal obligations, for they also
can be distinguished from the legal sanction which may or
may not be used to enforce them and whose infliction is
legally and perhaps morally justified by reference to the
broken obligation. If punishment is the infliction of
pain on an offender because he is an offender, then a
person's liability to punishment may be justified by the
fact that he is an offender, but his being an offender is
not to be equated with his liability to punishment.
Offences must be defined before we can speak of inflicting
pain on an offender, and an offender is, by definition,
someone who has broken a legal obligation.

We arrive at the same conclusion by considering how
to analyse the behaviour of a citizen who obeys the law

and does so because he believes that he has a moral duty
to do so. No calculation of the punishment that he might
incur if he breaks the law enters into his decision to
abide by it, nor does any judgment about the morality of
that particular law. He obeys simply because he knows
that it is a law and he believes that he ought to obey all
laws irrespective of their content. We may say of such a
person that he believes that he morally ought to fulfil
his legal obligations. Sanction theorists, with the possible exception of Austin, do not deny that such cases
occur, but they hold that legal obligations are identified as those actions whose non-fulfilment renders the
individual liable to punishment. But is it intelligible
to think of our 'moral' citizen having a belief that he
morally ought to abide by those rules which he will be
punished for breaking? This would indeed be a bizarre
moral belief. It must therefore be the case that he at
least does not operate with the sanctions definition of
law.

The distinction between an obligation and the sanction
supporting or encouraging the fulfilment of that obligation is, by and large, so clear and so necessary to give
substantive meaning to so many common beliefs about the
law (such as that it is right to punish people who violate the law) that it could only be the attraction of
having a simple theory which fits in with a certain
(empiricist) methodology and particular theses about
human motivation that can adequately explain its popu-
larity and persistence, particularly after the demise of
the imperative theory of law and its replacement by
normative theories according to which law is essentially
a system of norms laying down what people ought to do or
are required to do. Sanction theories of legal and other
types of obligation fit readily into command theories of
law, for commands, orders, threats and punishments are
all easily conceived of as the activities of a powerful
person or group directed towards getting other weaker
persons and groups to conform to their wishes. Yet while
command or imperative theories of law have been subjected
to prolonged and devastating criticism, sanction theories
of obligation remain in modified forms in the writings of
many legal theorists such as H.L.A. Hart and Hans Kelsen.
Why this should be so is a question of interest in itself
and of great significance for our inquiry into the logical
possibility of the idea of uncoercive law. For if law is
no longer considered as commands of a sovereign, but as a
set of behavioural norms, why should it still be insisted
that legal norms involve an essential reference to coercion? It is easy to see that it is readily believable

that since laws apply to all those living in a certain
territory some of them will not be universally obeyed and
may not even be widely obeyed unless legal norms are
backed by coercive sanctions, but this is an empirical
claim which cannot be made unless we can distinguish between legal norms and the sanctions which may be used to
back them up. If this empirical point is all that remains
of the sanctions theory, then it can be argued that in a
different type of society laws would be either universally or tolerably well obeyed without the use of coercion. Socialists project a type of society in which many
of the sociological 'truisms' about existing societies do
not apply, therefore no empirical claim about the necessity for law to be supported by sanctions can be used to
argue that this must be so in a society which has attained
socialism. I will argue that this is a conclusion which
can be drawn from Hart's analysis of a legal system, but
first consideration must be given to the less tractable
and still highly influential theories of Kelsen who, far
from loosening the connection between law and coercion,
has propounded a theory of the nature of legal norms which
not only maintains but develops the logical thesis of the
essential coerciveness of law. Kelsen himself explicitly
acknowledges that his theory implies that in the type of
socialist society predicted by Marx law would lose its
legal character. (12)

KELSEN'S PURE THEORY

Law is, for Kelsen, a coercive order, not because laws
are orders backed by force but because laws are orders to
use force. These orders are addressed not to the ordinary
citizen, but to the officials whose task it is to inflict
sanctions on those who act or do not act in specified ways.
A law is thus essentially a sanction-stipulating norm.
Coercion is necessary to law not because obedience to it
must be achieved through the psychological pressure of
threats, but because the content of laws is such as to
prescribe a penalty for certain types of behaviour, the
delict: (13)

> The law is not, as Austin formulates, a rule 'enforced'
> by a specific authority but rather a norm which pro-
> vides a specific measure of coercion as sanction.
> The law is a decree of a measure of coercion, a sanc-
> tion, for that conduct called 'illegal', a delict....
> This conduct has the character of a delict because and
> only because it is a condition of a sanction.

There can be no question, then, of a non-coercive law,

since it is not that a sanction is authorised in the
event of an offence or delict, but rather that an action
is a delict if a sanction is authorised for its non-
performance.

On examination, it is apparent that Kelsen echoes many
of Austin's tenets in a modified form, but he differs from
Austin in holding that laws are norms, that is, prescriptions of the form 'A ought to do X' rather than imperatives
tives (although he constantly uses imperatival language and
and holds that imperatives may be norms if they are part
of a valid legal system). A norm is a rule forbidding,
prescribing (or, perhaps, permitting) (14) certain behaviour; such rules establish duties or obligations. Like
Austin, Kelsen holds that all obligations involve sanctions
although he agrees that conformity to norms may arise
from a variety of motives and indicates that it is
the function of sociology, not of the science or 'pure'
theory of law, to study the causes of conformity and non-
conformity. So, while his definition of the law as a
normative order and his efforts to separate questions of
what the law is from questions about why it is obeyed
could be used in a non-coercive theory of law, by assuming
that all obligations must be sanctioned and that coercion
is part of the content of each legal norm, he operates
with the tightest possible connection between law and coercion. What he calls the primary norms of law are by
definition laws which are addressed to officials laying
down the sanctions they can impose if the so-called
secondary norms addressed to the individual citizen are
not complied with: (15)

> The Pure Theory of Law is only drawing an obvious con-
> clusion when it formulates the rules of law (using the
> term in a descriptive sense) as a hypothetical judge-
> ment, in which the delict appears as an essential con-
> dition, the sanction as the consequences. The sense in
> which condition and consequence are connected in the
> legal norm is that of 'ought'. If one steals, he ought
> to be punished, if one does not make good tortious
> damage, civil execution ought to be issued against him.
> In this way the science of law describes the relations
> which the legal norm, issued by the legal authority,
> establishes between delict and sanction. It is pre-
> cisely by establishing this relation that the legal
> norm imposes duties and confers rights upon the indi-
> viduals subject to the law.

Kelsen defends this theory of law as a coercive order by a
variety of routes, some short, some long. None of them is
without difficulty and some reveal major confusions of the
type that he himself set out to avoid.

Kelsen's shortest and most direct justificatory route
is an appeal to the ordinary meaning of the word 'law':
(16)

> What is the law as an object of a particular science?
> Proceed from certain usage in language ... the usual
> meaning of the word by which its object is designated.
> One must see whether the social phenomena termed 'law'
> present a characteristic in common distinguishing them
> from other social phenomena - a characteristic suf-
> ficiently significant to constitute a general concept
> for the rational understanding of social life. If the
> Pure Theory of Law assumes that coercion is an essen-
> tial element of law, it does so because a careful
> examination of the social orders termed 'law' in the
> history of mankind shows that these social orders, in
> spite of their great differences, present one common
> element, an element of great importance in social life:
> they all prescribe coercive acts as sanctions ...
> [this is] the meaning of the term 'law' in the history
> of mankind.

This argument rests on the essentially empirical claim
that all known systems of law involve coercion, a claim
that it is not necessary to dispute but which, if established, is insufficient to demonstrate that this is a
conceptually necessary matter or one which follows from
the existence of legal systems in societies as we know
them. It may be, for instance, that we can think of legal
systems as bodies of rules which require universal
adherence from those to whom they apply, in that it is
part of the meaning of 'law' that the individual is not
permitted to opt out of following such rules because, for
instance, he does not wish to do so, or because he thinks
the law to be morally objectionable. If law is a non-
optional system of rules whose raison d'être is to establish regular and predictable patterns of behaviour, then
in a situation in which some people are not willing to
conform to the law it may be necessary to use coercion in
order for the law to fulfil its various functions and so
to be law. It may also be that in using coercion it is
deploying a method which it does not normally permit to
be used in enforcing non-legal rules, and to this extent
coercion can be picked out as characteristic in the sense
of being unique to the law. As an empirical claim, this
can be called into question without appealing to the existence of non-coercive international law or the 'legal'
systems of primitive societies. Many educational and
economic systems as well as organised games permit a measure of force to be used, as is the case, of course, in
many types of criminal organisations. If it is replied

that the former cases the state authorises the use of force, this is to allow that force is legitimately used in non-legal systems, and if it is then asserted that what is unique to the state is that it alone may authorise the use of force, then, of course, force is far from the only thing that a sovereign state alone may authorise (levying taxes is another for instance) so that force is hardly the unique characteristic for defining the nature of law that it was set up to be.

In fact Kelsen's appeal to the past history of legal systems does not establish what ordinary usage as distinct from the traditional definitions of legal theory would develop to describe a 'legal' system in which the element of coercion had disappeared and the 'compulsory' norms were obeyed because citizens appreciate the need for conformity to authoritatively determined common rules. And, perhaps recognising this, Kelsen falls back on the sociological claims that the law is a 'specific social technique', that is, one which uses coercive rules to alter human behaviour. This is why coercion is 'a characteristic sufficiently significant to constitute a general concept for the rational understanding of social life'. (17) Thus, despite his claim to have depsychologised Austin and his admission that law remains law even if the motives for compliance are not psychological pressure, he appears in effect to be assuming that coercion is the major legal method and that this somehow explains why laws are sanction-prescribing norms: (18)

> Positive law ... is an order by which human conduct is regulated in a specific way. The regulation is accomplished by provisions which set forth how men ought to act. Such provisions are called norms and either arise from custom, as do the norms of the common law, or are enacted by conscious acts of certain organs aiming to create law, as a legislature acting in its law-making capacity.

This seems to raise the possibility of defining legal norms according to their sources or origins, but later on in the same essay he makes clear that behind his dogmatic claim that legal norms are sanction stipulating lies a sociological view of the nature and function of law: (19)

> Looked at from the sociological point of view, the essential characteristic of law, by which it is distinguished from all other social mechanisms, is the fact that it seeks to bring about socially desired conduct by acting against contrary socially undesired conduct - the delict - with a sanction which the individual involved will deem an evil.

True, he goes on to add that analytic jurisprudence is not

concerned with the exploration of the causal forces at
work here or with how successful law is as a social technique, but the belief that it is essentially a correct
sociological view must lie behind his confidence that the
science of law can take as a datum that legal norms are
sanction-stipulating. In other words, he is expressing an
Austinian theory of law which only makes sense on Austinian
assumptions about human motivation. He may not himself be
engaging in the sociology of politics (as he calls the
discussion of value questions about the law) but he is
certainly assuming a social-psychological theory according
to which the systems commonly called legal systems are at
core techniques for controlling behaviour through the use
and threat of use of force. The form of law is as it is
because the techniques of law are what they are. Why
otherwise would laws be best 'represented' as sanction-
stipulating norms? What if the vast bulk of a population
does not commit any delicts without any fear of sanctions –
a possibility which Kelsen allows in particular cases?
Would the 'primary' element in legal norms not then become
redundant and why then would he stick to it as the defining feature of law? Such lines of thought do not appear
to concern him, perhaps because he is confident of the
soundness of what he calls the sociological view of law,
namely that law operates by what he calls psychic coercion.
    Yet this theory is not intrinsically more sociological
than the theory that explains majority law-abidingness in
terms of non-sanctioned self-interest (that is, calculations of self-interest which do not incorporate reference to
possible sanctions), rationally applied benevolence, or
moral conviction. And if it is indeed the case that laws
are often obeyed for such reasons, this would explain –
assuming some sort of 'fit' between the logic of legal
norms and the social context in which they operate – why
so many existing laws do not readily assimilate to Kelsen's scheme. For instance, the laws stipulating that
officials ought to enforce sanctions given the occurrence
of a delict are not themselves sanctioned.
    Kelsen's theory is not, therefore, so 'pure' as he
might like it to be since it seems to rest on a possibly
false sociological theory of law. He cannot, therefore,
allow for a different representation of law more in accord
either with actual or projected social systems. The same
point comes out in the crucial concept of effectiveness
which Kelsen uses to bridge the gap between the normative-
ness of laws and observable conformity to them. Kelsen
argues, intelligibly enough if we consider some of the
rationales for having laws which were outlined in the previous chapter, that laws oblige only in so far as the

system of law of which they are a part is effective.   He
himself presents this as a presupposition of legal science
(that is the process of coming to know what the legal
norms are), but it is more plausible to argue that the
norm 'obey only if the law is part of an effective legal
system' is a fundamental norm within the law. We can see
why this might be so if at least some of the benefits of
law come only if there is general compliance. It is far
from clear that this is a norm within law rather than a
moral norm indicating the limits of our moral obligation
to obey it, but assuming that it is a fundamental legal
norm, in itself it implies nothing in particular about the
coerciveness of the law. Yet Kelsen simply goes on to
assume that effectiveness could not exist if it were not
for the application of coercion, so that the connection
between coercion and effectiveness makes it intelligible
that legal norms are sanction-stipulating. Here, as
elsewhere in Kelsen's work, it is hard to see why he
reaches the Austinian conclusions he so often endorses
without assuming Austinian utilitarian behavioural theory.

Kelsen avoids the direct challenges as to why sanction-
stipulating is the primary type of legal norm by claiming
that his task is confined to exhibiting the nature of
validity in law, not examining the sociological basis of
its effectiveness. It is in his account of legal validity that Kelsen makes his major contribution to legal
theory, but his thesis on the coerciveness of law is in
principle separable from his theory of legal validity
since although validity, as we shall see, may presuppose
the effectiveness of a legal system, effectiveness, as we
have already seen, does not logically require coercion,
and Kelsen's account of law as a hierarchy of norms does
not require that the content of those norms always be
sanction-stipulating. This is not clear in Kelsen's system because of his tendency - despite his protestations
to the contrary - (20) to coalesce the validity, the obligation and the existence of law:

By 'validity' we mean the specific existence of norms.
To say that a norm is valid, is to say that we assume
its existence or - what amounts to the same thing - we
assume that it has 'binding force' for those whose behaviour it regulates. Rules of law, if valid, are
norms. They are, to be more precise, norms stipulating
sanctions. (21)

Validity of law means that the legal norms are binding,
that men ought to behave as the legal norms prescribe,
that men ought to obey and apply the legal norms. (22)
Here and elsewhere Kelsen makes it appear that the

existence of a norm depends on its validity and its validity makes it obligatory, but these concepts can be prised apart and hence the connection of validity and bindingness with coercion, which is made through the notion that effectiveness is required for the existence of law, can be broken.

Validity as applied to law on the model of authority ascribing norms expounded by Kelsen means that the ground-level norms are valid if they have the authorisation of a higher norm according to which the secondary norms are recognised as being laws. Ordinary legal norms which are valid are so in relation to the constitutional norms from which the 'valid' norms may, given certain facts, be deduced. Thus if the constitutional norm is that Acts of Parliament are laws, then, given that we know how a particular rule originated, we can tell whether or not it is valid law within that system. On such matters judges may be called upon to give a ruling, a phenomenon which is most evident in the function of the Supreme Court of the United States of America when it decides whether or not a putative law is constitutional and hence valid law. Legal science then presupposes a basic norm requiring adherence to the constitutional norms. This basic norm is not itself valid because it does not follow from, or is not validated by, any higher norms, hence legal systems as a whole are not valid. One system of norms is not, therefore, any more or less valid than any other system

Why should this illuminating but rather limited notion of validity be linked to legal obligation? It cannot simply be that the content of a legally valid norm is an ought statement as this is true of all norms including legally invalid ones; rather it seems to be that no norm is binding within a legal system unless it is part of that legal system and that if a person is in some way committed to acknowledging or accepting a given legal system, then its valid norms and only its valid norms are binding on him. In other words, legal validity cannot be equated with legal bindingness or obligation except in the sense that it is part of the meaning of law that a law obliges those to whom it applies in a descriptive sense; hence a 'valid' law can be analysed as imposing a 'valid' obligation, but this means only that according to that law certain persons are obliged to behave in such and such a manner. (23) That is what laws mean: they state or prescribe that certain types of person have certain obligations, a valid law is therefore legally binding in the sense that a person cannot accept that law without accepting that it obliges the persons to whom its prescriptions are directed. But this is true of any system of law

whether or not it is actually adopted or followed in any
society and hence in this sense exists. We can speak of
such obligations, as of legal validity, in relation to
entirely imaginary systems of law for, in so far as the
notion of obligation depends on that of validity, the
validity presupposed may exist only on paper or in the
mind of the deviser.

But Kelsen obviously means something more than this by
legal obligation since he insists that the individual is
not legally obliged to obey a non-existent legal system or
one that is only partly existent in that it is only partly
complied with. Why is this? Perhaps because no purely
theoretical set of hierarchical norms could actually bind
anyone since it is part of the content of such norms that
certain procedures have to be followed in the recognition
of making of law and these procedures will not have been
gone through in a purely paper system. But let us assume
that this hurdle is overcome perhaps because our hypothetical system refers in its basic norms to some practices which already exist independently of the existence
or non-existence of that legal system (e.g. that any commands uttered by the oldest person alive are to be
regarded as laws). We now have valid norms in relation
to no doubt crude but in some sense existing systems. In
the only acceptable sense in which validity gives rise to
obligation the orders of the oldest person create obligations; if the system of law in question is accepted, then
those to whom the 'valid' laws are addressed have a legal
obligation to obey them.

This is to accept that Kelsen is right to connect legal
validity and legal obligation (although there is a problem about the obligation to obey the system as a whole)
provided that the legal obligation in question is regarded
as being purely descriptive. Within a given system certain persons can correctly be said to have obligations
without implying that there is any reason why such persons
should fulfil these obligations; or, alternatively, we may
say that these obligations are prescriptive only from the
'internal' point of view, that is in the eyes of someone
who accepts that system of law. (24) But this does not
connect with another common meaning of 'legal obligation',
namely, the idea that people have obligations to obey the
law in a sense which goes beyond the tautology that
according to the law they ought to do what the law
requires of them. This idea of legal obligation which
concerns our extra-legal obligation to obey laws is more
often referred to as political obligation since it raises
politically relevant moral questions about our obligation
to obey particular laws or whole systems of laws. To this

question the notion of legal validity has connection only in that it is needed to say what a legal system is and hence to explicate the nature of the system of which we may ask as a matter of political obligation whether we ought to conform to its dictates.

Kelsen's explicit position is that he is confining himself to legal obligation in the narrow or first sense and eschewing questions of political obligation or our extra-legal obligation to obey laws, but in fact it is clearly to the political question that he addresses himself when he puts forward the normative principle that a person is obliged to obey valid laws only if they are effective, that is, generally obeyed by those to whom they are addressed. True, he masks this by confining validity to those systems which are effective, but there is nothing in the notion of validity as he expounds it to justify this move; we can readily distinguish between valid and non-valid legal systems that do not exist in the sense that they are not efficacious. What he appears to be saying is that we are not really obliged to obey a law unless it is part of a system (so that we are able to distinguish valid from invalid laws in terms of the basic norms of that system) and it is generally obeyed or efficacious. This seems a sound moral point if the purposes of law include those outlined in the previous chapter, and a sound political principle when considering post-revolutionary situations, but it is hardly to be wished on the content of every genuinely legal system as if, from the internal point of view, a legal system presents purely hypothetical obligations of the form: do this if most other people do so as well. Kelsen himself only speaks of this normative principle of efficaciousness as being presupposed by legal science, but this is a mysterious claim, quite different from the claim that a basic or ground norm must be presupposed in any system of law, for while it is plausible to claim that we cannot in the end make sense of legal validity without erecting some idea of a hierarchy of norms with, perhaps, one single norm at the peak, there is no difficulty in making sense of the idea of a legal system or a legal science without the normative principle of effectiveness. What we cannot conceive of is actual people accepting legal obligations if the systems in question are not largely efficacious, but that is a different, and sociological-cum-psychological, point outside the scope of the pure theory.

It is only through the extra-legal principle of efficaciousness that Kelsen can link the existence of legal systems on the ground with the notion of legal obligation and legal validity, for when he gets as far as efficaciousness

he can draw on his prior assumption that law requires
coercion and so in a sense is coercive. Hence the coerciveness of law seems to follow as part of his concepts
of validity and legal obligation. But if the concepts of
validity and of legal obligation in the narrow sense have
meaning and application to systems which are not effective
and so do not in Kelsen's word 'exist', then we are able
to accept the insights of his presentation of law as a
normative system without accepting that the content of
these norms must, if they are to be legal norms, stipulate
sanctions.

   To see that this can be done, consider the fact that we
are able to speak intelligibly of the validity or lack of
validity of a norm under a system which has ceased to
exist or which we are contemplating the prospect of putting into effect, or the norms of a legal system that is
in the process of being overthrown by a political revolution. We can distinguish between valid and invalid laws
simply from knowledge of the secondary or constitutional
norms and information about the processes by which
allegedly valid norms have come or will come about. Of
course, there cannot actually be any valid norms, if the
constitutional norms specify law-making processes, unless
these law-making processes have been carried out, so in
that sense there can be no valid laws without certain historical happenings, but these historical happenings do not
amount to 'efficacious' in Kelsen's sense since there is
no requirement that the laws once made should be obeyed.
And so, although validity is dependent on some constitu-
tionally proper historical events taking place, this does
not make validity part of efficaciousness and we can
meaningfully talk of a valid law in a non-efficacious
system, just as we can speak of the legal obligations of a
system to which nobody conforms. This is not the sort of
legal obligation that in itself generates any reasons for
action since it is possible to note the legal obligations
under a particular system but deny that the mere fact that
they are obligations in terms of that system gives any
grounds whatsoever for conforming to that system. All
this will depend, as Kelsen sometimes admits, on your
point of view, be it that of a participant, a communist
critic, an anarchist or a professor of law. This will be
particularly evident in non-efficacious systems, but it
applies to efficacious ones as well unless one presupposes the non-legal principle that a person ought (morally
or prudentially), and therefore has reasons, to conform to
a system of law widely followed in the geographical area
where he happens to be. In other words the sort of bindingness that Kelsen gets out of his concept of a legal

system as a hierarchy of norms is logically independent of
the existence of that system and is not able of itself to
establish bindingness in anything other than a hypothetical or descriptive legal sense.

Of course, the premise that in the case of general non-
compliance the laws of a system are no longer legally
binding may be included in a legal system, (25) but it is
hardly a necessary part of a legal system. Kelsen's view
is that this premise is presupposed by the idea of the
validity of norms but his argument does not establish
this. All he can demonstrate is that there is no point in
following the dictates of a legal system if it is not
generally adhered to, but this rests on an assessment of
the purpose of legal science, and the awareness that the
benefits of law follow only when there is general compliance, and a moral or prudential judgment concerning the
desirability of bringing about these benefits.

The same point can be made clear by considering Kelsen's favourite example of the contrast between a valid
legal obligation and the sanctioned command of an armed
robber. The latter threatens, the former is entitled to
threaten, the meaning of the entitlement being that the
command is validated by a sanction-stipulating norm in a
hierarchy of norms. This explains how we can speak of
validity in one context but not in the other. But Kelsen
seems to think that we can do more than this and somehow
legitimise the law but not the robber on the basis of the
validity of the law. But validity means no more than
being in conformity with constitutional norms and, unless
we introduce a supposition of the extra-legal 'validity' or
justification of these norms validity is not sufficient to
make the legal commands of an official in any way morally
superior to the illegal commands of the robber. (26)

If we drive a wedge in this way between the legal
validity and the obligation to obey the law in any except
a descriptive sense in which valid norms are synonymous
with valid ought statements, and allocate the principle
that one is obliged to obey only efficacious systems to
the realm of morals or, for Kelsen, politics, then, even
if efficaciousness is assumed to require, in the strictest
logical sense of 'require', coercion, legal validity can
be explicated without reference to coercion and hence the
idea of a legal system does not necessarily bring with it
the assumption that such systems must always involve an
element of coercion.

I have dwelt long enough on Kelsen's system to demonstrate the confusion between the internal conceptual relations of any legal system in which we can speak of legal
validity and legal obligation in the non-moral and

non-political sense, on the one hand, and the allegedly
necessary sociological conditions for the existence of a
legal system on the other. It is pure conceptual dogmatism to assume that the two are necessarily related. In
fact no purely analytical study of the law can demonstrate
its coerciveness. Certainly, Kelsen's pure theory does
not in itself give us any reason to endorse the sociological assumptions with which he starts out. Whether or not
law is coercive can thus be seen as essentially a sociological dispute concerning the possibility of a non-
coercive society. And since socialists of the radical
sort are committed to the idea that such a society is
possible, they at least cannot use the sociological thesis
on the relation between law and coercion to argue that law
always will be coercive.

H.L.A. HART'S CONCEPT OF LAW

Within Hart's system, which is similar in many respects to
Kelsen's Pure Theory, basic conceptual moves are made
which clear the way for a non-coercive theory of law.
Hart's distinction between being obligated (that is, being
under a legal obligation) and being obliged (that is,
forced or coerced), the former depending on the existence
of a valid legal norm and the latter simply on threatened
sanctions, frees in principle the idea of law from that of
coercive sanctions and so enables us to speculate, without
logical impropriety, on the possibility of an effective
system of law which does not use force and perhaps does
not inflict any painful consequences on those who break
the law. (27) Indeed, Hart allows that this situation is
approximated to in the case of officials whose 'internal'
attitude to the law involves the acceptance of second
order rules as valid non-sanctioned obligations. And,
presumably, if officials can act in this way, then
ordinary citizens may also do so, obeying the law because
they recognise the first order rules as valid and because
they have an attitude of respect towards valid norms.
Hart assumes, because of certain 'truisms' about human
nature, that some violations of valid laws are inevitable
and argues that if these violations are not met by sanctions then benefits of law will be lost. Hence there is a
'natural necessity' for the use of organised sanctions, at
least in municipal legal systems. (28) But if we are
speculating about a form of society to which these truisms
do not apply, we need not accept either that there must be
significant violations or that, if there are, these must
be met by sanctions. From the point of view of logical

analysis, the most that can be insisted is that violations must be noted and criticised, although this need not be so in each and every case, for it is not part of the idea of the violation of a rule that this violation always be criticised.

As Hart's criticisms of Austin's imperative theory (29) and his treatment of international law as a sanctionless legal order (30) make clear, his conception of law has the advantage of limiting the role of sanctions in law to marking the existence of legal obligations and encouraging compliance with them. Hart analyses law as a system of rules or behavioural norms amongst which he distinguishes between primary or first order rules, directed towards the regulation of the behaviour of the ordinary citizen, and secondary or second order rules, which determine the validity of primary rules. These second order rules lay down who has the power to make first order ones. They may thus be regarded as constitutional rules in that they relate to the processes of making law, but they are wider than that in that they also incorporate norms as to how the question of what rules are primary rules is to be decided. Thus a primary rule is a norm of conduct indicating how persons are required to behave, e.g. 'no citizen ought to steal', and it is a law of a given system if it is recognised as such by reference to the secondary rules of that system. Second order rules are of various types, some relating to how new laws are made, others how existing laws may be annulled, and others setting out the procedures for authoritative identification of the laws of the system, but what makes them second order is that they do not apply directly to the behaviour of ordinary citizens but feature in the 'recognition' of the laws that do. (31)

Hart's view of the law as a union of primary and secondary rules has been enormously influential and is very effective at meeting the standard objections lodged against imperatival versions of positivism. It enables the positivist to give sense to the idea of the legitimacy or validity of primary rules as those recognised by the secondary rules of the system. And the existence of such valid primary rules establishes a meaning for the idea of legal obligations as those actions or inactions required by valid primary rules. Moreover, in itself this idea of legal obligation involves no reference to sanctions or coercion and we therefore seem to have a normative theory of law which could serve as the basis for a non-coercive legal theory. The validity of obligations established by primary rules does not appear to depend on the existence of coercion, and the obligations of officials to apply

the second order rules need not be sanctioned either. As
Hart says, officials and citizens may have an internal
relationship to rules, that is, they may have an attitude
of critical acceptance of first and second order norms.
    Nevertheless, Hart does not follow out the logic of his
position by relegating coercion to the status of a purely
contingent extra-legal support for legal systems. His
positivism leads him to assert, quite correctly, that for
a rule or a system of rules to be valid in a given terri-
torial area it must be generally obeyed within that area.
No positivist can accept that a law which was not acknowledged as law in the sense of being effective in guiding
behaviour, really is law. To exist as a legal system, a
set of rules must be efficacious and only when a system
exists does it generate obligations. This means that
officials must routinely follow the second order rules and
the rules they recognise must be widely followed. No reference to coercion is involved so far. But Hart has to
allow that in existing systems conformity is incomplete.
He therefore adds to the requirement of general conformity that the minority of non-conforming acts must be met
by some form of official reaction. This is where reference to sanctions comes in. Violations must be met by the
application of sanctions, or, in the case of non-legal
social obligations, deviations must meet with serious critical reactions which are seen to be justified by the
fact of the deviation. All this is assumed to be a necessary element in all legal system, hence the spectre of
coercion does not seem to have been fully exorcised from
the notion of legal obligation and hence from rights, for
a legal obligation remains analysed partly in terms of the
efficacy of the system of which it is a part and this
efficacy apparently requires that violations of obligations are standardly met by the use of some type of sanction. So, although we have come a long way from cruder
versions of sanction theories, the conceptual connection
has not been entirely severed if non-compliance must be
met with coercion. There is, however, no need to make
this empirical condition for the efficacy of a legal system. Once it is allowed that some individuals obey laws
because they regard legal duties as a species of moral
obligation (the obligation being to obey those rules which
are adopted as non-optional according to recognised procedures), then there is no reason why this should not hold
for all individuals. And even if conformity to law is not
universal in a society, it is not at all clear that, were
a small number of deliberate violations of these rules to
be marked by no more than social criticism, this would
mean that a system of rules loses its legal character. In

practice it may be that violations have never, in the
past, been kept within reasonable bounds without coercive
measures but the radical socialist's hope is that the
future will not resemble the past in this respect. Hart
provides us with no definitive conceptual vetoes on
cherishing the ideal of a non-coercive legal order and in
fact provides us with the conceptual apparatus required to
anatomise its operations and distinguish it clearly from
custom and morality.

NON-COERCIVE JURAL AGENCIES

It can be argued that in the unlikely event of the emergence of a non-coercive society there would be societal
rules but not laws. Such a conceptual dogma has little
basis in standard attitudes to existing legal systems. If
we are positing a system in which there are clear 'second
order' rules, that is, legislative procedures for creating
binding rules and various judicial and administrative
agencies for authoritatively applying the rules in disputed cases, then we have a system which is far closer to
existing legal systems than to any set of societal rules
which lack such explicit logical structures and jural
agencies. The absence of a coercive agency to see to the
enforcement of decisions and the administration of punishment is, however striking, a marginal difference compared
with the basic logical and institutional similarities between coercive and non-coercive 'legal' systems. If there
were a system of rules, both primary and secondary, applying to and generally followed in a given geographical area
and involving the standard legislative and judicial agencies with the exception of a police force and a prison
service with the authority to use force, then it is far
less misleading to speak of a no doubt untypical legal
system than a system of societal norms. (32)
    What we may take from the suggestion that non-coercive
'laws' are really just societal rules is that the sanctions of these so-called laws are of a non-coercive sort,
in that they do not involve the use or threat of physical
force and perhaps not even the threat of economic or other
loss. The attraction of this conceptual move is that we
could then discuss what to put into the void created by
the withdrawal of coercion from legal systems. In a non-
coercive legal system instead of the arrest of unco-
operative offenders and their forced punishment there
would remain only such 'sanctions' as the loss of benefits
previously conferred by social agencies and fellow citizens, or perhaps only exposure to criticism and

exhortation, and this not for the purpose of inflicting suffering on the guilty (either for its own sake or for deterrence), but merely to persuade them that they ought to change their ways irrespective of whether or not their future behaviour will lead them to 'suffer' further criticism. This accords nicely with theories sometimes put forward in socialist countries that their systems of law rely less on punishment and more on education and persuasion. (33) Whether or not such claims reflect actual legal realities in these countries does not affect the argument as to whether or not, were such a situation to be realised, we would cease to have a recognisable legal system. It would be odd indeed to claim that the more coercion deployed in support of a system of law, the more legal or law-like that system is and similarly, the reduction of the incidence of physical enforcement of laws to vanishing point seems an arbitraty stage at which to refuse to call a system of primary and secondary rules a legal system.

There is no doubt that, given the reasons outlined in the previous chapter for having rules, there will be a need for some sort of procedure in any rule-governed society for monitoring the degree of conformity to certain rules and taking measures to minimise any non-conformity there may be and rectify any damage caused by it. Thus, if the object of having rules is to prevent harm which would otherwise occur and promote co-operative activities which would not otherwise take place, this means that behaviour which conforms to these rules does not always take place 'naturally', that is, without efforts being made to see that they are followed. At the very least it is necessary for those whose actions are meant to be rule-governed to be made aware of the rules and to have some reason or motive to follow them. On the Austinian view, this means that the individual must be aware not only of the rule but of the unpleasant consequences that will follow upon his breaking it. But this follows only if the dubious utilitarian behavioural theory of psychological egoism is accepted. If we allow the possibility of a prior desire or moral conviction motivating the individual to refrain from harming his fellows and prompting him to look for ways of benefiting others, it may be sufficient for the individual to be made aware of the consequences of conformity to rules for human welfare for him to have a sufficient motive to abide by rules which do have these beneficial consequences. And if it is the case that obligation-imposing rules are to some extent restrictions, in that they are incompatible with other things that those obliged might wish to do, so that conformity to rules is a

cost incurred for the sake of benefiting others, then
there may also be a sense of the unfairness of an individual failing to fulfil his obligations in a situation
where others are conforming. Thus, given that those
affected have grasped the idea of legal obligation, that
is, the point of having non-optional rules, and have a
desire or moral commitment to the objectives which these
rules serve and a sense of the immorality, both in terms
of unfairness and of harm done or benefits not attained,
of failing to play their part in the co-operative effort,
we can conceive of people conforming to behavioural norms
without being coerced, where these are norms to which they
would not have consistently conformed unless rules had
been made known to them and their function or purpose explained and understood.
     Even so, complete conformity is not to be expected un-
less we discount the normal human frailties of inattention, carelessness, forgetfulness, lack of foresight and
sustained energy, any or all of which may explain failure
to abide by rules without recourse to the explanation of
selfishness or the preference of the individual for his
own interests over those of others. We do not need to
resort to ideas of egoism and ill-will to explain all
failures in rule-following. As long as there are intellectual, psychological and physical weaknesses in human
nature, there will never be complete adherence to a set of
rules requiring any degree of care and effort on the part
of those to whom they apply. Such lapses are bound to
detract from the advantages of rule-following, especially
where the benefits require the participation of large
numbers of people in co-operative processes, and in order
to minimise and prevent recurrences and where possible put
right the damage done, agencies will be required to record
them, rectify any remediable ill-effects which resulted
from them and endeavour to prevent recurrences. We can
therefore envisage a role in every complex society for
monitoring, rectifying and preventative agencies. Monitoring agencies would be concerned with the identification
of breaches of the rules, establishing the facts about
each alleged breach and examining the consequences of such
as are proved to have occurred. In this their function
would be similar to that of the investigative activities
of police forces and the role of the courts in deciding
whether or not the law has been broken. Rectifying agencies would have the task of putting right, where possible,
any damage that is shown by the monitoring agencies to
have occurred and taking ad hoc steps to make the best of
the resultant situation in the light of the objectives of
the rules. This would, to an extent, be similar to the

functions of the courts in civil cases where non-
punitive damages are awarded in order to return the situation to the status quo ante, or compensatory payments are
made to those who have been harmed as a result of the un-
lawful acts of others.   Finally, preventative agencies
would be concerned with endeavouring to ensure that the
same or similar persons do not violate the rules in future.
This may involve no more than drawing the violation to the
offender's attention, but it could include a variety of
educational measures designed to show the offender or
others in his situation the damage done by non-conformity
and perhaps seeking to awaken a partly dormant moral
sensibility.

    Some such agencies would be an inevitable part of any
rule-based society to which the reasons given for having
rules apply, and their existence could conceivably take
the place of coercion and perhaps of all sanctions in the
functioning of legal systems.   Indeed, it is not difficult
to make a convincing case for the claim that they apply to
a large extent in most existing legal systems since sanctions are by no means the sole motivating force affecting
the law-abidingness of most individuals in non-socialist
systems of law.   Socialists might contradict this by saying that willing or 'moral' conformity to law in such
societies is the result of false consciousness imposed by
the ruling ideology of their society so that 'willing'
behaviour is in an important sense coerced since men are
not free to change their attitudes in the light of a correct apprehension of their social and economic situation.
But if we either deny that this apparently willing conformity to law is based on false consciousness or hold
that it is misleading to extend the idea of coercion so
as to make ignorance coercive, then the move from existing
legal systems to genuinely socialist ones is simply a
matter of degree.   Moreover, the argument that law and
coercion are separable concepts does not depend on
establishing whether or not legal conformity in non-
socialist countries which is not literally coerced is in
fact the outcome of societally induced repression of
individual awareness and freedom of choice.

5 The individualism of rights

Significant progress has been made towards securing a place for rights within the socialist ideal if I have established that to endorse the institution of rights is not necessarily to commit oneself to the view that the rules which are logically inseparable from rights need be coercive or authoritarian. But this is not yet sufficient to justify the claim that there would be rights in a socialist society. For, although there cannot be rights without societal rules, there may be societal rules which are unconnected with rights. Not all behavioural directives or authoritative requirements for human action can be interpreted plausibly as involving the rights of others. While it can be argued that every right correlates with some obligation to respect that right, (1) it is much less convincing to say that every obligation correlates with a right. A socialist may, therefore, contend that the rules of a socialist society will offer authoritative guidance as to how citizens should act in furtherance of social objectives, and may even place obligations on the members of society, but insist that these obligations will not correlate with the rights of individuals. This would make duty, not rights, the essential concept of socialist community life. (2)

The rationale for stressing obligations and excluding rights is rooted in the third aspect of the socialist critique of rights: rights are to be rejected because they are an integral part of liberal individualism, the central ideology of capitalism. Rights, it is argued, are only of importance to those who are seeking to protect their self-interest against the predations of others; they express the ground-rules of a type of society which consists of isolated or atomic individuals in perpetual conflict with each other in a struggle for wealth and domination. Selfishness, competitiveness, acquisitiveness – these are

83

the characteristics of capitalist man. The function of
rights is to legitimise and regulate conflicts between
such individuals. (3)

This attack on the individualism of rights is supported
by an analysis of the language of rights: people 'stand
on' their rights, 'insist' on their rights and enforce
their rights against others, all of which appear to be
self-regarding activities. (4) The close tie between a
person's rights and his self-interest is also said to be
reflected in the moral assumption that, whilst for someone
to waive his rights is praiseworthy and to violate the
rights of others is blameworthy, for him to insist on his
rights is neither praiseworthy nor blameworthy. This is
explained by pointing out that although unselfishness is
generally admired and excessive selfishness blamed, a certain degree of self-interested behaviour is regarded as
blameless. For the same reason, a person is said to be
imprudent but not immoral if he fails to exercise his
rights, but he is reprehended if he infringes the rights of
others. This makes sense in a content of authorised competitiveness carried on within authorised bounds. The language of rights expresses these authorisations. In particular, liberty-rights provide the justification for right-
bearers'pursuing their own interests while the claim-
rights of others mark the boundaries of legitimate self-
interest. To remove this context is, it is argued, to
remove the meaningfulness of rights. (5)

There is an immediate plausibility in this perspective
on rights, but it is possible that the association of
rights and competitive individualism is a contingent feature which serves to distinguish capitalist from socialist
rights. Clearly, we would expect that in a society of
self-centred persons attitudes to rights would be ungener-
ous and grasping. But this does not establish that pos-
sessive and selfish attitudes are presupposed by the
institution of rights. Altruists might be expected to
take a very different attitude to their rights. Nevertheless, it is clear that rights do have a close connection
with individualism if only because they characteristically
belong to individuals and all relate in some way to those
aspects of rule-governed behaviour which centre on benefiting specific persons. What needs to be argued by the reformist is that this does not necessarily embroil rights
in the sort of individualism which accepts or glorifies
conflict between selfish and self-sufficient persons.

From the point of view of the logic of rights, a crucial
issue here is the interpretation of what it is for an obligation to be 'owed to' another person, for it is the
notion of an obligation being owed to the person with the

correlative right that enables us to distinguish those obligation-imposing rules which do correlate with rights from those which do not. Therefore, it is through the analysis of what it is for B to owe to A the fulfilment of an obligation that we can explore the nature of the connection between rights and individual interests.

CONTRACT AND POWER THEORIES OF RIGHTS

I shall discuss three competing theories of what it is that marks off those obligations which are owed to other people (the right-bearers) from other obligations. According to the contract theory, only those obligations which can be construed as arising from promises or contracts create rights. In contrast, the power or will theory is that right-correlating obligations are those which subordinate the will of the obliged person to the will or legal power of another. Lastly, the interest theory is that a right exists when an obligation is directed towards and grounded in the satisfaction or protection of the interests of another person, the right-holder. In this section I argue that the first two theories are inadequate even within the assumptions of liberal theory and in the next section it is contended that there is a form of the interest theory which is both in itself a more satisfactory theory and also the only theory congruent with the moral and sociological assumptions of the socialist ideal.

A paradigm example of a right is one arising from a promise, and by extending the notion of promising there have been erected contractual theories of rights which explicate what it is for an obligation to be owed to A by saying that a right arises from an agreement or contract in which another person B binds himself by giving his word to A, often in exchange for some reciprocal commitment; A, as the promisee or contractee, is the person to whom the obligation is owed, the person who has the right that B do or refrain from doing something in relation to the object of the right. The obligation is owed to A because B has made his promise to A, in consequence of which A has the right that B fulfil his commitment, but may, if he chooses, release B from his obligation. (6)

Although the notion of promising is itself problematic, it would be foolish to deny the attraction of the contractual approach to the understanding of rights, particularly when discussing justificatory theories about what rights people ought to have, or to underestimate the subtle developments of the crude theory outlined above to take in tacit and hypothetical promises. But simply as an attempt

to say what we mean by an obligation being owed to A, the
right-holder, it is clearly inadequate, if only because we
can readily understand and make clear what it is for A to
have a right without invoking the concept of promising or
contracting. The right of the hungry to be fed, the right
of children to be educated, the right of a citizen to a
fair trial in respect of any charge brought against him –
all these make no essential reference to a prior promise-
like commitment on the part of those with the relevant
correlative obligations: they may be claimed, asserted,
upheld and in general understood without involving the
notion of contract in any way, yet they are just as much
rights as the rights of any promisee. The contract theory
seems particularly inapplicable to liberty-rights,
although it is common to avoid this difficulty by taking a
natural law position on the right to liberty and a con-
tractarian position on obligations which diminish liberty
by establishing correlative positive rights. (7)

Of course, the enactment or adoption of a rule or law
laying obligations on B towards A could be regarded as a
promise or understanding given to A, but since the
authority which initiates the rule is not necessarily the
locus of the obligation established, it is not clear how
this alleged or tacit promise explains the relation between B and A. Thus when a government enacts a law which
obliges B to do X for A, the promise, if there is one, is
made by the state and not by B and so, on this theory,
A's right is against the state not against B, so that we
have not explained what it is for B to owe the obligation
to A.

To reject the contract theory as explaining the very
nature of what it is to have a right is not necessarily to
adopt the view that there are 'natural' rights which exist
prior to the establishment of 'conventional' ones, for it
may be that there are non-contractual positive laws which
confer rights. In fact, the notion that all rights must
originate in contracts can be cited as an example of the
sort of individualism to which socialist theorists object.
(8) The idea that we have no obligation to our fellow
creatures except those that we have voluntarily agreed to
take upon ourselves, presupposing as it does that the
individual is an independent being who has an existence
and self-sufficiency in abstraction from his social relationships, is totally opposed to the socialist concept of
man as a social creature whose being is closely involved
in the lives of others at a level of integration far
deeper than that of the relatively superficial institutions of promising and contracting. While revolutionary
socialists may, therefore, seize on the contract theory to

demonstrate the unsocialist nature of rights, it is not a
theory which has strong socialist credentials.

The second standard solution to the problem of expli-
cating what it is for B's obligation to be owed to A, the
right-holder, is the 'will' or 'power' theory, according
to which A has a right only if there is a rule that makes
A's choice or will pre-eminent over the actions or will of
others in certain specified ways and circumstances. On
this theory to have a right is to be able to require
others to act or refrain from acting in a certain way so
that A is to be in a position to determine by his choice
how B shall act and in this way limit B's freedom of
choice. (9) The obligations correlative to rights are
owed to those persons who have the legal or quasi-legal
power to require that obligation to be fulfilled. Thus
only when there is an identifiable person A who can
require B to act in certain ways and have at his discretion whether or not so to require B's action or inaction can we speak of rights. Rights are discretionary
powers; powers of a legal or quasi-legal type which the
holders may or may not deploy as they wish. To have a
right is to be able to require the correlative obligation
or to waive it, hence we speak of B having an obligation
to A.

The power theory has the advantage of having a straightforward positivist content which enables us to determine
who has a right by consulting the relevant laws or rules
rather than by inquiring into alleged past events, such as
contracts (although such inquiries will be germane to
establishing whether particular contractual rights exist).
It also has the advantage that it enables us to distinguish clearly between analysing and justifying rights.
Further, it has to its credit the capacity to explain a
good deal of the standard language of rights, in particular the notion of waiving rights, but also the vast array
of ways in which we speak of claiming rights, insisting
upon, demanding, standing on, neglecting, exercising,
defending and using rights, all of which accord with the
idea of the right-holder having discretion over the use
of legal-type powers over others. In this respect, it
explains why rights are regarded as valuable possessions,
for rights can be used to defend ourselves and carry out
our wishes in a variety of circumstances, should we choose
to do so; they are all gain and no loss. (10)

We can also use this idea of rights as discretionary
powers over the actions of others to develop a positivist
interpretation of rights by describing the practices
characteristically used to enforce rights, the procedures
for settling disputes about the existence and

interpretation of the relevant rules and the use of
enforcement agencies to require the fulfilment of such
obligations as the right-holders legitimately demand.
The right-holder is then seen as the person who has the
legal standing which enables him to raise an action to
compel the conformity of B to the rule in question or, in
the case of social rights, to call on the forces of public
opinion in his support. Thus we can see how particular
rights are part of a wider institution or practice of
rights with recognised ways of claiming, assessing and, if
appropriate, requiring the fulfilment of correlative
obligations or obtaining compensation for non-fulfilment
of obligations, all initiated by the acts of the right-
holder and directed towards the satisfaction of his claims
as established by the relevant authorities.

It is, however, even more obvious in the case of the
power theory than in the case of the contract theory that
such an interpretation of the nature of rights is too narrow to encompass all rights. There are rights for which
there are no capacities on the part of the right-holder
either to claim or to waive his rights. Even excluding
the rights of animals as being too controversial, we must
allow the rights of children, of the mentally retarded and
of the aged. Indeed, in general we would not want to exclude the idea of rights of the powerless, including the
legally powerless who cannot activate the legal or public
processes on their own behalf, or make demands and waive
obligations; beings who do not have the will to possess
the sort of rights which accord with the power theory. (11)

Now it is, of course, possible for rights to be enforced or waived on the behalf of right-holders, so it
might be argued that the idea of a right as a power is
thus extendable to all rights. What is it to say that
children have rights other than to say that specified persons have the legal power to compel the actions of others
with respect to children? But this would mean that children's rights concern children but are not owed to them,
for, on the theory under consideration, the essence of a
right is the power of demand and waiver. If we separate
the right-holder and the right-waiver (who we may call the
administrator of the right) so that to have a right it is
not necessary to have the power of claiming and waiving,
then it becomes a contingent fact about rights that the
right-holder is normally the person who may either insist
or not insist on his rights. In this case it is quite
clear that when we speak of the correlative obligation
being owed to A we are not simply indicating that A has
this discretionary power over B, for we still say that the
obligations of parents are owed to their children even

when the discretionary power of enforcement is lodged else-elsewhere, perhaps in the state. Generalising this point, the thesis that A can choose whether or not to exercise a right presupposes that this right is something which can be described and analysed in isolation from A's legal cap-acity to exercise the right. Moreover, it makes perfect sense to say that A does not have the right to waive his right, indicating that the power of waiver is additional to, and may be separated from, the right itself. It would appear that the power theory is still in the shadow of the contract theory for it is in connection with promises and contracts that we normally assume a power of waiver on the part of the promisee or contractee.

For the reformist, the power theory is equally suspect from the point of view of ideological neutrality, since it has the implication that we should cease to think of the rights of those who have no capacity to make demands on others and limit the distribution of these valuable com-modities to beings with rational wills capable of com-prehending and involving themselves in quasi-legal pro-cedures: the possessions of the intelligent, informed autonomous beings of the sort who make good entrepreneurs and lawyers. And it is the power theory which most fre-quently serves to explain the revolutionary's doubts about rights. Thus Hirst minimises the significance of rights for socialism on the grounds that rights exemplify an area of claim and counter-claim. (12) In this he is only fol-lowing Kelsen's thesis that a right (in the technical sense of a type of legal power conferred by a legal order to raise a suit for the execution of a sanction) is a 'specific technique' of the capitalist legal order 'inso-far as this order guarantees the institution of private property and considers especially individual rights'. (13)

In fact, both the contract and the power theories of rights can be regarded as bourgeois theories in that they emphasise the legal role of the autonomous individual who has purely external and voluntary relations with other similar individuals entered into and maintained on the initiative of those involved. This model has particular relevance to the commercial exchanges which occur within capitalist societies where each individual, from the eco-nomic and legal points of view, is an independent owner of property (including the property he has in his own labour power), free to enter into any commercial trans-action he chooses, transactions enforceable at the behest of those with whom he has contracted. Contract and power theories of rights are, on this view, a theoretical ex-pression of bourgeois society in which the role of each individual as a property owner is that of a subject of

rights. The idea of the rights of the individual, by
which is meant primarily the equal right of all to buy and
sell their labour and their products, is thus a feature
of capitalism but not of the feudalism which preceded
capitalism or the socialism which will supersede it.
This is why the bourgeois revolutions of the eighteenth
century championed the rights of man and why these same
rights will cease to be relevant in post-capitalist
society. (14)

The influential Soviet legal theorist E.B. Pashukanis
(1891-1937) applies this theory of individual rights to
the entire 'form of law', arguing that all legal (as distinct from administrative) rules have the form of commodity exchange. (15) Pashukanis's theory is a bold attempt
to develop Marxian ideas concerning the essentially bourgeois nature of law and its incompatibility with socialist
society. Pashukanis does not rest his case against law on
its oppressive or coercive nature as an instrument of
class rule but proposes the more subtle idea that law is a
type of social relationship specific to capitalism. (16)
From our point of view the interesting aspect of his
theory is that he regards law as a relationship between
equal jural subjects who are the bearers of rights: (17)

> The legal system differs from every other form of social
> system precisely in that it deals with private, isolated
> subjects. The legal norm acquires its *differentia spe-
> cifica*, marking it out from the general mass of ethical,
> aesthetic, utilitarian and other such regulations pre-
> cisely because it presupposes a person endowed with
> rights on the basis of which he actively makes claims.

Arguing on Marxist lines, Pashukanis identified legal
relationships as a type of economic relationship. (He
therefore rejects the idea of law as a system of rules or
norms.) The basic economic relationships in capitalist
society hold between those selling their labour (the proletarian class) and those purchasing it for the purpose of
organising mechanised production (the capitalist class),
and between the producers of commodities (that is, goods
manufactured for sale in an open market) and participants
in the market-place. Law provides a framework for such
exchanges, particularly in the resolution of disputes
about commodity exchanges. (18) This is why law is
adjudicative rather than administrative. In doing this,
it treats each individual as a legal person entitled to
the full (standard) compensation for his labour-power and
the freedom to exchange his goods at whatever price he
can obtain. Private law, especially the law of contract,
which represents the essential form of law, assumes that
each jural person is a distinct or isolated being, with

interests opposed to other such beings, who is engaged in
competition with all other owners. (19)   Contract is thus
integral to the ideal of law.   The point of this system is
to make possible the economic exchanges necessary for
capitalist production, but the form of law is apparent in
other social relationships, even in the family, all of
which are viewed as involving the exchange of commodities
at market prices. (20)   Legal relationships are, at base,
relationships between the possessors of commodities,
therefore he treats law, not as an appendage of human
society in the abstract, but as a historical category
corresponding to a particular social environment based on
the conflict of private interests. (21)

Despite certain grave internal weaknesses in Pashukanis's theory (such as his difficulty in distinguishing
between facts, such as possession, and legal norms such as
ownership), (22) his limitation of the concept of rights to
rule-governed exchanges of a capitalist nature illuminates
certain features of private law.   But it has little application to legal relationships between the state and the
citizen and is strained to breaking-point in its interpretation of criminal law as a process whereby a crime is
'exchanged' for a punishment of equivalent 'value'. (23)

The evident purpose of Pashukanis's theory is to vindicate a Marxian interpretation of law and to do so he,
like so many revolutionary critics of rights, draws selec-
tively on theories emanating from an alien ideological
background.   Such theories are evidence only of the sort
of rights current in the types of society that Pashukanis
wishes to contrast with socialism.

There is, in fact, little reason to accept Pashukanis's
arbitrary refusal to regard as law the non-bourgeois
systems of societal rules.   His conclusions follow only if
we accept contract and power theories of rights and give
them a very special locus in certain economic relations of
capitalism.   He himself allows, following Engels, that
where there are no clashes of commercial intersts there
will still have to be administration, that is, the organisation of joint activities on the basis of agreed objectives, as in an army, a religious order, or the running of
a railway system. (24)   We have already seen that such
organisational activities generate rules and noted that
some of these rules will include provisions for entering
into agreements and having some legal powers over others.
The fact that these institutions are not used for the purposes of bourgeois commerce is an insufficient reason to
decline to call them legal, or refuse to regard them as
establishing rights, for we still have to take into
account the prospect of a theory of rights which is not

confined to contractual and power rights.

Moreover, it is evident that Pashukanis assumes that bourgeois (and hence all) rights are pre-legal relationships to which law merely gives expression. This means that he is taking over for the purpose of his critique something like the theory of natural or moral rights according to which the idea of the individual as an equal bearer of rights is a metaphysical doctrine underlying law rather than a statement about the content of law. This is a point which has relevance to the revolutionary's view of human rights, which is discussed in the next chapter, but it does not have direct bearing on the concept of positive rights which is the object of our present analysis.

THE INTEREST THEORY OF RIGHTS

The inability of the contract and power theories to explain, at least in some cases, what it means to say that B has an obligation to A, leaves as the main contender the 'interest' theory of rights according to which to have a right is to have an interest protected or furthered by the existence or non-existence of a rule, law or understanding requiring action or inaction in ways which are designed to have a bearing on the interests of the right-holder; obligations, under these rules, are owed to the right-holder because they are obligations to further or protect A's interests, this being of the essence of the right in question rather than a secondary consequence of the fulfilment of the obligation. (25)

The strength of the interest theory is that it can cover all types of rights and explains the limited plausibility of contract and power theories. The protection that is given by rights may sometimes be afforded by giving A legal power over the wills of others (as the power theory contends is always the case) or it may involve practices such as the institution of promising or contracting whereby B undertakes to further A's interests in some specified way (which is how the contract theory construes all rights). But neither of these devices is essential to rights. As long as it is possible to interpret a positive obligation, like the obligation to feed the starving, or to leave adults alone to make their own decisions, as being for the interests of A, then such an obligation may be said to be owed to A, and A may be said to be the right-holder, his interests being the objective of the obligation. On this theory, not only are particular rights to be seen as ways of furthering the interests of right-holders but the whole institution of rights is regarded as having the function of protecting interests of right-holders.

Further elucidation of what it is for a right to be for the protection of an interest requires us to distinguish the strictly legal or positivistic content that can be given to this conception from the background assumptions which go along with this understanding and application of rights, legal and non-legal. The specific consequences which flow from ascribing a right to A vary according to the type of right in question but they can be spelled out in terms of the processes and assumptions which affect the application and interpretation of the correlative obliga- tions. Where rights are explicitly mentioned in positive rules this has the function of expressing either the legislator's intentions or the traditional understanding of the purpose of societal rules in a way which indicates that A's interests are to be considered as relevant in such judicial matters as (a) who may raise issues in court about the non-fulfilment of the obligation (normally the right-holder or person authorised to act on his behalf, but perhaps any person in a position to show that A's interests have been detrimentally affected by B's behaviour); (b) how the content of the obligation is to be interpreted where this is in doubt (namely from the point of view of the interests of A which the rule is designed to protect); (c) how serious the violation is to be regarded when an obligation is not fulfilled (perhaps in proportion to the degree to which A's interests have suffered); (d) where questions of compensation or damages arise, who should benefit therefrom; and (e) the judicial creation of new obligations to protect interests previously protected by other obligations in different circumstances involving the same interests.

Quite apart from the specific implications in matters of procedure and application which the identification of whose rights are at stake in a particular situation may have, all of which may be seen as ways of ensuring that A's interests are safeguarded by legal or quasi-legal pro- cesses, the use of rights terminology in everyday discourse carries with it the connotation of the defence of right- holders' legitimate interests which affects the whole approach to political and legal issues in those cases where the rights of those involved are explicitly stated to be at issue. Not only is the legal meaning of 'rights' cashable in terms of various mechanisms for taking A's interests into account in applying and interpreting rules, but the assumption that rights are for the protection of the interests of right-holders also points the whole pro- cess in the direction of protecting the interests of those

who are shown to have rights relevant to issues before
courts and permeates the background political and moral
assumptions of the language of rights.

The general orientation which is introduced into the
legal process by the concept of rights is continuous with
the assumptions which go along with how we regard right-
conferring rules in the course of non-legal social interactions independently of any issues which arise in the
judicial process. Where rules employ the notion of rights
this is taken to mean that the purpose and hence the correct interpretation and significance of the rule is to
assist or protect the right-holders in the pursuit of
their interests. It indicates that it is A who has the
warrant for action, or entitlement to receive or decline
certain benefits or burdens and that it is A's interests
which are the raison d'être of the required correlative
obligations. This is not to say that there can be no
ulterior purpose for ascribing rights to A. But to understand what it is to ascribe a right we must see this
ulterior purpose as being served by a mechanism which
gives precedence or standing in a stated manner to the
relevant interests of the right-holder in specified circumstances. We can best understand the meaning of B's
obligation to A (the right-holder) by saying that B's
obligation is to act or refrain from acting so as to further or protect the interests of A in a way indicated by
the content of the right in question, such that in the
application and interpretation of the rules requiring B's
activity or inactivity it is the interests of A that are
to be taken into account.

The stress on individual interest in this analysis may
seem to allow the revolutionary critic of rights all that
he seeks or fears. It seems that rights are simply a way
of institutionalising the overriding priority given to
certain interests of competing individuals in situations
of conflict: an institutionalisation of limited selfishness. (26)

But this is so only if 'interest' is taken as being
synonymous with self-interest, or selfishness, and it is
assumed that obligations must be performed unwillingly.
Neither of these contentions has to be accepted, although
both are made naturally enough in a society in which individuals are primarily or even exclusively concerned about
their own welfare in contrast to that of others and in
which assistance is given to others only grudgingly, under
coercion or in order to obtain reciprocal benefits. These
assumptions are not, however, a necessary part of the conceptual tie between rights and interests. It is true that
much of the history of the development of rights can readily be seen as reflecting successive attempts by one group

after another to secure what they felt to be in their interests by imposing obligations on other groups with conflicting interests: historically many rights can be seen as
practices created for the regulation of conflicting self-
interests and the imposition of the interests of the
dominant group over those of others. Moreover, if we do
take 'interest' to mean 'self-interest' and 'self-interest'
to imply 'selfishness', then this accounts as well as any
other theory for the typical associated terminology of
rights: demands, claims, insistance, enforcement, imposition, and so forth, and the idea that it is proper to
waive one's rights but not to neglect obligations. It is,
however, possible to detach 'interest' from 'selfishness'
and 'obligation' from 'burden' and so open the way for a
socialist concept of rights which retains the individualism inseparable from the idea of obligations being owed to
others, but interprets the relevant interests in such a
way that they do not amount to self-regarding behaviour
and the correlative obligations in such a way that they
are not typically viewed as burdensome.

While it is tautological to say that a person's interests are *his* interests this is not so to say that his
interests are directed towards his own welfare, and while
the 'selfish' interpretations of 'interests', in which it
is assumed that a person's interests are self-regarding
(that is, directed towards benefiting himself) are characteristic of a society in which 'individualism' implies
the propriety of each seeking his own benefit except in so
far as he is constrained by custom or law from harming
others in the process, it would not be so in a society
such as the socialist envisages. To allow for the possibility of unselfish 'interests', a more neutral and
potentially more helpful way to regard 'interest' as it
relates to the concept of rights is to concentrate on the
idea of a person being 'interested in' something, rather
than on the bare notion of something being in someone's
interests in the sense of his welfare or wellbeing. (27)
This enables us to produce an analysis of the concept and
institution of rights which is adequate to existing systems and permits the development of a theory of rights
which avoids the criticism that they are inherently and
inevitably tied to the pursuit of self-interest or legitimate self-centredness and at the same time maintains the
essential connection between rights and the interests of
their 'owners'.

For a being to have interests in the sense of being
'interested in' X or Y it is necessary for that being to
be in some sort of conative relationship to an object,
that is, to have some sort of desire, care or concern

about that which he is 'interested in'. This may be relatively passive, as when an object attracts or holds the
attention of A, or relatively active, as when A has hopes,
fears, aspirations, cares or concerns which prompt him to
action or inaction in relation to the object of his interest. Having interests in this sense, therefore, depends
on the arousal of his attention and usually also of some
affective or emotional attitude towards features of his
environment or of himself which are sufficient to motivate
efforts towards or away from the objects of interest in
appropriate circumstances. A person's interests are not
simply those things which he considers in an abstract way
significant or valuable, but items to which he devotes
his own concrete attention and activity, the things he
wants and cares about as part of his own way of life. They
are the things in which he is disposed to be interested in
that, given particular, usually recurring, circumstances
of his life, he manifests attentiveness to, concern for
and activity towards them, according to the nature of the
objects and the opportunities available to him.

It is important to note that the idea of being interested in something does not necessarily carry the implication of self-regarding concerns which goes with the
narrow idea of interests as that which is for the benefit
of A. What a person is interested in may often be some
condition of himself, but it need not be. He may be
interested in the development of knowledge, the welfare of
others, artistic conceptions, sports, animals, foreign
countries, and so on, none of which can be seen as tied up
with his self-interest in the sense of self-regarding
interests.

The theory that what is common to all rights is that
they relate positively to what the right-bearer is interested in is, in part, a descriptive generalisation about
actual rights. As such, it is vulnerable to the readily
available evidence that the social and legal rights of
particular individuals do not always have direct bearing
on what they are concerned about. A person may, for
instance, have a legal right to a pension but, perhaps
because he is wealthy, be entirely indifferent whether or
not he receives that pension. The theory can, however,
readily be developed to take account of such superficial
objections.

In the first place, the ascription of A's right to X
although it presupposes that A is interested in or is concerned about X, often does so on the basis that the interests and concerns in question are dispositional. To be
interested in X it is not necessary to be constantly
thinking about X or always manifesting wants and desires

about it, but simply to be disposed to have such thoughts, wants and desires on appropriate occasions. Thus if I have a right to sell my labour, this does not imply that I always wish to do so but only that it is a wish which I have from time to time in appropriate circumstances.

We also speak of the right of A to X when A is a member of a class of beings all of whom are capable of being interested in X even although they do not all in fact have such an interest. This means that we sometimes ascribe a right to a being on the basis of the interests which he could have, in the sense that he is capable of having them, on the grounds that they are the sort of interests which ought to be protected and furthered by rights. This would, of course, normally be pointless if it is certain that the being in question never will have these interests, and the close relation between rights and interests can be seen from the fact that it would be misconceived to ascribe rights to X to a class of beings none of whose members are likely to be interested in X. Thus I, as a human being, can have a right to freedom of speech even if I am not interested in free speech, for it is clearly the sort of thing that I could be interested in and which many human beings are interested in. The point of ascribing this right to me, as a person who is not interested in free speech, is to establish that if and when I do come to have such an interest, then my freedom to speak is something which ought to be protected by rights. Many rights are ascribed to persons in this way because of the interests which they are capable of having.

We could regard these 'capacity rights' as being purely hypothetical rights which beings have if they have the appropriate interests but not otherwise, which preserves a close tie between rights and actual interests. This has the merit of bringing out the rationale for ascribing such rights to anyone although it is not a formulation that is likely to help with the drafting of readily applicable rules. It is also worth noting that there is another way in which what I have called 'capacity rights' are related to actual interests in that it is common for people to be concerned about the existence of rules imposing on others duties which will protect interests which they believe they are likely to have in the future; when this is the case it is not misleading to speak of A's right to X even although A has, at present, no disposition to be interested in X, provided that X is the sort of thing in which A could be interested.

Another way in which the connection between rights and interests is not always as direct as my formula suggests is that a person's right to X may not depend on his

interest in X itself but in that to which X is causally
related, or can be used to obtain. Thus a person's right
to a certain monetary income may be based not on his
interest in having money as such, but on his interest
in having those things which money can be used to buy.
And a mentally subnormal person's right to medical treatment, about which he neither knows nor cares, may depend,
for instance, on the fact that this treatment will help to
make his life more comfortable, which is something in
which he is interested. Thus the connection between
rights and what right-bearers are interested in may not
always be immediately apparent because it may be mediated
by an assumed causal or instrumental relationship.
Strictly speaking, therefore, we should say that to
ascribe a right to X presupposes that the right-bearer is
either interested in X, or in something to which X is
causally or instrumentally related. Alternatively, it
could be said that, where X is only indirectly related to
what A (the right-bearer) is interested in, A has not got
a right to x as such, but to that to which X is causally
or instrumentally related. The point of putting it in
this way would be to draw attention to the fact that the
correct ascription of such 'instrumental rights' depends
on the existence of the relationship which is said to hold
between X and that in which A is interested. If money
cannot be used to buy things which A is interested in having then there is no basis for saying that he has a right
to it. Instrumental rights may therefore be regarded as
secondary rights which presuppose the existence of prior
and logically more fundamental rights to those things to
whose protection or furtherance the instrumental rights
are directed.

Despite these developments of the 'interested in'
theory of rights it would be difficult to claim that it is
entirely successful as a description of all actual linguistic uses of rights language. In particular, legal
systems have evolved the concept of a legal person to
cover states, corporations, and other inanimate things
which cannot be literally concerned about anything since
they lack consciousness and desires. The rationale for
such usages is generally that such rights indirectly, but
in effect, have to do with the concerns of sentient beings.
In the case of associations, for instance, the 'interests'
of the collective entity can be given meaning in terms of
the interests or concerns of its constituent members,
assuming, that is, that these members are individual
beings. But it is more difficult to accommodate the
extension of rights to purely inanimate things such as
deserts and trees, as is sometimes proposed. (28) Many

natural entities can be regarded as having interests in
that they can be benefited and harmed, but they cannot be
said to be interested in anything.

The reason for confining the literal use of rights
language to those cases where the right-holders have concerns is in the end an evaluative one which rests on the
proposition that only the concerns of conscious, sentient
beings have the moral significance to serve as the ends of
a rule-governed order. That inanimate objects do not have
this standing is ultimately as much a moral as a conceptual point, although the awkwardness of speaking of the
interests of non-sentient entities indicates that it is an
evaluation which is enshrined in the informal logic of our
practical discourse.

The superiority of that version of the interest theory
which interprets interests as concerns rests also on the
extent to which it systematises at least some powerful
intuitions to do with the proper criteria for membership of
the class of possible right-bearers. (29) If we adopt the
sense of 'interests' in which it means only the benefit of
a thing, then we may plainly speak of the interests of
flowers, buildings and rocks, for in each of these cases
the entity in question may be preserved, and it even makes
sense to think in terms of their protection and improvement. In this case anything that can be benefited or
harmed, improved or damaged, may be said to be a potential
right-bearer. All that is required is that there be good
or bad specimens of the type of thing in question and we
are then able to speak of benefiting or harming it and
thus of doing or not doing what is in or against its interests. This would mean that if any rule-protected interest
constitutes a right then any inanimate object might have
rights. This cannot be said to be without sense, or without relevance in law, since legal systems have no difficulty in extending the application of legal personality to
whatever type of entity it is expedient so to regard, but
such extensions to entirely inanimate objects are so out
of line with ordinary assumptions as to cast doubt on this
interpretation of 'interest' as a criterion for demarcating
the class of possible right-bearers. Indeed, it is one of
the strengths of the 'interested in' theory of rights that
it gives us a plausible criterion for defining the class
of possible right-bearers. The requirement that right-
bearers satisfy the condition of conative consciousness is
broad enough to encompass nearly all human beings who are
biologically alive and gives us some sort of guideline to
apply to such borderline cases as animals (the 'higher'
animals clearly being included as potential right-bearers),
human 'vegetables' (who may be defined as lacking

consciousness and therefore as not having rights, and
human foeti at various stages of development. Thus we
would have some basis for saying, on the suggested criterion, that foeti at the early stages of development can
have no rights, and that whether or not they do so at
later stages will depend on empirical assumptions about
the emergence of consciousness. It has, further, the
acceptable consequence of excluding from the class of
right-bearers all inanimate objects including those 'living' things like plants and microbes, which it is possible
to regard as being benefited but not as themselves having
concerns, while at the same time allowing that there is an
analogical basis for extending the range of right-bearers
to include at least this limited category of rights-
bearers, and allowing that the grounds for not doing so
are as much moral as conceptual in that the boundary between those entities which may have rights and those which
do not is in the end to be decided by reference to the
prior decision as to what sort of things are the proper
objects of moral concern for their own sakes.

In chapter 7 I shall deal with the question of precisely which interests socialists take into account in
arriving at right-conferring rules, but it is already
clear that taking the interests which are protected and
furthered by rights as species of 'interests in' is sufficient to break the alleged analytical tie between rights
and self-interest since men may be interested in the welfare of others as much as in their own wellbeing and concerned about the realisation of a multitude of objectives,
such as the production of material goods, or the growth
of knowledge, which may have no direct connection with
any condition of themselves. This is particularly true in
the case of the concerns which people have as the occu-
pants of social roles, such as those of mother, teacher or
worker.

The 'interested in' theory of rights appears to have
the consequence that a person's rights may not relate to
his own welfare. This might be thought to introduce an
unacceptable gap between a person's rights and that which
benefits him. Surely it cannot be the case that A has a
right that the welfare of B be furthered simply because A
wishes B well. Rather, would we not say, more naturally,
that it is the person who benefits who has the right?
Indeed, is it not badly askew to say, for instance, that
an environmentalist has a right that an endangered species
about whose future he is concerned should be saved or
that a football supporter has a right that the team of his
choice win their match.

It is not being argued, however, that just any interest

in a person or event will be an adequate ground for the acquisition of a right, but only that such interests are candidates for having the protection of right-conferring rules. And in those cases where the interests in question do not relate to a condition which involves the right-holder it still remains the case that the right is his because its justification relates to the fact that it is his interest in the person or event that is the grounds for establishing and maintaining the right. This is compatible with the existence of other rights relating to the same desired outcome which do belong to those directly involved in its realisation. It is not hard to give examples of existing rights which are based on the individual's concern for others, such as the rights which parents may have for support in the care of their children. The rights which arise under the institution of promising and contracting provide plenty of illustrations of one person's right that others be treated in certain ways. The fact that it may seem strange to regard the standard right as arising from a non-self-centred interest may derive more from the fact that in the societies with which we are most familiar self-directed interests are those which are most prized and protected. But there is no logical reason why this should be so. It makes perfect sense to say that there is a societal rule such that A owes it to B that C receive a certain benefit so that we may say that B has a right against A that C be benefited. This will be so where A's obligation to benefit C is grounded in B's interest in C's welfare rather than directly in B's welfare. The difficulties involved in multiplying this type of right will be taken up later, but the conceptual propriety of grounding B's rights in interests of this sort is a first step in countering the argument that a system of rights necessarily institutionalises competitive individualism. What it does presuppose is that the concerns of human beings are, at the very least, a factor of major moral importance. This form of individualism is inseparable from rights. It also accords well with the socialist ideal of man as an active, project-pursuing and creative being.

The proper target of the socialist onslaught on individualism is not on the institution of rights as such but the prior assumption that human nature is irredeemably egoistic. To reject the Hobbesian model of man as an unchanging bundle of desires for the pleasure of the desirer as no more than a historically conditioned image which is approximated to only at certain periods and in certain types of society, is not to reject that form of individualism which gives a central place to the satisfaction of

desires and concerns. If we allow that man may develop a
limited, even an extreme, altruism, this does nothing to
downgrade the significance of so arranging organised
social existence that the fulfilment of human interests is
its central objective. The Marxist model of man as, at
least potentially, a social being whose creative agency is
most fully developed in co-operative productive enterprises centres as much on the flourishing of the concerns
and pursuits of individual human beings as any other
social ideal. Indeed, the image of man as an agent or
labourer whose fulfilment is attained through work fits
neatly into the assumption that many societal rules are
designed to encourage and defend the concerns of human
beings. The individualism of rights requires no more than
an acceptance of the organisational significance of some
of the concerns and projects of sentient beings.

6   Socialism and human rights

The ambivalences and tensions in socialist attitudes to
rights are heightened when it comes to the evaluation of
the concept of human rights. (1) Ideologically, socialism
is in two minds as to whether the rights of man are a
historically conditioned expression of bourgeois interests,
an underpinning of the legal preconditions of capitalism,
or, properly understood, the ground-rules of a genuine
socialist community.

For the revolutionary socialist the modern idea of
human rights is no more than a refurbishing of the concept
of natural rights, which was closely associated with the
rise of the bourgeoisie and their struggle with feudal
authorities. For the reformist, human rights are detach-
able from the historical context of the natural rights
tradition and are capable of being developed into an
important element in socialist practice.

No socialist accepts as a definitive the lists of
natural rights formulated in the seventeenth and eighteenth centuries. At the very least the right to property
has to be limited to personal possessions or eliminated
altogether, and the new social, economic and welfare
rights appended to the traditional, civil and political
ones. Whereas eighteenth-century rights were predomi-
nantly rights against oppressive actions by governments,
modern human rights, in general, include claim-rights
which correlate with the duties of government to take
positive, economic and administrative action on behalf of
their citizens. The reformist embraces these developments
and encourages the incorporation of yet further rights to
promote the wellbeing of all. The revolutionary, in common with orthodox liberal theorists, argues that these
new positive rights are quite different in kind from the
traditional negative ones and should be clearly distinguished from them, leaving the old list of natural rights

to serve as the basis for our assessment of the worth of
human rights. Liberal philosophers, like Maurice Cranston, (2) who have resisted the inclusion of these so-
called 'socialist' (social, economic and welfare) rights
in modern declarations of human rights, on the grounds
that they are quite unlike the original and genuine
human rights, share certain assumptions with those radical
socialists who reject the whole institution of human
rights, even although the former's arguments are directed
towards the enforcement of purified and more traditional
notions of human rights, while the latter's intentions are
to reject the entire tradition as ill-adapted to the expression of socialist ideals and methods. Against both
these positions the reformist, or democratic socialist,
maintains that socialism represents a major updating of
the content and pursuit of human rights and is the only
effective means of assuring that human rights are respected in practice. (3) We have, then, in the controversy
over human rights a sharpened and dramatised form of the
ambivalence of socialist theory towards the idea of rights.
I shall draw on critics from both Left and Right in an
effort to clarify the question of whether socialism is
conceptually revisionist or revolutionary in its implications for human rights.

If social and economic rights are excluded from the
class of human rights then it becomes much less plausible
to locate human rights within a socialist philosophy. For
this reason I will, in this chapter, take some cognisance
of the content of human rights, but the important issues
on which I will concentrate have more to do with the concept of a human right than with its content, for it is
the very notion of 'innate' or pre-social rights possessed
by all individuals in all societies, which are 'inalien-
able', 'imprescriptible', or 'absolute', that has drawn
the heaviest fire from socialist philosophers in their
general criticism of rights. I have already conceded that
there is some force in many of these criticisms, without
allowing that they are the sole preserve of socialist
theorists. What remains to be investigated is whether
there is a defensible concept of human rights which
clearly distinguishes human rights from other sorts of
rights and, if so, whether this concept fits readily into
socialist theory.

An immediate obstacle to the acceptance of the idea of
human rights is that they are a species of moral rights.
In chapter 2 it was argued that the concept of moral
rights is highly questionable once they are detached from
natural law, in itself an implausible moral theory.

This problem can be overcome quickly, however, by

adopting the analysis of 'moral rights' proffered in chapter 2, according to which they are the rights which ought to
to be constituted by positive societal rules. This then
leaves open the moral questions of what these positive
rights should be and excludes the epistemologically naive
method of answering these questions by asserting the existence of a moral law containing a list of rights which can
be known by all men in all ages through the exercise of
their powers of rational intuition or common sense. This
was, indeed, the dominant doctrine of the eighteenth-
century moral theory used to vindicate natural rights, but
socialists are not alone in suggesting the datedness of
such a moral epistemology. Theorists as disparate as
Edmund Burke and Jeremy Bentham join in casting doubt on
the value of this type of moral philosophy and in this at
least they are in agreement both with Marxian and contemporary socialist critics of rights who regard moral or
'innate' rights as obscure metaphysical entities whose
existence or non-existence is beyond the scope of empirical observation or rational criticism. (4)

The revolutionary socialist critic of rights contends
that the idea of human rights cannot survive the demise of
the old rationalist moral ontology. Once the universalism
based on the existence of an intuited objective moral
order is abandoned what basis is there for insisting that
there are positive rights which all men in all societies
ought to possess? Is this not the sort of ahistorical
fiction which served to legitimise the egoism of capitalist society by dignifying it with the halo of eternity or
universality? (5) If there are to be rights at all,
should these not be varied in the light of social and
economic circumstances? Did Marx and Engels not reserve
their strongest sarcasm for the notion of such eternal
rights as a prime example of ideological thought dis-
guising class interests as universal truths? (6) Is the
notion of universal human rights not tied up with the
absurdities of a pre-social state of nature in which men
lived as isolated self-sufficient individuals each
possessed of rights which they could not 'alienate' on
entering society, hence the notions of innateness and
inalienability? Is this not the type of egoistic individualism which, despite the arguments of the previous
chapter, stands as an insuperable difficulty for the
socialist who wishes to accommodate the idea that there
are certain positive rights which ought to be the possessions of all men in all societies? If the essential
individuality of each person is identified with that which
we possessed as self-sufficient independent beings, can
this have any role to play in a community based on the

assumption that man's nature is inseparable from his
social relationships? For the revolutionary critic, the
answer to these questions is clear: human rights, the
natural and imprescriptable rights of man, are the
embodiment of an ahistorical bourgeois individualism.
For the reformist, the task is to identify what aspects of
the universalism of rights he wishes to defend. Once this
is settled, we can ask whether the remnants of universality which remain are sufficient to mark off a set of
rights as universal or human rights which are of sufficient importance to be given a fundamental place in socialist philosophy. I shall, therefore, approach the analytic
problems raised by socialist doubts about human rights
through an examination of what it is for a right to be
universal, a highly ambiguous notion which covers a wide
range of characteristics only some of which are incompatible with socialist theory.

PRE-SOCIAL AND AHISTORICAL RIGHTS

The idea that there are rights possessed by all persons in
every age and situation is historically linked to the belief that men have these rights in a state of nature which
is not only prior to the existence of a state but actually
precedes the formation of society. An examination of the
state of nature, abstracted from all the arbitrary conventions of actual societies, will start to reveal exactly
what these natural or human rights are. (7) Hence the
central significance of the rights to life, liberty and
possessions, that is, the right not to be killed or enslaved and to retain for one's own use those things on
which one had laboured, all of which, it is imagined, are
necessary for human survival and can be enjoyed by independent individuals living outside society.
     In our analysis of rights in general we have seen that
this concept of natural rights is incoherent if such
rights amount to anything more than negative liberties,
that is the total absence of obligation, which would mean
that the right to life would be no more than the absence
on the part of others of a duty to kill the right-holder.
(8) If we are talking about positive or full liberties
which correlate with the duties of others not to infringe
our life or liberty then we are entering the realm of
rule-governed behaviour and hence presupposing, as the
pre-socialist theorists did, a law of nature or a primitive
form of social order which is inconsistent with the
theory's postulates. It is this background theory to the
idea of pre-social rights that is most inimical to

socialist thought for it assumes a pre-social human nature with fixed human attributes carrying over into life in society. Such a nature can at best be non-social and is more often assumed to be anti-social and the whole contextual assumption that individuals can be independent of others and so 'owe' nothing to others, is, from the point of view of normative theory, pernicious in its encouragement of the notion that those who flourish within societies do so because of their own merits rather than as the result of the communal effort and setting.

The definitive socialist response to the pre-social concept of universality is to deny the possibility of a pre-social human condition. Human life is inherently social in that it is unthinkable outside a social group, just as the notion of a right is incoherent except in a context of shared norms regulating human interactions. This is not to deny the universality of human rights but to deny that there is a pre-social state so that the question of the rights which pertain in such a state does not arise. Human rights may be universal and as a matter of fact still be applicable only within a society.

This move frees the concept of human rights from the individualistic assumptions of state of nature theory which in any case is best regarded as a justificatory theory rather than an analytic one in that it was historically an attempt to provide a basis for the justification of the rights which men ought to have in society. (9) For this reason it is easy to see why state of nature theory has survived the collapse of a belief in the reality of an actual state of nature and remains as a device for thinking how societal rules may be assessed and criticised. There is, however, no need to accept this particular justificatory device which is logically separable from the idea that there are such things as human rights. For the socialist this must be a relief since modern hypothetical forms of state of nature theory are still closely associated with the liberal assumption that individuals owe nothing to their fellows beyond that which they have voluntarily undertaken to perform. What needs to be explored, then, is the force of the claim that there ought to be universal positive rights in some further sense of universal than that which incorporates the idea of pre-social rights.

Closely allied to the notion of pre-social rights is the interpretation of the universality of human rights as indicating that they are rights which are, or ought to be, enjoyed by men and women at every stage of social development, from the most primitive form of hunting group to the largest and most complex technological states.

This 'ahistorical' idea of human rights takes no account of the differences between types of society in either material or cultural terms. If adopted, it excludes as possible human rights all those which are inconceivable or impracticable in any one type of society. It may therefore include the rights to life and liberty but hardly rights to take part in the government of a country, to have full legal personality, to enjoy the protection of the rule of law, to have freedom of movement within a state, to possess a nationality, to receive social security benefits, or to have the opportunity to enjoy some leisure, all of which rights are part of modern declarations of human rights and most of which are incorporated in the traditional Bills of Rights. (10)

To the socialist ahistoricity seems particularly absurd because of the enormous impact of economic and social circumstances on the values and expectations of men. The disquiet with the attempt to give special significance to those features of human life which are the same in all societies evokes similar criticisms from non-socialist thinkers. (11) In fact, the only way in which this ahistorical view of human rights can have any plausibility is by restricting human rights to a few highly general requirements which are presupposed by every form of human good. The only obvious right of this sort is the right to life, for without life man cannot achieve or enjoy anything (some may argue that this is true of liberty as well), (12) but even in the case of the right to life what this right actually amounts to will vary from society to society with the dangers and protections that are present and possible in these societies, and in the case of liberty what is to count as liberty will vary enormously in the forms of enslavement or oppression which are characteristic of particular societies.

If human rights are to remain in this very general, unspecific and underdeveloped form then no socialist would have much difficulty in accommodating them, allowing the universal right to life and liberty and perhaps adding to these rights the right to creative and productive activity, since if there is an unchanging element in the socialist concept of man it is along the lines that all men are producers or workers and that fulfilment involves participation in some form of active exchange with nature. However, such highly general rights have very little significance in actual social situations and require in practice to be filled out by a concretisation of what they require in the light of particular circumstances and social values. At this point the socialist must deny that such specification can proceed by reflecting on the nature of man

abstracted from his particular historical circumstances.
At the stage of elaborating the contents of highly general
rights and making them into significant behavioural
requirements, the socialist rejects entirely the ahistorical approach, preferring instead to concentrate on the
needs of man as they arise in each type of economic system
and in terms of the available resources in a society. No
special store is set by those factors which happen to be
common to many different societies for there can be no
assumption that what men in different types of society have
in common is any more important to them than those features
which differentiate them. Just because disease is a minor
problem in one society does not make it less significant in
another society any more than religious freedom must be
important to all men because it is important to some.

It is hard to believe that the ahistorical approach to
detailed conceptions of human rights is a necessary or
even central feature of the concept of human rights. Certainly, any theory which allows for the inclusion of rights
which are unthinkable outside a modern industrial state
(such as the right to social security benefits) and wishes
to incorporate new rights, such as the right to privacy,
in response to the specific dangers of a bureaucratic and
technologically advanced society, must allow for the
elaboration of general formulations of human rights in the
light of circumstances which do not apply across the
historical spectrum. The right of a people to self-
determination may make no sense in a primitive tribal
society but this does not necessarily render it less
important for those experiencing colonial rule. Ahistorical universality is separable from the significance of a
right for human welfare in particular settings.

Moreover, both the pre-social and ahistorical readings
of universality have the drawback, for the socialist, of
encouraging the unthinking acceptance of the erroneous
assumption that the rights which it makes sense to ascribe
to man in a primitive or undeveloped type of economy must
be the rights which are fundamental for human beings living in totally different economic and social circumstances.

GENERAL AND FUNDAMENTAL RIGHTS

An alternative conception of the universality of human
rights is to regard them as the rights which ought to be
the possession of all citizens or all members of society.
On this view, some rights (human rights) ought to be
secured for all without regard to such status divisions as
class, rank, race, sex, religion, colour or nationality.

Some rights, special rights, apply to particular persons (such as members of parliament), other rights, general rights, belong to all (such as the right to stand for election to parliament). This interpretation accords with the origin of natural rights in the critique of the feudal system which had different sets of rules for different orders of society. Eighteenth- and nineteenth-century statements of the rights of man were in large part demands that all should be entitled to participate equally in the economic and political life of a society irrespective of birth and religion. Modern human rights simply extend this sort of demand to exclude racial, sexual and national discrimination in the belief that all inhabitants of the state ought to have some identical rights, the arguments being about what, precisely, these rights should be. (13)

The proposition that the universality of human rights is equivalent to their generality in a society may not go beyond the liberal idea of everyone being treated with equal consideration according to the same set of laws (a principle which is compatible with highly discriminatory practices when the content and effect of these laws is taken into account).(14) Or it may be given a more socialist or egalitarian flavour by association with the view that there are no grounds for different treatment other than differences of need. This latter position, which will be explored in the next chapter, involves the abolition of status groups and in particular of economic classes so as to bring about genuine equality of situation, a distinctive socialist tenet which provides the reformist with his strongest argument for defending the applicability of 'human' (in the sense of 'general') rights to socialist societies.

However, the generality of human rights does have its own problems, for there are few rights which are clearly equally applicable to all persons. Rights to medical treatment apply obviously to those who are sick, the right to education (but not the right to vote) is particularly relevant to children. These considerations may prompt us to reformulate general rights so that they become hypothetical; their standard form would then be 'If any person is in condition X then he is entitled to Y.' But this formulation seems to open the door for incorporating all special rights however few persons they apply to in practice. For instance, it would make 'If anyone is a member of parliament then he has absolute privilege in respect of his utterances in parliament' a possible example of a general and hence a human right. One answer to this problem is to confine such rights to hypothetical conditions which all people are in, or are very liable to be in, at some stage of their lives: birth, upbringing, employment, sickness, marriage, and so forth. These conditions generate course-of-life needs which might serve as a basis for the general rights which we call human. It is not easy, however, to see why such rights are necessarily more important than others simply because they are commonly experienced. Personal peculiarities such as abnormal sexuality or injuries arising from accident or congenital defects might have more significance to the individual than some of his course-of-life needs. Moreover, many course-of-life needs - such as the need of young people for fashionable clothes - may appear too trivial to serve as a basis for human rights. What seems to be missing in the idea that human rights are general rights is some reference to their importance or significance. It may be that most important rights do relate to interests which all men in particular societies have in common but there must at least be some reference to the significance of the rights in question in any adequate statement of what it is for a right to be a human right. In fact, generality only matters where it is a question of extending a valued right to other persons on the grounds that they also are human beings with similar interests. Behind the generality of human rights lies an assumption of their overwhelming significance for all human beings. Not to be imprisoned without trial, to have enough food, clothing and shelter, to be equipped to take part in the economic life of one's society, to participate in the control of those in political authority, all these general rights have a grounding in their overriding importance for human beings. In terms of the analysis of the previous chapter, we may say that all members of society have in common certain interests, in the sense of concerns, which require the special protection and support of societal rules.

This criterion of overridingness or fundamental importance helps to explain some aspects of the controversy over the new social, economic and welfare rights. Socialists support the inclusion of such rights because they view them as being just as fundamental as the traditional civil liberties. Freedom from government interference or the right to security of property are of little significance to the person who is unable to find work or to support himself or his family. To make such claims is not to reject the idea of human rights as such, but to proffer a different view of what rights are important. It follows that the reformist socialist, in advocating the adoption of social and welfare rights as human rights, is endorsing the view that the universality of human rights indicates that they are rights which ought to apply to all men in a

society because they are important for everyone in that
society.

There is no difficulty in incorporating this more precise notion of universality within a socialist philosophy
of rights for one of the objectives of socialism is to
achieve a society in which the division of labour is
reduced in scale and significance to the point where all
men share in the various aspects of economic and social
life on the same footing. While this does not imply an
identity of work and leisure involvements it does assume
that all members of a society will play some part in the
major aspects of social existence. Whatever diversity
there might be in a socialist society, all would be in a
position freely to engage in purposeful communal activity
of a creative and fulfilling nature unencumbered by divisions of class, wealth, sex, race or religion. This
social ideal readily generates the assumption that certain
things are very important to all members of society
including the resources which are available in that
society to enable individuals to take an equal part in the
current forms of social activity. We will see when we
come to discuss the justificatory principles of socialism
that the full and equal participation of all in the political and economic activities of a community may involve unequal distribution of material resources but the equality
of importance presupposed in the idea of human rights
remains in the thesis that all should receive that which
is necessary for them to play their full and equal part in
their society. This conception of human rights can thus
serve to articulate the essential preconditions of socialist society.

Importance is not, however, a formal characteristic of
rights since it refers to the significance attributed to
their content. This importance gains formal expression in
the idea that very significant general rights are overriding in that they take priority in any clash of rights
which may arise in the course of social interaction. For
instance, the right to have a promise kept gives way
before the right to life, if the keeping of the promise
endangers life. All rights, we have seen, serve to exclude or require certain forms of behaviour and enable the
individual to justify his activities without further reasons being given, unless other rights are involved. (15)
The scope of this exclusionary aspect of rights varies
from right to right and the force of the exclusiveness
changes with the right in question. It is a feature of
human rights that the degree and scope of the exclusionary
force is stronger than normal rights, this being a formal
reflection of the importance of their substantive content.

Institutionally, the important thing about human rights
is that they are rights which have special protection, a
status which recognises their relative importance in the
hierarchy of rights. In practice, this may mean having a
Bill of Rights or other entrenched constitutional provisions which give human rights priority in the courts over
normal law, in such a way that if any provision of ordinary law is in conflict with the requirement of the constitutional provisions it can be put aside. (16) Fundamental laws of this sort can be protected from the normal
processes of legislative alteration so that they are not
vulnerable to transient shifts of political opinion.
There are many alternative constitutional devices which
can be used to give legal force to the overriding status
of human rights. These vary from the acceptance by nation
states of the jurisdiction of international courts with a
special brief to enforce a convention of human rights,(17)
to a general acceptance by political activists of certain
long-standing rights as fundamental in that special reasons must be given for any legislative or administrative
decision which appears to run counter to them. (18)

Arguably there might be no need for fundamental laws in
a socialist society since the rules protecting general and
important interests are unlikely to be violated or altered
in such an ideal community, although the likelihood of un-
foreseen consequences of legislative change and the possibility of conflict between rights requiring clear priorities to be established would count against such a view.
It might be expected, therefore, that the status of human
rights in a socialist society would be protected by a
general consensus as to their significance rather than by
specific constitutional provisions. However there is
clearly no incompatibility between a socialist idea of the
function of law and the existence of special constitutional provisions to protect general and important interests. If we assume that the furtherance of important
human concerns is the consequence of foresight and skill
rather than chance or haphazard goodwill then there is a
place for the notion of general and fundamental rights
even in a socialist Utopia. What is not evident, however,
is whether the ideological role of the concept would remain unchanged, a point to which I shall return at the end
of this chapter.

More controversial, from the socialist point of view,
is the idea that the priority given to human rights is so
strong as to be impregnable. This goes beyond the simple
overridingness of human rights over ordinary rights to a
further notion of universality, namely the absolute or
imprescriptible status that is sometimes accorded to human
rights, to which I now turn.

ABSOLUTE RIGHTS

An undoubted element in the idea of natural rights was the
factor that such rights cannot be overridden by governmental or any other human action, even that they cannot be
surrendered voluntarily by their possessors (the idea of
inalienability). This means, in particular, that there are
certain things that governments are never justified in
doing to individuals or certain benefits that they are
always required to provide for them. Human rights are universal in this sense if they can never be forfeited or
surrendered. (19)

The importance of the absoluteness of human rights is
obvious in the light of the traditional role of natural
rights in providing a justification for rebellion against
governments. Any state which violates human rights, it is
said, loses the right to be obeyed. Human rights thus
express the basis for morally legitimate political authority. This means that the protection of human rights is not
at the discretion of governments since if they fail to fulfil this function, political obligation ceases in that
society. No reason is adequate to justify, for instance,
arbitrary killing of innocent persons, torture or the
suppression of religion and perhaps opinion. (20)

It is in the light of this criterion of universality
that socialism is often alleged to be an inadequate doctrine in that, it is argued, socialists are prepared to
sacrifice important general rights of individuals for the
sake of the general welfare or the progress of society as
a whole. Socialists, it is said, override free speech in
the interests of political change, sacrifice the lives of
those who represent the old order in times of social transition and, in general, withdraw human rights from those
who oppose the policies of socialist governments. (21)

The short answer to such criticisms is that they are
based on empirical generalisations about what happens in
so-called socialist states more than on an examination of
socialist theory. In addition to which, it can be pointed
out that most of the rights in modern declarations of
human rights, as they are adopted by governments, allow
for such rights to be limited or suspended according to
processes of law in times of national emergency. For instance article 29, Section (2) of the Universal Declaration of Human Rights states: (22)

> In the exercise of his rights and freedoms, everyone
> shall be subject only to such limitations as are
> determined by law solely for the purpose of securing
> due recognition and respect for the rights and freedom
> of others and of meeting the just requirements of

morality, public order and the general welfare in a
democratic society.

This is, of course, to deny the absolute nature of human
rights, a denial which can be said to be implicit in the
most basic of all human rights, the right to life, which
is often thought to be compatible with capital punishment.
Clearly most, if not all, rights with the possible exception of the right to a fair trial, may be forfeited for
criminal behaviour and some disorderly social situations
are generally thought to justify the withdrawal or suspen-
sion of some human rights, such as the right to freedom
of assembly, without calling into the question that they
are human rights.

Judged by these standards, socialist theory has no
difficulty in incorporating the 'absoluteness' of human
rights, but it is arguable whether the let-out clauses of
declarations and conventions of human rights which are
ratified by states rather than those which are formulated
in the course of revolutions against governments, are in
fact compatible with the traditional idea of natural
rights. In particular, those provisos which permit
'morality' and 'the general welfare' to overrule fundamental rights are suspect since it is part of the function
of human rights to protect minorities against the prevailing moral consensus and the dominance of the interests of the majority.

However, some limitations of human rights can be made
congruent with a useful notion of absoluteness. For
instance, if we allow that a person may forfeit his human
right to X only if he violates another person's right to
X, thus permitting capital punishment for unjustified
killing but not for opposing a government, this is compatible with the way in which the absoluteness of human
rights has been interpreted in the past, although some
rights, such as the right not to be subjected to torture
or degrading treatment, could be regarded as exceptionless
and thus absolute in the strongest sense. (23)

It can also be allowed that where human rights conflict
with each other (as when A's right to privacy thwarts B's
right to free speech), or with themselves (as when A's
right to choose the kind of education that is given to
his children cannot be reconciled with other people's
choices regarding the education that their children
receive), such rights cannot all be upheld in every circumstance. While this sort of difficulty arises even in
the case of old-style civil liberties, for not everyone
can exercise their rights of free speech and assembly at
the same place and at the same time, the problem of conflicting rights is exacerbated by the multiplication of

so-called absolute rights in modern attempts to render the
content of human rights more specific and more extensive,
for it is in a rough and ready way true that the more
rights that exist, the more conflicts are liable to arise
within and between them. (24) The Universal Declaration of
Human Rights acknowledges this problem by adopting the
formula that no one may 'arbitrarily' be deprived of this
or that human good (see articles 9, 12, 15(2), 17(2)),
but if 'arbitrary' means 'except by due process of law'
this is too weak to count as constituting a human right,
for human rights are intended to protect the individual
against certain types of legislation, and if it means
'unreasonable' it is equally unhelpful as a protection
against the prejudices and interests of the majority. The
caveat 'arbitrary' may, however, serve to indicate an
order of priority or hierarchy of human rights by making
a distinction between those that are absolute and those
that are only prima facie rights, subject to modification
in the light of practical conflicts within and between
human rights. This has, however, the disadvantage of
instituting different classes of human right and thus
blurring the distinction between human and other types of
rights.

Another approach to the same problem is to specify in
detail the circumstances in which a right may be forfeited or put aside with the assumption that the right, so
qualified, is exceptionless. Thus the Nigerian Constitution of 1963 lists six reasons why a person may be deprived of his personal liberty after due process of law
and four types of 'forced labour' which are excluded from
the right not to be required to perform forced labour. (25)
The logical terminus of such a process of making rights
more specific in order to make them more 'absolute' could
be to destroy the boundary between ordinary law and fundamental law since it is part of the normal process of
legal development to establish comprehensive and precise
laws which can be applied with clarity and certainty to
all specific circumstances. However, a significant degree
of specificity is perfectly compatible with the role of
fundamental law in the judicial review and in political
criticism of legislation and other governmental activities.

The complexities engendered by conflicting human rights
are undoubtedly particularly acute when typically socialist rights to social and economic benefits are appended to
the standard civil and political liberties. Even after
certain property rights are excised and various caveats
explicitly provided for, the very multiplicity of the new
rights is a threat to their allegedly absolute nature.
This threat is increased by the fact that socialist rights

are frequently positive in form, requiring action on the parts of governments or social agencies to provide for the needs of their citizens. Normally, but not always, inaction is easier to achieve than action and therefore more suited to rules which allow for no exceptions. There is also the special problem of the scarcity of resources, which can put the provision of adequate health care, education and material subsistence beyond the reach of some governments. Scarcity of resources is not, however, irrelevant to the protection of well-established human rights, such as the right of accused persons to a proper trial, or the right to participate in democratic processes, both of which cost money. Moreover, since the socialist is not committed to an ahistorical view of human rights he can readily adjust the standards of adequate material provision to the economic capacities of each society. Further, when governments plead incapacity to provide benefits in line with minimal standards of welfare this can be an assertion of lack of political will rather than a literal incapacity. The point of insisting that social and economic rights are human rights may often be to give them that priority of political status that makes their fulfilment an overriding governmental priority. More specifically, many socialists would, if a conflict is assumed, wish certain social and economic rights to override even those traditional liberties that he wishes to see preserved.

Further discussion of the practical difficulties of providing a socialist concept and content of human rights which are both absolute and implementable requires a closer look at socialist analyses of capitalist welfare which will be discussed in the final chapter of this book. It also requires us to note that socialist views on human rights are relative to the stage of historical development which applies, a point which will be touched on at the end of this chapter. But some further consideration can be given at this stage to the charge that socialism is particularly prone to take advantage of the proviso in the Universal Declaration that human rights can be sacrificed to the 'general welfare' (article 29(2)).

Arguably the most important aspect of the 'absoluteness' of human rights is the idea that they cannot be set aside simply because it is in the majority's interests that this is done. Hence the constant tension between utilitarianism, as the doctrine which dictates the maximisation of happiness and the minimisation of harm, and human rights, for utilitarianism seems to license the sacrifice of innocent minorities for the general happiness. (26) Similar points are made about socialist theorists who are said to be more ready than liberal theorists to place the interests of the masses before those of individuals who stand in the way of social objectives. It is said that socialism, even in normal periods, is inclined to flout the absoluteness of human rights by giving scant respect to the fundamental interests of minorities where these conflict with the general interest. The view is that socialists are thorough-going utilitarians in their approach to the general interest and therefore have no need for institutionalising basic human rights as a protection for minorities against the side-effects of actions which are for the general welfare. Not only are the bourgeoisie to be sacrificed to the proletarian class, but any minority that wishes to establish a competing and different way of life from the socialist norm is seen as a threat which must be suppressed in the general interest. I have noted that this unfavourable view of socialism may in part be due to the fact that socialists give a higher priority to social, economic and welfare rights than to civil and political rights, and that this is not in itself a rejection of the absoluteness of human rights. The answer to the more general question of the weight given to individual interests where these conflict with the general welfare must to an extent wait upon the discussion of the next chapter which deals with the justifications which socialists can offer for the rights that they wish to see adopted. Specifically, it depends on the relative weight which socialists give to the egalitarian as against the aggregative or maximising aspects of their overall normative theory.

Assuming for the moment, that egalitarianism predominates, and that this involves giving equal weight to the interests of all members of a society, this does not necessarily imply the absoluteness of the rights of specific individuals or classes, since, as we have noted, there may be practically insoluble clashes between rights and, where this occurs, it may be rational to prefer the interests of the many to those of the few. Thus, even if it is not the case that major interests of a minority are neglected in favour of minor improvements in the lot of the majority, egalitarianism may not in practice entail the inviolability of specific rights. To the extent that socialists take seriously the welfare of all members of a society and accept that in non-socialist societies irreconcilable clashes of interests arise, particularly as between the ruling elite and other members of society, there is always a likelihood, for instance, that positive liberties which in effect benefit only the wealthy will assume less significance than the organisational measures which must be taken to remedy the deprivations of the poorer sections of society. Thus, if the choice has to be made, socialists will be inclined to prefer promoting the social and economic rights of the proletariat over the civil and political as well as the economic freedoms of the bourgeoisie. Socialists differ from liberal theorists on this matter mainly in acknowledging that such choices may sometimes have to be made since they assume no prior guarantee that the basic interests of any one individual or class is always compatible with the basic interests of all other members of a society. (27) But this does not mean that socialism is in principle in favour of sacrificing present interests and rights for the sake of future benefits or licenses, the sort of trade-off between the basic interests of minorities and the less basic interests of majorities which it is one of the purposes of the institution of human rights to prevent. It simply reflects the fact that socialists are very aware of the impracticality of preserving the absoluteness of an adequate list of human rights in non-socialist societies, and are highly suspicious of the tendency to use appeals to traditional human rights in order to veto reforms designed to protect fundamental social and welfare rights. (28)

CONCLUSION

In this chapter I have in the main defended the reformist socialist position on human rights by outlining an approach to human rights which takes them to be general rights of fundamental importance to all members of a society which can only be overridden when they clash with each other or with other human rights, but allowing that such clashes are a frequent and inevitable aspect of human rights in non-socialist societies.

   This is sufficient to justify upholding the conceptual compatibility of socialism and human rights but further analysis is likely to be fruitless unless it is related to a consideration of the uses to which statements of human rights are put. The crucial functional difference here is between the use of declarations of human rights to establish a consensus on political ideals, and their deployment to assert the minimum standards of attainment which render a government or societal organisation legitimate in the sense of being deserving of loyalty and obedience. Are governmental failures with respect to human rights simply a matter for censure and regret or also grounds for disobedience and rebellion?

Part of the ambivalence of socialists towards human rights stems from a lack of clarity on this issue which is compounded by the factor of historical relativity. In a fully socialist society there would, ex hypothesi, be no need to invoke violation of human rights as a basis for civil disobedience and rebellion (although there is no reason why the justification of such a system could not be couched in terms of human rights). Moreover, due to the aspirational nature of such societies there is liable to be an escalation in the content of human rights in order to establish worthy objectives for co-operative social enterprises (although this is a process which would be held in check if such rights were given the institutional protection of the status of fundamental law enforced through procedures allowing for judicial review of legislation and appeal by the ordinary citizen to a supreme or constitutional court charged with the guardianship of human rights). Overall, the role of human rights within socialist societies will tend towards the model of an ideal blueprint for social and economic arrangements. For these reasons the revolutionary critics of the idea of socialist rights, having in mind the traditional function of human rights discourse in establishing the criteria of political obligation, can argue that the idea of human rights is not central to socialist philosophy, thus confirming the suspicions of liberal critics concerning socialist revisions in the content of human rights.

The revolutionary socialist adds that it is pointless to apply the idea of human rights to non-socialist societies since there is no way that such societies can provide satisfactory implementation of any adequate list of these rights. (29)   At the most he will allow for the tactical use of appeals to human rights in order to further basic economic changes towards the transformation of that society, but the notion that violations of human rights per se 'justifies' rebellion smacks too much of the idea that individuals and groups are able to make radical political changes as and when they choose to do so. (30)   The right of rebellion makes little sense for the revolutionary if it is abstracted from the ripeness of a society for major social and economic changes.   The model of human rights as embodying the minimal requirements of political obligation is therefore insufficient to solve the problems of pre-socialist societies.

A modified version of the revolutionary position is provided by Istvan Mészáros's interpretation of Marx's attitude to human rights as involving a clear distinction between the use of human rights discourse (1) to reject 'the ruling sectional interests and the advocacy of

personal freedom and individual self-realisation, in opposition to the forces of dehumanisation and increasingly
more destructive material domination or reification';
(2) in societies in transition towards socialism to enable
discrimination 'positively in favour of needy individuals,
in order to redress the inherited contradictions and inequalities' in contrast to; (3) the 'higher phase of communist society', in which there is no need to talk in
terms of 'enforcing rights' since 'the free development
of individualities' is 'integral to the social metabolism
and acts as its fundamental regulating principle'. (31)
For most reformists Mészáros shows too little awareness of
how socialist ideals are to be put into practice. A 'fundamental regulating principle' to be socially effective
must, they could argue, be instantiated in specific
societal rules, as was contended in chapter 3. He also
manifests the common positivistic assumption that 'enforcement' means coercion, which was criticised in chapter 4.
But the reformist does go along with Mészáros's evaluation
of human rights in relation to capitalism as a basis for
rejecting that system if not for the futile justification
of premature rebellion, and also in relation to transitional societies as the basis for making radical demands
on governments on behalf of deprived sections of the
population as part of the move towards social transformation. Here there is a socialist role for human rights
discourse as presenting more than mere aspirations for
a transformed society but the minimal standards to be
achieved by any government entitled to political allegiance. It is, of course, far from clear precisely what a
'transitional' society is, but assuming that this term
covers those societies in which it is possible to meet
something approaching to the norms set forth in the Universal Declaration - which cover such social and economic
rights as the right to work (article 23(1)) and the right
to rest and leisure (article 24) as well as such civil and
political rights as freedom of thought, conscience and
religion (article 18) and the right to take part in the
government of one's country (article 21) - and in which
the state has achieved some measure of control over the
powerful economic forces which shape social relationships,
then there is scope for the traditional deployment of the
idea of human rights as the basis of political obligation
provided that considerations of moral right are tempered
by calculations of historical possibilities.
   This is, however, to go beyond our primary task of
demonstrating the compatibility of socialism and rights,
human and otherwise. It is a theme to which we shall
return in the final chapter. First, we must consider

the justificatory basis for socialist rights (chapter 7) and illustrate their application in conditions of social- ist perfection (chapter 8).

7   Justificatory principles

I have argued that any form of socialism, as a form of
social organisation, will require authoritative rules, if
only to facilitate co-operative and educational activities,
and that some of these rules will be directed towards the
protection and furtherance of the concerns of individuals,
thereby constituting rights. It has been contended, further, that this affirmation of the social significance of
the interests and therefore the rights of the individual
is distinguishable from the assumptions of liberal individualism that society is an aggregate of competitive and
essentially egoistic individuals both separated and held
together by a combination of economic self-interest and
coercive sanctions. We have also seen that this broader
form of individualism readily accommodates the conception
of human rights according to which all members of a
society ought to have certain of their interests protected
and enforced by relatively inviolable or overriding rules.
   To complete the argument against the revolutionary
critique of rights it is necessary to proceed from a discussion of the form or concept of rights to a consideration of the principles which socialists use to commend
specific rights. Without such justificatory principles to
provide a basis for decisions about the material content
of particular rights, the defence of the purely formal
idea of socialist rights is without point. In this chapter I shall examine some central justifying arguments
relating to substantive rights from the point of view of
socialist values and consider the most helpful way in
which they can be analysed and presented so as to bring
out their continuity with and differences from non-
socialist ideals.
   A major advantage of the legalistic interpretation of
rights in terms of legal or societal rules which lay down
obligations for the protection and furtherance of

interests (or make explicit the absence of rules detrimental to the realisation of interests) is that it frees the concept of rights from any necessary tie with a particular type of justificatory theory. Given the distinction between questions about what rights there are and questions about what rights there ought to be, the former can be answered by reference to positivistic criteria and the latter are then open for moral discussion untrammelled by any prior assumptions about the nature of the relevant moral justifications.

Two dogmas in particular can thus be shed. First, it becomes unnecessary to insist on the logical connection between rights and justice, unless by 'justice' is meant simply the formal justice of impartially administering rules. Formal justice, as we have seen, is inseparable from the institution of rights as a rule-governed system, but the logical connection between rights and formal justice does not entail that the content of rights has any exclusive connection with material justice. In fact, in any study of the reasons commonly given in support of specific rights, it is clear that many rights are based on considerations of utility, or the promotion of general welfare, rather than the wellbeing of the particular individuals whose rights they are, and utility is standardly opposed to justice. There is thus reason to be dubious about the central place of the concept of material justice as a rights-justifying consideration. (1)

The logical separation of rights and material justice enables us to discount a second traditional dogma, the doctrine that there is a fundamental conflict between rights and utility. In fact, the chronic opposition between rights and utility features only when issues of formal justice arise in the application of right-conferring rules. In the application of rules, including right-conferring rules, the formally just decision is one which takes into account only the relevant rules and is unaffected by considerations of the social consequences of the particular decision being made. In this respect rights are inseparable from formal justice and are opposed to utility as a criterion of judicial decision-making. To this extent 'taking rights seriously' does involve rights overriding utility; anything else would be to abandon the practice of rule-governed organisation. (2) But the idea that utility is in itself necessarily inadequate for the determination of what rights there ought to be, so that rights and utility are at this level fundamentally opposed, is profoundly misleading. The mistaken idea that rights present a veto on purely utilitarian reasoning in the processes of justifying societal rules may have something to

do with socialist reservations about rights which sometimes appear to protect the vested interests of favoured
individuals and classes to the clear detriment of the welfare of society at large. But when the utilitarian
criterion is applied, as it can be, to the choice of
material rights then conflict between rights and utility
is neither inevitable nor incorrigible. (3)

What, then, are the moral principles commonly considered to be relevant to deciding which interests or concerns ought to be protected by rules and hence what rights
are justified? From what has been said it would appear
that these principles are likely to be indistinguishable
from moral principles in general, and this is partly correct, for rights are not to be distinguished from other
phenomena by the fact that they have a particular sort of
moral support. But the question of what rights ought to
exist is far from identical with the question of what
forms of behaviour are morally right and wrong. In making
decisions about rights we are not simply determining how,
as individuals, we ought to behave, but deciding how other
people are required to behave. Instituting any right and
its correlative obligations inevitably curtails other
rights. One person's claim-right limits another person's
liberty thus reducing his negative rights. Although this
restriction need not involve the use or threat of force or
other coercive measures, it does call for the moral
acquiescence of those whose liberties are at stake and who
may not agree with the requirement in question. For this
reason special considerations arise in assessing the
reasonableness of asking for such acquiescence.

While, therefore it is proper to draw on the wide range
of moral reasons to determine what rights there ought to
be, it is important to be clear that this question has
features which distinguish it from non-legal moral questions where each person is 'legislating', if at all, for
himself alone. It is this fact, for instance, which has
led many theorists to argue that in the case of rights
(as, indeed, of law in general) certain distinctions, like
that between benefiting and harming are of central significance, for while it may be morally praiseworthy for
people to benefit others it is said to be morally unacceptable to require them to do so, which is not the case with
seriously harmful behaviour from which we may reasonably
call on others to refrain. (4)

This is not, in the end, a distinction which has a
strong appeal for socialists who are likely to look for a
'higher' level of moral performance than mere restraint
from harmful activities as the expected social norm, but
it does illustrate the potential implications of the fact

that in deciding on the content of rights we are making
moral choices of a political rather than a private nature.
   Classifying justificatory principles is ultimately an
arbitrary matter better assessed by its intellectual utility in clarifying the value choices at issue than as an
attempt to be faithful to all the obscurities and ambiguities of ordinary political debate.   It is, however,
within at least some traditions of political discourse if
we adopt a scheme based on the concepts of desert, utility
and need, to represent the main types of consideration
relevant to the determination of rights.   This trio of
distributive criteria does not include allocation in
accordance with choice or consent, which may seem out of
line with the emphasis placed on obtaining the acquiescence and support of participants in binding schemes of
rules, but we are at present considering the principles on
which individuals be invited to make such choices, not
whether they should be required to abide by rules to
which they have not consented.
   I distinguish, then, three types of moral reason for
the enactment and maintenance of specific rights: securing
material justice, satisfying human needs, and promoting
utility or general welfare.

(1) Material justice

Material justice has to do with the distribution of benefits and burdens in accordance with desert or merit.
This involves formal justice, or accurate rule-application,
only as a means to the further end of achieving an allocation which is fair in meritorian terms.   This specific
conception of material justice distinguishes it from the
unhelpfully general use of 'justice' to cover any treatment or state of affairs that is thought to be right or
justified.   In its narrower sense I take material justice
as analytically tied to pre-legal or natural desert; not
what a person 'deserves' according to established rules
and procedures, but what his acts and personality merit
independent of any positive entitlements.   Material justice is based on the autonomous premise that the benefits
and burdens a person receives should bear some relationship to what he merits or deserves, his good or bad
qualities and deeds in so far as he is able to claim
credit for them.   Applied to rights, the principle of
material justice implies that the rights a person enjoys
should reflect his natural merit or have bearing on his
opportunities to acquire such merit.

(2) Human need

The principle of need states that the rights of persons
ought to be determined by their needs or requirements.
The presumption of this principle is that beings cannot
flourish if they do not have certain things or if they are
not treated in certain ways. Such requirements are
regarded as needs in that they are prerequisites for the
attainment of certain individual objectives. What these
needs are is an open question which requires to be
answered before the principle can be assessed. An upholder of the need principle has to make clear what is to
count as a need in the application of the principle, just
as any advocate of the principle of material justice must
indicate what is to count as merit in its application.

(3) Utility

According to the principle of utility, the rights of the
individual ought to be based on calculations of the general
welfare or happiness, that is, on the effects which the
implementation of right-conferring rules will have on the
lives of all those affected by their operation (not simply
the interests of the right-bearers). In contrast to the
other two criteria, this principle centres less on the
characteristics of the putative right-holders than on the
assessment of the effects which the existence of rights
will have on the welfare of others. If a rights-based
distribution is efficient in that it makes for maximal
benefits within the jurisdiction in question then the
principle of utility is satisfied. Enormous scope remains,
of course, for the determination of what counts as benefit
and harm.

These three principles may not, in the end, be entirely
distinct, either practically or conceptually. Thus a
utilitarian distribution of rights could turn out to be in
accordance with justice. For instance, if merit is
defined in terms of the contribution of an individual to
the general good then there are unlikely to be major
clashes between utility and justice, even although justice
is backward-looking in that it considers only past per-
formances, while utility is forward-looking because it is
concerned primarily with future benefits. Similarly, a
distribution of rights in accordance with need may be the
best way to maximise the general interest if the needs of
right-holders dominate in the assessment of general welfare.
   Despite these, and other possible convergences, the

three principles represent distinct approaches to the
justification of rights and, depending on the more precise
content given to them and the circumstances in which they
are applied, they may give rise to radically different
policies. My discussion will centre on how socialists
might choose between these competing criteria and attempt
to render more specific their particular versions of these
principles and the implications of this for the general
form, content and tone of systems of socialist rights.

MERITORIAN JUSTICE

Conceptually, the most controversial element in the trio
of justificatory principles is the use of desert alone as
the basis for material justice to the exclusion of other
criteria, such as need. (5) The connection between justice and desert has historically been very close and is
analytically tight enough to make it difficult to conceive
of a conception of justice which has no place for desert.
However, despite the respectable philosophical ancestry
of a meritorian analysis of justice (versions of which
were held by John Stuart Mill (6) and Henry Sidgwick (7)),
most present-day theorists assume that desert is, at the
very most, one amongst many possible criteria for justice.
The standard contemporary view is that 'the central idea
of justice is not the requital of desert but the exclusion
of arbitrariness' (8) a formula which has no difficulty in
accommodating almost any principle distribution in some
terms or other. Such formulae are largely empty, in that
they take us no further than the requirements of formal
justice, and offer little guidance as to what makes justice a specific right-making consideration. Moreover,
once we have put aside the usually unargued dogma that
justice must always override all other moral considerations, (9) the major stumbling block to the acknowledg-
ment of the conceptual force of the association of justice
and desert is removed.
    It is only sensible to take up the meritorian position,
however, if we have a clear idea of natural or pre-legal
desert on which to ground this analysis of material justice. One reason why philosophers have tended recently to
play down the meritorian interpretation of justice is
their perplexity about the notion of natural desert. (10)
As we shall see, this is a perplexity which is shared by
many socialists and one which becomes out and out hostility when merit is given its substantive content in terms
of the values of the capitalist societies in which the
meritorian concept of justice has dominated.

Natural merit or desert is best thought of as referring
to those qualities and actions of an individual which are
the proper objects of praise and blame, gratitude and
resentment, or, in some cases, reward or punishment. It
therefore involves an assessment of the worth of individuals' conduct and characters as exemplified in their past
behaviour. This requires an evaluation of both rightness
and goodness, that is, of both the moral rightness of the
behaviour in question and the reasons or motives for which
it is undertaken, that is, of moral goodness. A meritorious person not only does what is right but does it either
because it is right or from some other admirable motive,
such as benevolence.

Now it is true that a great deal of praise and blame,
gratitude and resentment, or reward and punishment is
meted out simply on the basis of the evaluation of conduct
in relation to external conformity with accepted social
norms, and it is difficult to envisage patterns of praise
and blame where such conventional norms do not exist. But
if we consider what is involved in praising and blaming on
the part of persons endorsing the conventional social
norms or by reference to their own modified versions of
these norms, and distinguish these from the award of
prizes and punishments simply for the achievement of present goals, then we can appreciate what is meant by
natural desert. Such desert is attributable only to
actions, actions which must display a commitment and
effort on the part of the person praised (or the absence
of these qualities in the person blamed) directed towards
the prosecution of goals approved of by the person assessing the conduct. As such it does presuppose that those
praising and blaming have standards by which to judge the
worthwhileness and worthiness of human behaviour, but
these standards need not accord with any prior legal or
societal norm, and may in fact serve as a basis for setting up or defending such norms. For instance, if we can
make sense of the idea of praising someone for saving the
life of another out of a desire to save that life for its
own sake and irrespective of the existence of a societal
norm requiring the saving of life, then this is an adequate illustration of the idea of natural merit which can
then be used to argue for the institution of a right to
receive a reward for saving life, or for any other naturally meritorious form of behaviour.

There are, however, major difficulties in the idea of
natural desert as a justificatory base, despite its grounding in the spontaneous impulse to reward those who do us
good and retaliate against those who cause us injury.
These difficulties are not remarked on by socialists alone

but they are often used by socialists to discredit the meritorian concept of justice. I shall argue that such objections are often based on misunderstandings engendered by an over-readiness to take over non-socialist concepts of merit.

First, I shall deal with the more fundamental objection to the principle of meritorian justice: that it is based on an erroneous concept of individual responsibility.

It is often said that the whole idea of desert pre-supposes that individuals are free to choose how they behave, for otherwise it would not make sense to select such phenomena as choice and effort as in some way indicative of individual worth. If all action, including choice and the capacity to try hard, are equally determined by prior psychological, sociological or biological factors, then it must be misguided to make these characteristics the basis for rights-allocation on the grounds that they demonstrate some mysterious quality of moral goodness. It may be rational to attempt to change human behaviour by inducement, punishments and any other form of behaviour modification, including praise and blame if this has a causal effect on actual behaviour, but this can be sub-sumed under the principles of utility or the principle of need, both of which may direct us to control the actions of others, but it must be mistaken to think that there is any deeper meaning to the idea of desert than conformity to the social norms to which sanctions are conventionally attached. Similarly, gratitude and resentment may serve useful functions in aiding social control but there is no hidden quality in human action which makes it inherently more rational to express such emotions towards conduct rather than towards, for instance, natural events or accidents.

Despite all that has been written to the contrary, there is much to be said for the view that applying cau-sal determinism to human behaviour does indeed undermine the moral rationale for praising and blaming actions and hence the moral significance of the concept of natural desert. (11) Clearly, this has important implications for those socialists who see human conduct as an expression of social, and in the end, economic factors rather than as the outcome of free rational choices. Arguably this is the position adopted by Marx in his analysis of capitalism as the product of changes in the means of production, since the actions of capitalists and proletarians alike are determined by their relationships to the means of pro-duction. Consistently with this approach, Marx refrained from blaming capitalists and praising proletarians. (12) It is, in fact, a common view amongst socialists that the

rich no more deserve their riches than the poor deserve
their poverty: both are equally the result of a system
over which neither group has any control. Distribution in
accordance with desert is seen as a purely ideological
maxim which has the function of providing a rationalising
justification for those who are successful in market economies, a position which is in line with the interpretation of desert in terms of the contribution which the
individual makes to the economic system as measured by
the wages for which he can sell his particular skill, and
the justifying assertions that relative success in a
capitalist economy is the consequence of wise choices and
hard work, and that, in any case, those with valuable
capacities require incentives if they are to make their
required contributions.

The idea of natural desert need not, however, be tied
to capitalist values. In particular, it is possible to
arrive at a more purely 'moral' view of desert which dis -
counts the significance of scarce capacities and economically fortunate qualities which are not themselves the
consequence of admirable choices and individual effort.
Moreover, unless a wholly determinist position regarding
human behaviour is adopted, and such a position is hard to
sustain in practical attitudes, there is no a priori reason why a socialist conception of desert should not be
deployed as a guide to the appropriateness of responsive
attitudes of gratitude and resentment, and hence, without
absurdity, reward or punishment. (13) Such a conception
would stress effortful, altruistic activity in the furtherance of communal objectives.

Even if we go along with the view that Marx himself had
no time for such reactive attitudes in his analysis of
capitalism this cannot be the last word as far as socialist society is concerned, for it is part of the same
interpretation of Marx that in a communist society men
will be free of economic determinism and able to mould
their lives and characters according to their own spontaneous choices. (14) In such a society the language of
meritorian assessment would be natural and untainted by
charges of false consciousness and assumptions regarding
incentives. It can, therefore, be argued that only in a
socialist society would it be proper to apply the meritorian conception of justice.

Nevertheless, the informal use of desert-based conceptions would not necessarily become institutionalised if it
is used as a criterion for the distribution of rights.
It could be argued that to bring desert within the confines of societal rules is to destroy its assumed basis
for, by giving individuals an entitlement to rewards when

they are in some rule-determined way deserving makes it inevitable that they will endeavour to satisfy the rules in order to obtain the rewards (or avoid the burdens), thus rendering impossible the purity of motive which is necessary for the qualities of moral goodness that is the only proper basis for reward and punishment.

This problem, and the equally formidable practical difficulty of knowing how to go about assessing moral goodness when this depends on knowing the motives and situation of the individual concerned, raises serious doubts about the practical applicability of justicising criteria. It is difficult enough for laws to take into account the intentions of individuals without also having to consider their motives or ulterior objectives. It is possible, however, to achieve some sort of rough justice by establishing rights on the basis of average standards, that is the degree of moral worthiness or fault the citizen normally exhibits by undertaking certain types of behaviour, and seeking to ensure that the relevant benefits and burdens are not so substantial that they would of themselves induce conduct of the preferred type thus making it less likely that rewarding desert degenerates into straightforward inducements and deterrents. It has already been argued that the fact that conduct is authoritatively required does not mean that it cannot be undertaken willingly, and, if socialist optimism concerning the eventual emergence of socially responsible attitudes in a socialist society has any substance, then the coincidence between admirable motivation and conformity to socially required and laudable standards would be the rule rather than the exception. The point of such a system would be to give public recognition to the worth of certain activities and the desirable qualities that are required to undertake them. This would satisfy a meritorian sense of justice which may not be fundamental to socialism but is perfectly compatible with it.

HUMAN NEED

There is something like a consensus among those who accept that socialism has a moral basis that the principle of distribution in accordance with need is the foundation of socialist entitlement. Marx's use of the slogan 'from each according to his ability to each according to his need' (15) is often taken to license the view that in a fully socialist community need, not desert, would determine the allocation of any resources which require to be distributed. This would seem to indicate that the

socialist criterion for the ascription of rights is that
of need.

The concept of need is, however, one of the most elu-
sive and open-ended to be found in the arena of political
discourse. (16) In its broadest sense a need is something
required for the fulfilment of any purpose or objective
whatever. Thus, a human need is anything necessary for
the attainment of a human condition or goal. There are,
therefore, few things which cannot be regarded as needs in
virtue of their role in the attainment of some objective
or other and consequently people can be said to have needs
for the means necessary to carry out evil as well as good
activities and to attain conditions of luxury as well as
bare subsistence. For these reasons the need principle is
highly implausible as a general political criterion unless
it is presented in conjunction with standards for choosing
between possible human objectives or wants. In any normative principle, needs must be taken as applying only to
those things which are requisite for the attainment of
particularly valued human goals.

Further, for the principle of distribution in accordance with need to form the basis for a systematic allocation of rights it would be necessary to establish a hierarchy of needs in line with their moral priority, so that
the criteria for being 'in need' are specified in a way
which enables us to select which interests are to have
priority in settling entitlements. One attempt to do
this distinguishes between 'adventitious', 'functional'
and 'course-of-life' needs. (17) These distinctions can
be used to specify what it means to be 'in need' in the
strict and relevant sense of lacking those things necessary to achieve, not just any morally proper goal, but a
certain condition of living defined in accordance with
some norm setting out what constitutes a minimum tolerable
level of material existence.

'Need' in this restricted sense does not cover 'adventitious needs', the term used to refer to the requisites
for transitory goals which, in David Braybrooke's words,
'come and go with particular contingent projects', nor
does it take in 'functional needs' which arise in the
course of a person's job or social role, such as the sol-
dier's need for a gun, or the entertainer's need for an
audience. Braybrooke gives more weight to 'course-of-
life needs' which 'people have all through their lives or
at certain stages through which all must pass', like the
need for shelter or health care. For many theorists of
social policy, it is course-of-life needs which are
written into the need principle.

However, it is not clear that all course-of-life needs

have significant moral import. Such pervasive requirements
as those for delicious foods and entertaining friends do
not seem in themselves to merit major justificatory status.
For this reason a distinction is made within course-of-
life needs between those which relate to the attainment of
certain minimum basic standard-of-living conditions and
those which merely arise out of the common range of human
desires. Exactly what constitutes this minimum standard
will vary with the economic condition of the society and
the values of its members, but the principle of need can
usefully be interpreted by reference to some such selected
basic course-of-life needs. The frequently asserted
'objectivity' of statements about human need is then
understood as an expression of the belief that there is a
range of basic human requirements far narrower than the
total shape of wants and desires which has a great deal
more moral significance than any other type of 'need'.
This assumption is encapsulated in the idea of being 'in
need' and the standard contrast between needs and wants.
This prescription, that each person ought to receive or
be left in possession of that which is necessary to meet
his or her basic, course-of-life needs, I will call the
'welfare principle'. (18)

Do we, then, have in the idea of allocation in accordance with basic course-of-life needs, the central socialist rationale for the justification of the content of a
system of rights? Does the welfare principle express the
essence of socialist political morality in the commitment
to the elimination of suffering by the institutionalised
response to such needs in proportion to their gravity
irrespective of the deserts of those in need or the
demands of aggregate utility? If so, this would appear
to have, for the socialist, the advantage of being a
genuine principle of humanity with clear egalitarian
implications in contradistinction to ideologically suspect meritorian justice and the impersonal calculations
of utility.

One problem which the socialist has with the welfare
principle is that it seems to presuppose the existence of
universal human needs which, as we have seen in the discussion of human rights, conflicts with his view of human
nature as a historically variable phenomenon. But, given
that what is to count as minimum physical and social conditions for a tolerable human life will vary in accordance with historically conditioned circumstances, the
goal of meeting such needs would be accepted by many
socialists as an essential element of socialism. Within
these limits Marx, for instance, points to a distinction
between real and artificial needs which embodies the

necessary relative evaluation of the experienced range
of human wants. (19) Certainly, making the relief of such
needs a matter of right, so that there are specific obligations laid upon those able to alleviate need, accords
with the socialist impulse to organise the relief of dis-
tress and ensure that the receipt of the necessities of
life is a matter not of charity but of entitlement, and
thus both effective and dignified.

It is, however, very doubtful whether such a minimal
principle of need is adequate to a developed socialist
society. The welfare principle seems characteristic of an
ideologically mixed type of polity called the welfare
state, which is designed to cope with the exigencies of
the 'needy' while leaving the normal operation of the economy to run along entirely different, market lines.
Socialists typically wish to go beyond this half-way house
to make a strengthened version of the welfare principle
the basis of all social relationships. This is typified
in the attempt to use the concept of need as a basis for
a principle of equality or egalitarianism in accordance
with which, from the point of view of all valued goods and
services, individuals are all essentially in the same
position, irrespective of their capacity to purchase goods
in a market place. 'Need' is here used to represent
that degree to which the individual falls below the sum of
goods he would possess or enjoy if the resources of his
society were divided so as to give equal satisfaction to
its members. This is not an equality which involves identical holdings or treatment since individual differences
in health, strength, taste and capacity are taken into
account. Nor does it require that equality be reached for
the purpose of eliminating envy or greed, for such emotions are either absent or have no standing within a
socialist scheme. Rather this more radical version of
the welfare principle aims at something approximating to
equal enjoyment and fulfilment for all. In this version
of the principle 'need' is taken to refer to that which is
required if those 'in need' are to reach a level of equal
benefit. For this reason rights based on the need principle do not come up against Marx's criticism that all
rights, by setting up an equal standard of treatment,
produce inequalities, for the principle uses inequalities
to justify making people equal with respect to the desired
benefit. Unequal needs may lead to different treatment,
but the result is not a situation of relative inequality.
(20)

What is to count as a benefit (and burden), and how
equality is to be measured within and between benefits
(and burdens) are major problems for the socialist, as for

any egalitarian. To settle such issues there are characteristic socialist norms to which reference may be made:
the full development of creative productivity, equal participation in co-operative or communal activities, the
fulfilment of spontaneous, 'natural' or non-artificial
desires, to say nothing of the more basic goal of the
satisfaction of basic course-of-life needs. Although precision and agreement are not readily obtainable in this
area, the role of the concept of need in the articulation
of egalitarianism is clear: it points to those ways in
which individuals (or groups) fall short of the currently
attainable average condition. It is for the removal of
these deficiencies that a system of socialist rights would
be, at least in part, deployed, so that where, for instance, inherited individual differences, lack of health
care, education, material goods, or the environment necessary for the development of creative talent and communal
activity contribute to any person falling below an average
level of attainable satisfaction, there is a prima facie
case for establishing rules laying down obligations to
remove the deficiencies, thus instituting rights on the
basis of human need.
     A second way in which the limitation of 'need' to basic
course-of-life needs may be thought inadequate to express
how a thorough-going socialist might interpret the need
principle becomes evident when we consider the distribution of the rights that are bound up with fulfilment of
each person's place in co-operative enterprises. Given
that socialism has to do with the organisation of complex
industrial societies in such a way as to ensure that
individuals are fully participant members of communal
productive methods, some form of acceptable division of
labour must exist to ensure the efficient organisation of
economic and social relations in a manner compatible with
giving each individual a satisfying role to perform.
(Such division of labour need not involve the individual
being confined to one role which, as Marx points out,
would inevitably be stultifying). This is to bring into
the picture the functional needs which Braybrooke considers irrelevant to distribution in accordance with need.
But clearly functional needs, such as those things which
a person requires to carry out his co-operative function,
could not be entirely overlooked in any allocation of
socialist rights. This has nothing in particular to do
with differential rewards, rather it relates to those
things (be it tools, space or time) essential to the performance of socially approved roles, including the right
to loyalty and obedience for those who are given the no
doubt limited task of creating and enforcing societal
rules.

The notion of rights exercisable in the pursuance of duties is neither unusual nor contradictory and the usefulness of the notion is not dependent on the associated duties being regarded as burdensome. It can be projected therefore that some rights in a socialist society will arise out of the functional inter-relationships of those engaged in co-operative activities. In so far as such rights are decided upon with a view to promoting the efficiency of an enterprise which is assumed to be for the benefit of all, then the criterion for rights-allocation could, as we will see, be regarded as a utilitarian one. This in itself carries no implication that the content of these rights is affected by the device of enticing the able to perform socially desirable tasks. Indeed, many of these rights would relate to social functions - such as parenthood - open and welcome to most members of a society. Nor need the instrumental connection between role-related rights and the general welfare be seen as an 'invisible hand' process which turns self-interested or wicked actions into utility-maximising ones. (21) Such rights may be equally well-grounded in the determination of which altruistic interests or concerns should be favoured with the protection and facilities of societal rules. In this area of social organisation at least the demise of burdensome duties does not entail the redundancy of rights.

Functional needs, and hence functional rights, have wide and, to an extent, inegalitarian implications, although these will vary with the scope and range of the division of labour in society. Some socialists, impressed by the evils of coerced division of labour in capitalist systems, assume that the division of labour is tied to monetary differences in rewards and must result in a very restricted development of the individual's potential capacities. They therefore argue that there will be no organised division of labour in a socialist society. Even in these circumstances it must be assumed that all citizens would have approximately the same tasks to fulfil, and would therefore have the same functional needs and consequently the same functionally dependent rights. However, a more likely scenario is that socialist citizens would each develop a range of different economic, social and political roles, with varied creative and productive features, so that there would be differing functional needs in a socialist society reflecting the variety of capacities and interests. Such needs would be as 'basic' as the course-of-life needs we have already considered, in the sense that it is part of socialist doctrine that fulfilling and productive co-operative activity is an

essential requirement for a satisfying and genuinely human
life. (22)

A third socialist modification to the welfare principle
is to render it more positive in content so as to make explicit the moral imperative to maximise need-satisfaction.
The normal connotation of the concept of need expresses a
double lack or deficiency, the absence of a necessary
means to an objective and the fact that failure to reach
the objective is itself a condition of deprivation or below average benefit. In its ideal and aspirational import
the socialist concept of needs extends beyond this second
form of deficiency to cover those things which are necessary for the fullest possible development of all desirable
human activities and experiences. There are, therefore,
needs for such things as scientific equipment to realise
people's potentialities for original research and in general for special training and opportunities to develop
physical, artistic and social skills. Since there are
inevitable individual differences in the potential of
individuals with respect to the variety of worthwhile
human attainments this element of the need principle has,
strictly speaking, inegalitarian implications even
although development of each individual's capacities is
given equal weight, but its basic import is to require
egalitarian need-satisfaction at the highest possible
level.

It would seem, therefore, that socialism goes beyond
the welfare principle to an ideal of distribution in
accordance with need which is substantially egalitarian
and takes into the conception of human need whatever is
requisite for the fullest possible development of human
nature under the particular social conditions which pertain. This will, no doubt, involve singling out for priority those needs which are 'basic' in the sense that they
must be satisfied before other human activities can be
engaged in - as Marx writes, men must eat, sleep and be
housed before they can make history (23) - but beyond such
prerequisites there has to be some selection of those
forms of human interest and concerns which most fully
express the ideal of co-operative, creative, and productive activities and enjoyments. The welfare principle is
thus transformed into an ideal-regarding and open-ended
need principle which is at once more comprehensive and
more central to the general ordering of social relationships, but which leaves for further disposition precisely
what is to count as needs in contrast to mere desires.

UTILITY

In taking the principle of need to involve the distribution of rights so as to achieve the objective of maximal equal need-satisfaction by giving individuals rights to that which they require to live a fully human existence, we have moved some way towards turning the principle of need into a version of utilitarianism according to which acts and institutions are right or wrong in so far as they further or retard human happiness, conceived of as the absence of pain and the presence of pleasure. (24)

There are, however, several reasons for not presenting socialist political principles in the utilitarian format, despite the fact that Marx is sometimes regarded as a utilitarian. (25) It may seem natural to think of an ideology which is committed to relieving the suffering of the largest social class as utilitarian in outlook, and the introduction to the principle of need of functional needs is specifically consequentialist in form. Moreover, no socialist would deny that the satisfaction of need is conducive to human happiness. But happiness is the by-product rather than the goal of socialist ideals which centre more on the idea of free purposeful activity than on the concepts of pleasure and pain as such.

Some of the reluctance of socialists to adopt the utilitarian maxim relate to its historical association with the egoistic psychology of Hobbes and Bentham and the related assumption that men must be threatened or bribed into refraining from harming others and making their contribution to the general good. The functional rights of socialism have to do with those things which are internally necessary to fulfil a socially useful role rather than with artificial or external incentives to perform unwelcome tasks. Thus the scholar has a right to books, not a higher than average standard of living, and the administrator has a right only to command the resources necessary for the performance of his task. Such rights are socially beneficial but not in the manipulative way envisaged by classical utilitarianism.

A further historically explicable source of socialist hostility to utilitarianism relates to the tendency to translate happiness into monetary terms thus contributing to the topsy-turvey world in which an artificial device to aid economic activities in commercial societies becomes the measure of human satisfaction. Money does provide an easy standard for comparing the situation of different individuals and it is certainly common to think of money as being translatable into any other valued human possessions and experiences thus enabling us to rank preferences on the same scale of values. But this clearly does not apply to such objectives as the establishment of the sort of human relationships which socialists regard as a prerequisite of human happiness and takes no account of the nature and limitations of the goods which are available for purchase.

More generally, the major objection to the utilitarian principle is that - when utility is measured in terms of individual preferences - it gives equal weight to all preferences or satisfactions whereas socialism, as we have seen, values certain types of human activity and concern above others. The pleasures of isolated indulgence are not equated with those of active communal creativity.

This difficulty is exacerbated by the fact that utilitarians, often in the interests of simplicity but also to exclude discrimination, (26) seek to exclude other-regarding preferences from their calculations in that they discount in computing the general happiness A's preferences about what is to happen to B and C. (27) If there is a socialist utilitarian principle it must be compatible with socialist ideals of human nature in which such other-regarding preferences and concerns are of central importance. While it is formally compatible with the utilitarian maxim to include all human preferences, social, non-social and antisocial, the standard utilitarian proviso, limiting recognition to the desires of self-interested individuals, unfits it for the effective communication of socialist principles.

One of the most frequently recurrent points made against utilitarianism is its apparent indifference to the fair distribution of benefits and burdens. (28) Socialists share this general unease. Bentham's dictum that each is to count for one and no more than one entails only that every person's pain and pleasure is to be taken into account and measured on the same scale, but this does nothing to veto distributions in which the sufferings of some are outweighed by the pleasures of the majority. In practice, some mitigation of this fault may be allowed on the basis of the economist's 'law of diminishing returns' or 'diminishing marginal utility', according to which the effect of benefit deriving from one unit of resource varies positively with the extent of the relative deprivation so that, as an individual becomes better off, so the degree of benefit he derives from additional units of resource is proportionately reduced. The suspicion remains, however, that the relative importance of relieving suffering is underestimated when it is traded off against the general happiness.

In contrast, the principle of need has a more stringent

egalitarian requirement in that the concept of need incorporates an element of comparative assessment according to which those in greater need should receive more. The principle of utility, on the other hand, even where it is deployed in the service of maximising need-satisfaction, will tend to provide a more agreeable and fulfilling way of life for those who have no particular deprivations, thus tending to a certain inequality.

There seems little question that inequalities of this sort are justified provided no one suffers as a result, and certainly Marx gave no encouragement to a lowest common denominator form of egalitarianism that allows for no conceivable relative advantages, (29) but this leaves open whether the utilitarian objective should be to maximise average satisfactions or discriminate in favour of specific groups, such as the least advantaged. One possibility, recently canvassed by Rawls and subjected to much subsequent criticism, is the idea that inequalities are justified only if they benefit the worst-off representative individual. (30) This is obviously to some extent in tune with the egalitarian aspects of the socialist need principle although Rawls's use of his 'maximin principle' to justify the use of incentives is not applicable in a socialist society. But Rawls's principle leaves unresolved a whole host of other comparisons that have to be made between the relatively better-off groups which are important objects of social concern for the socialist who is unwilling to leave such matters to the mercy of individual competition and good fortune. General priority must doubtless go to those in greatest need, but other differentiations in the rights afforded to individuals could also be justified on the grounds of equalising need-satisfaction at the highest possible level. This somewhat vague formula does not, of course, give any clear guidance as to the priority of aggregative over equalising considerations but it does, more forcefully than the utilitarian maxim, suggest a general bias in favour of distributions designed to correct inequalities as much as to increase satisfactions.

In sum, socialists differ from traditional utilitarianism over the nature of the valued things that are to be distributed, the manner in which this distribution is productive of the general welfare, the identification of what constitutes human happiness and the relative importance of equality in distribution. It is therefore best to subsume the acceptable remnants of utilitarianism under the rubric of functional needs and the general idea of maximising need-satisfaction within the constraints of egalitarian considerations, and to resist the temptation to present

socialist ideals as a variety of utilitarianism distinguished by its distinctive factual beliefs about the
perfectability of human nature and the sources of human
happiness.

SOCIALIST PRINCIPLES AND SOCIALIST RIGHTS

Summarising the previous section, we may say that the
characteristic justificatory principle of socialist
organisation is the equal satisfaction of need at the
highest level of fulfilment. It is admitted that this
involves an unresolved tension between maximising and
equalising considerations since it is by no means clear
whether all socialists would acquiesce, for instance, in
a small loss of equality in return for a large gain in
quantitative need-satisfaction. Moreover, we cannot discount the possibility of a socialist normative theory
incorporating an element of natural desert into its distributive system although this fits rather more readily
into non-regulated areas of social relationships that are
outside the sphere of rights and duties. Further, the
concept of need requires to be given specific content in
relation to the socialist ideals of fulfilled or 'unalienated' human existence. Slogans concerning free creative
activity or the full development of essentially human
capacities in co-operative social relationships are insuf-
ficiently detailed for the determination of rights.
    However, without claiming that this egalitarian version
of normative need-satisfaction is adequately precise, or
that it will satisfy all socialists, it does provide us
with a sufficiently distinct socialist approach to justificatory issues to enable us to make some fairly concrete
points about the relationship between socialist principles
and the concept of rights.
    Most fundamental is the point that socialism can be
expressed partly in terms of normative principles of social
organisation applicable to the determination of the rights
that ought to exist in an acceptable society. The principle of distribution in accordance with need can be
brought to bear on determining liberties, claim-rights and
powers. It is therefore false to say that there is no
place for the concept of rights in a socialist society.
While it may be, in abstraction from realistic sociological considerations, just conceivable that such principles
as the equal satisfaction of needs be applied directly and
de novo to a social situation (provided some content is
given to the norms relating to which 'need' is assessed)
without the intermediacy of a set of rules directed

towards the satisfaction of interests, even the consistent application of the simplest distributive criteria, as in the allocation of available food according to the degree of hunger felt by the distributees, involves following a rule which can be expressed in terms of rights, in this case the right to a share of food proportional to one's hunger. And since the concept of need gives rise to a whole series of 'claims' of this sort it must inevitably generate a complex system of such rules which, if they are to be consistently applied, must be explicitly formulated and communicated as authoritative guidelines, at least to administrators. Thus any remotely adequate implementation of the need principle must give rise to a range of rule-governed distributive procedures which cannot be departed from without infringing the rights of recipients. This is not to say that rules will not have to be subject to alteration in the light of the outcome of their application, but to change particular rules is not to abandon rule-governed process.

Interpreting the need principle as having primarily to do with the allocation of pre-existing resources for the satisfaction of human needs, the characteristic type of right that it justifies is one which places obligations on those in a position to provide the wherewithal for the satisfaction of the needs of others. Such rights will be positive or affirmative rights in that they correlate with obligations that others take positive steps to meet the needs of right-holders. This assumes the rejection of the liberal assumption that, while there is a general moral requirement not to harm others, there is no equivalent requirement to assist them, even when in need. According to the rough and ready socialist principle of equal need-satisfaction, there is always a prima facie obligation on the part of those with more than the average of benefits to help those below the average. Granted such a general-ised obligation, obvious practicalities require that it be discharged routinely in a socially organised way, that is, through a system of social rules designed to equalise need-satisfaction. A socialist society would typically be constituted by such positive obligations directed towards meeting the interests of those whose relative needs place them below the point which generates claims on the atten-tion and actions of others.

Even this sketchy picture of what would be involved in the implementation of the principle of equal need-satisfaction raises the question of the location of the obligations correlative to the rights of the 'needy'. The principle, it will be remembered, is not simply an equal-ising principle concerning the distribution of available

resources, opportunities and roles, but contains a maximising or aggregative element in relation to which all
people are in a sense 'needy' in that they all have
requirements which must be met if they are to approximate
to the level at which a socialist might say that they are
living a fully human existence. On whom do the obligations to meet these requirements fall? The answer must be
that they are obligations shared by all members of the
community, including the needy themselves, in that all
have the obligation to contribute within their capacities
to the creation of the means to satisfy approved human
needs. This is not to say that the obligations of all will
be identical in content or degree, for they will depend in
part on the roles acquired by the individual, their capacities, opportunities and the resources available to them.

Consequently, the relationships between right-holders
and obligation-bearers is not the simple one-to-one correlation which holds in the case of such typical liberal
rights as the right to freedom from bodily injury which
are primarily rights which all members of a society have
against all other members. The fact that meeting needs
requires the co-operative effort of many individuals,
involving public or collective procedures, means that the
fulfilment of typically socialist duties must be mediated
through social procedures. In this sense the individual's
rights in a socialist society are rights against society
and the correlative obligations can also be seen as obligations to society since their fulfilment does not depend
on the individual who has the obligation identifying and
acting directly towards the individuals who have the correlative rights. In this formulation 'society' is simply
a way of referring to the indispensable system of rule-
governed co-operation which forms the intermediary between rights and duties.

This model of societally mediated rights and duties
has, from the socialist point of view, the defect that it
seems to assume the activity of B (the obligation-bearer)
and the passivity of A (the right-holder), whereas the
socialist ideal is of a society in which individuals are
fulfilled primarily through the active co-operative creative ventures. In part this objection is met by pointing
out that any particular person is both an A and a B, both
a receiver of what he needs and a contributor to the
social mechanisms designed to see that he and others receive what they need. It can therefore be argued that
it is to obligations, not rights, that we should look for
the instantiation of active, productive socialist man.

However, this is not entirely satisfactory since, for
the socialist, one of man's essential needs is to be an

active participant in productive processes of a sort that call on a wide spectrum of his capacities. Thus one of the most important benefits to be distributed is the opportunity to play a part in the ongoing activities of productive social life: the 'needed' things are not, therefore, to be seen as sets of material goods for indi- vidualised consumption (although something of this is assuredly required) but involve the distribution of opportunities for productive activity in conjunction with others. This means that there is no sharp distinction be- tween the allocation of such producer-role rights and the obligations attaching to such roles. If there is a need to produce then in this respect rights and obligations coalesce: A's productive rights (such as the rule-guarded capacity to require the involvement of others and to be left alone to carry out obligations without interference from others) will go along with the obligations of role- fulfilment.

This is not to render the distinction between rights and obligations vacuous since the rights and the obliga- tions are separably describable (thus A may have an obli- gation to produce corn and a right to a tractor to enable him to do this). It does mean, however, that functional rights will have a central place in a socialist society. Moreover, many socialist rights limit the content of related obligations, since they have to do with the man- ner in which co-operative enterprises are conducted, namely in such a way as to further the human development of those involved and not simply the wellbeing of the external beneficiaries. But the point has to be made that socialist rights will include rights not simply to receive but rights to give or contribute, so that activity and not just passivity will be a feature of the rights as well as the obligations of the socialist citizen.

The ethos of a socialist system is declared to be co- operative rather than competitive in that the rights allocated will be designed to help each individual to con- tribute according to his capacities to the productive endeavours of a society designed to meet human needs rather than to enable each to compete on equal terms in the struggle for scarce resources. For this reason the purely formal liberties which are analysed as being equi- valent to the absence of duties to act or refrain from acting, will assume less significance, since their prime function is to license competition of the sort which will no longer exist under socialism. This is not to say that a socialist society would not uphold the principle that what is not forbidden is permitted, but it does mean that, given the no doubt questionable assumption that within socialism individuals will not be motivated to compete, the circumstances in which formal liberties are important will simply not arise.

The same cannot be said about substantial liberties or negative claim-rights which correlate with the obligations of others to refrain from interference with the right-holder's interests, since a sphere of unimpeded action is presupposed by all human activity, but such rights will be taken for granted rather than treated as exhaustive and will be curtailed by the overriding requirement that com-munal resources be used for the common benefit. Socialist man is not likely to regard this as an unwarranted restraint on his sacrosanct private interests.

It is perhaps this revolution in human motivation that renders it difficult to visualise a socialist system of rights in operation, particularly on a positivistic analysis of rights according to which all rights are in principle justiciable, that is, may be settled by an appeal to something like a legal court. This imaginative difficulty is increased if we assume an adversarial system of courts with claims and counter-claims, accusations of guilt, protestations of innocence and pleas of excuse. Such procedures presuppose one-sided and partial presenta-tions of evidence which are intelligible in the conflict between self-interested people but strikingly out of place in a dispute between altruists for whom their duties are of more pressing significance than their rights.

Court procedure can, however, be investigative rather than adversarial and it is interesting to note that states which claim to be socialist do tend to favour a non-adversarial system. (31) Moreover, there is no difficulty in conceiving of a massive extension of modes of legal representation which permit legal standing to be accorded to those seeking to defend the rights of others. Further, it need not be assumed that socialist man is altruistic in the sense of caring only for others and not at all for him-self. Impartiality or non-egoism is a more appropriate description of non-competitive man and this is compatible with the individual giving to his own interests equal weight to those of others, remembering also that his interests will involve a concern for the welfare of other people as well as his own. This will still generate con-flicts of interest to the extent that the different view-points and roles of varied types of individuals with dif-ferent responsibilities and involvements will give rise to alternative views of actual social situations and opinions about the meaning and application of the relevant rules, thus making some judicial intervention necessary. No such system could operate if no one was prepared to press their viewpoints, and given that no selfishness is entailed in doing so, it can be assumed that in many cases the person best able to present a claim of right would be the person whose rights are at issue. Self-representation and initiation of actions might be most economic and sensible in pursuing disagreements over the application of rights, but it is a virtue of the interest theory of rights that there is no bar, conceptual or practical, to adjudicative processes being initiated and pursued on behalf of those whose rights are at risk, although it is to be expected that such vicarious initiatives would themselves become a relatively specialised occupation subject to the normal framework of non-alienated yet divided labour.

It might seem that, given such radical changes in human motivation and expectations, legal disputes would be of a civil rather than a criminal nature and that the main purpose of adjudication would be declaratory in that disputants would be willing to accept the decision of any procedurally correct tribunal or court, so that the only remedial steps required would be a return to the status quo prior to the disputed events; hence compensation rather than punishment would be the appropriate remedy in every case, there being no need to inflict retribution or deter wilful wrongdoing. But, while it might well be the case that the sharp divide between the stigma arising from an adverse criminal decision and the more socially neutral consequences of civil proceedings would evaporate, the elimination of sanctions would not necessarily remove the guiding, educative and even the denunciatory functions at present fulfilled by the criminal law. No plausible social theory can project the disappearance of the need to direct, socialist and persuade, processes in which criminal law plays a significant part. Some rule-infractions will always require to be identified, proved and pronounced upon, so that criminal law of a non-punitive sort would be retained as one area in which the language of rights and obligations would have a prominent function.

The social function of the socialist concept of rights would not, however, be centred on courts of law. The chief purpose of societal rules designed to further the concerns of individuals would be within the normal administrative operations of whatever institutional arrangements were thought necessary to organise communal life so as to meet approved human needs. It is an essential corollary of the dominance within a socialist society of positive or affirmative rights that those entrusted with the tasks of societal organisation would be the primary initiators in the protection of individual rights and themselves the

bearers of significant power-rights to enable them to
carry out their functions. Socialist rights are more
typically directives and enablements than claims. They
signify the proper ends and capacities of organised co-
operative activity rather than the ultimate recourse of
aggrieved individuals. This places them at the conscious
centre of any human group organised to satisfy the needs
of socialised man.

8   Political rights: freedom of expression

When fears are expressed that socialism involves the negation of rights it is usually political rights, particularly democratic rights such as the right to participate
in elections, that critics have in mind. (1) Talk of the
end of law, the abolition of the state and the impotence
of 'bourgeois' institutions, such as free speech and free
elections, to prevent exploitation and alienation, as well
as the actual practice of so-called 'communist' countries,
all support the impression that socialism puts an end to
the previous civil liberties which are regarded in the
West as the bedrock of freedom. This chapter, which
examines the hypothesis that socialism, even if it does
not herald the end of rights in general, is at best un-
enthusiastic about the civil and political rights enshrined in Western democratic theory, concentrates on the
right to freedom of expression (2) as an example of the
old-style political liberties which socialism is alleged
to put at risk.

It will continue to be assumed that socialist claims
concerning the transformation of human nature and the
prospect of attaining socialist ideals are realistic, the
objective being to vindicate the reformist thesis that,
even in such Utopian circumstances, socialism has a place
for political rights. In the final chapter I shall turn
to the added complexities which arise in unravelling the
conceptual ambiguities and associated philosophical ambivalence in socialist attitudes to rights in non-socialist
societies.

Also taken for granted will be the arguments of chapter
3 concerning the need for societal organisation in fully
socialist communities, particularly in relation to the
organisation of the processes of production for the
attainment of equal need-satisfaction. Such organisation,
as we saw in chapter 5, requires rules, and it has been

contended that these rules generate rights when they are
directed towards furthering the interests or concerns of
individuals. In the main these rules apply directly to
the activities of the individual citizen, and are therefore what Hart calls 'primary rules'. (3) But a complex
society also requires 'secondary rules' granting power-
rights to certain persons to change and adjudicate on the
application of primary rules in accordance with established criteria which are specified in what Hart calls a
'rule of recognition'. (4) It is these secondary rules
which make up the most important political rights, the
constitutional rights which determine whether one, some,
or all persons are entitled to make law, and how these
laws are to be administered. The rights which primary
rules create are also political where, as in the case of
freedom of speech, these are relevant to the processes of
influencing the making and enforcement of societal rules.
The assumption, then, is that a socialist society will
have some such legal-political system. The questions
which then arise concern the nature and content of the
political rights embodied in that system.

It will be a recurring point in the course of this
chapter that, even when rights which feature in the philo-
sophies of non-socialist societies are carried over into
socialism, their justification is far from identical.(5)
This, as we will see, has significant implications for the
interpretation and possible limitations or extensions of
rights, particularly in situations where they conflict
with each other. Attention will be paid specifically to
the consequences of viewing rights as relating to societal
rules designed to further the joint self-realisation of
socially integrated persons rather than to defend the private space and conflicting interests of isolated and
antagonistic individuals. The same considerations will
also be used to examine what is involved in transforming
the negative rights of liberalism into the positive rights
of socialism and the differences in attitude and practice
which are brought about by regarding rights as being facilities within government rather than defences against
government.

'The right to freedom of opinion and expression' is
enshrined in article 19 of the Universal Declaration of
Human Rights (1948). (6) It also features prominently
amongst the fundamental rights of those countries with
written constitutions, (7) and is in general accepted as
a central, perhaps inviolable, human right. What the right
to freedom of expression amounts to in practice is predict-
ably variable. This is in part due to the non-implementa-
tion of paper rights and in part because of different

specifications of its content. Article 19 of the Universal
Declaration goes on to say 'this right includes freedom to
hold opinions without interference and to seek, receive
and impart information and ideas through any media,
regardless of frontiers', while article 11 of the French
Declaration of the Rights of Man and of the Citizen
(1789) states that 'unrestrained communication of thoughts
and opinions being one of the most precious rights of man,
every citizen may speak, write and publish freely'.(8)
This indicates that freedom of expression guarantees the
absence of legal penalties for holding opinions and pro-
hibits legal and perhaps other restraints on communicating
opinions. But, while the right not to be penalised for
holding opinions, whatever their content, is widely
regarded as inviolable, this is not the case with the
right to communicate them, although advocating an activity
is normally sharply distinguished from actually doing it.
In the United Kingdom, for instance, there are laws of
slander and libel which allow for civil remedies for false
and defamatory expressions of opinion about another person,
censorship laws which prohibit the communication of
classified information, laws against the public expression and display of obscenities, laws regulating what may
be shown in theatres, cinemas and in advertisements, copy-
right laws restricting unauthorised reproduction of certain materials, numerous regulations govern the use of
various means of communication, such as loudspeakers,
radio and television transmitters, and laws regarding the
use of public places as well as entry to and behaviour in
private meetings, all of which abridge freedom of communication either by making the expression or portrayal of
certain words and images illegal, or by enforcing penalties or damages after the event. (9)   Similar, although
much less sweeping, regulations exist in the United States
of America, and this is true to some extent of all modern
states.
     Some statements of fundamental rights make explicit
allowance for such restrictions on freedom of expression.
Article 11 of the French Declaration includes the caveat
'provided he [the citizen] is responsible for the abuse of
this liberty, in the cases determined by law'. (10)   The
Basic Law of the German Federal Republic, after stating,
in article 5, that 'there shall be no censorship', goes on
to make the proviso that 'these rights are limited by the
provisions of the general laws, the provision of the law
for the protection of youth, and by the right to inviolability of personal honour'. (11)
     It seems clear, then, that the apparently straight-
forward right to freedom of expression breaks down into a

collection of more specific and limited liberties, claim-
rights and powers. The practically important and theoretically interesting issues arise in the process of seeking to reach agreement on the precise nature and content
of these specifications and limitations. For this purpose
it is helpful to distinguish, in accordance with the
logical scheme outlined in chapter 3, those rights of
expression which are:
(i) purely formal liberty-rights, simply indicating the
absence of an obligation to remain silent;
(ii) substantive liberties or negative claim-rights
which lay obligations on others not to interfere with the
expression and communication of opinions;
(iii) positive or affirmative claim-rights which correlate
with the duties of others to provide the wherewithal for
effective communication of ideas; and
(iv) power-rights which give entitlement to use certain
means of communication or to be heard on certain specified
occasions, such as in legislative gatherings, public
places and court rooms.
    In general, liberal and socialist rights to freedom of
expression may be contrasted by saying that characteristically liberal rights are formal and substantive liberties (although they also include some power-rights) while
socialist rights to freedom of expression are more typically positive claim-rights and power-rights. The reformist socialist would claim that the right to freedom of
expression must involve being given the means and opportunity to communicate, a right which is spelt out in the
constitution of the USSR which states that 'These civil
rights are ensured by placing at the disposal of the working people and their organisations, printing presses,
stacks of paper, public buildings, the streets, communica-
tions facilities and other material prerequisites for the
exercise of these rights.' (12) This accords with the
suggestion, made in the previous chapter, that socialist
rights have an administrative more than a grievance
function.
    It is also useful to distinguish between those limita-
tions on rights to freedom of expression which are
designed:
(a) to prevent the violation of other rights, such as the
right not to be defamed, or the right to privacy, or to
a fair trial;
(b) to prevent offence being caused to others, as with
obscenity;
(c) to prevent corruption of the moral standards of
others;
(d) to prevent the communication of information which

could cause damage to the general welfare as it is protected by government, as in the case of military and
industrial secrets;
(e) to protect or enhance the moral, religious or political consensus in a society;
(f) to facilitate the orderly expression of opinions, particularly in the allocation of scarce opportunities and
means for effectively communicating with others.
     Very different considerations arise under each of these
headings. This chapter, in concentrating on constitutional political questions primarily concerning the
nature and content of secondary rules, will not deal
directly with the importance of limitations on free speech
in the spheres of religion, literature, entertainment and
education, and will therefore be concerned largely with
the last three types of consideration which have direct
bearing on the operations of societal organisation.

LIBERALISM AND FREEDOM OF EXPRESSION

The classic liberal defence of freedom of expression is
generally taken to be John Stuart Mill's essay 'On Liberty'
(1859) (13) in which consequentialist arguments about the
benefits to truth and progress of unrestricted discussion
are linked to claims about its importance for the encouragement of independently minded individuals with soundly
based opinions of their own. John Stuart Mill's position
is essentially a refinement of a purer and cruder utilitarian and more directly political theory in which his
father, James Mill, set forth more explicitly than his son
the Benthamite justification of free speech as a constituent part of a democratic system of government.
     James Mill applied to the theory of government, in a
rigorous deductive manner, the twin principles of Bentham's utilitarianism, (i) that every individual seeks to
obtain his own pleasure and to avoid his own pain, and
(ii) that society should be so organised as to produce
the greatest happiness of the greatest number. (14) This
was to be done by producing an artificial harmony of
interests by means of legal and other sanctions which make
it in each individual's interest to concentrate on
maximising his own satisfaction whilst refraining from
damaging those of others. In the sphere of government
this argues for a limited form of indirect democracy
whereby the interests of the majority are protected by
the communal use of force to back up laws preventing citizens from harming each other (particularly by taking away
each other's property, the fruits of their labours), a

power which can itself be controlled and hence limited to its proper function by the electoral process. Government is a necessary evil which involves giving some men power over others, a situation which is likely to be used by governors for their own selfish ends. By making rulers subject to re-election, (and assuming that their egoism means that they desire to be re-elected and that others wish to compete to replace them), this produces the mechanical synchronisation of interests between the rulers who wish to be re-elected and therefore act so as to please the majority of electors, and the electors who, knowing their own interests, vote for that candidate whom they have reason to believe will benefit them most. (15) This is essentially the 'economic' theory of democracy which has recently been up-dated to include the role of political parties and interest groups as mediators between electors and governors. (16)

According to the economic theory of democracy, freedom to communicate is essential if the democratic mechanisms are to produce the desired result. Only adequate information diffused throughout the system can ensure that rulers are able to act so as to maximise the happiness of the majority and that electors are in a position to know something of the abilities, performance and potential of rival candidates for office and so choose wisely in their own interests. Unless the individual can express his self-interested concerns, they will not be taken into the ruler's calculations, and if the activities of rulers are not communicated through the press, or by other means, to the electorate, then there is no incentive for them to rule according to the ethical principle of utility and no guarantee that their electoral fate will depend on their performance in office. Freedom of expression is thus essential for the defence of the individual's private interests in a democratic system.

James Mill's theory of free speech provides us with a paradigmatic instance of the apparently indissoluble relationship between rights, coercion and the individualism of atomic, self-centred beings. In this case, the right relates to the absence of a penalty or sanctioned obligation for expressing opinions which is designed to protect the individual's happiness against the predations of others. It is assumed, by James Mill, that people will use this right largely to criticise governments, an activity which, he agrees, is liable to get in the way of the smooth operation of government and can lead to disaffection and disorder, so that it would be better to do without the liberty of the press, for instance, if it were not so vital for the limitation of the abuse of power by

egoistic rulers. Indeed, Mill seems willing to agree
with his critics who regarded a free press as a cause of
discontent and rebellion that if it were possible to
establish a neutral and impartial authority to assess the
worth of a person's opinions, then censorship of political
views would be the better course. (17) His only real
argument against this is that there can be no such independent authority and that giving powers to governments
to restrict free expression for any of the good reasons
that there are for having such restrictions (such as
public order, protection of reputation, the efficient
operation of government) would mean that these powers
would be misused by governments to protect their own interests and subvert the democratic process. It follows that
James Mill is open to arguments for restricting freedom of
expression and political rights in general where these are
not demonstrated to be requisite for the operation of the
artificial mechanisms productive of general happiness.
Even true facts about individuals should not, he thinks,
be published with impunity if this does not serve to
correct behaviour which is harmful to others. (18) In a
similar vein he concludes that there is no need to give
voting rights to women or to men under forty since their
interests can be adequately protected by the votes of
their husbands or fathers. (19)
     The obverse of the Millite defence of freedom of expres-
sion is the thesis that men living in a society in which
individuals are working together in harmony and are not
prone to the deliberate infliction of pain on others would
not have any reason to concern themselves about free speech.
A revolutionary socialist critic of the right of free
speech could use James Mill's reasoning to argue that such
a right would be entirely without purpose in a socialist
society in which the individual would not have occasion to
voice his discontent, keep a constant surveillance on the
activities of elected leaders and issue threats of non-
co-operation and rebellion. He could also, on the same
basis, go on to argue that, given Mill's premises,
'free' speech and 'free' elections could not produce the
hoped-for utilitarian consequences. Each individual has
an interest in distorting the truth to serve his own ends,
and, in any case, ultimately political decisions are taken
by majorities of partial and prejudiced persons or the
minorities who are able to control the opinions of such
majorities. It would also not escape their attention that
Mill wished to limit the franchise which free speech is
intended to serve to males over forty and within this
group to those with some of the property which it is the
government's function to protect.

John Stuart Mill was exposed to arguments of this sort
and it is clear that, for a while at least, he had some
sympathy with socialist scepticism about the adequacy of
a minimal state and the crucial role of sanctions in human
affairs. (20) His novel line of defence was to stress the
argument that the conflict of opinion is necessary for the
generation of truth, since only views which have withstood
the onslaught on constant critical questioning have any
claim to rational assent. This theory of justified belief
has great plausibility in connection with matters of fact,
about which it is possible to gather empirical evidence
and in relation to which men's self-interest are not
directly involved. John Stuart Mill agreed with his
father that 'where there is no motive to attach a man to
error it is natural to him to embrace the truth', (21) but
in a society of self-interested men truth does not get
fair play and discussion will not, therefore, lead to
rational agreement. To get round this difficulty he has
to erect a complicated theory of representative government
whereby the major antagonist groups in a society (the
property owners and the proletariat) have roughly equal
voting strength, and the balance of power between them is
held by the minority of middle-class intellectuals, the
educated few who were detached from the basic class
struggle, in whose capacity for detached and balanced
assessment of competing views Mill put great trust. In
any political dispute victory would go to that group which
could appeal successfully to this enlightened minority
for, 'assuming that the majority of each class, in any
difference between them, would be mainly governed by their
class interests, there would be a minority of each in whom
that consideration would be subordinate to reason, justice
and the good of the whole'. (22) It is this situation
which he has in mind in 'On Liberty' when he says that the
truth in practical matters is usually a combination of
'half truths' advocated by those who represent 'the standing antagonisms of practical life'. (23) His hope was that,
given a balance of employers and employees in the legis-
lature, truth and justice would emerge from its discussions. This, plus the development of a 'constitutional
morality' which inculcates a sense of interdependence and
'unselfish sentiment of identification with the public',
(24) would produce a political consensus in which it would
be possible to allow the expression of any sort of wild
opinion without the danger that this would result in
foolish and immoral political decision. (25)
John Stuart Mill's defence of freedom of expression is
complex and many-sided and includes many elements not
dealt with here, but it is noteworthy that the

modifications he felt impelled to make to his father's position involved, first, an attempt to justify elaborate constitutional provisions in a way which presupposes that constitutions can be decided by an influential educated minority of people like himself, and second, by modifying the one-sided analysis of human nature on which the whole theory rests by incorporating community sentiments. Neither approach would seem particularly realistic to anyone holding radical socialist beliefs about the causes of political change and the transformation of human nature. The standard socialist comment on Mill's programme is to draw out the implications of the presuppositions of self-interest in a commercial society by showing how differential access to the means of communication (which relates ultimately to the differences in ownership of the means of production) makes a nonsense of the idea that individuals and classes can find adequate outlets for their opinions. Moreover, even allowing the Benthamite view that each individual knows his own interests best (which ignores the phenomenon of false consciousness) John Stuart Mill is said to be wildly optimistic in the influence he attributes to rational and moral considerations in determining the outcome of the political process in a capitalist society. The way is then open for an ideological analysis of the Millite theory of government in general and his views on freedom of the press in particular, according to which they are in effect, if not in intention, a justification of the transfer of power to the bourgeois class which were accepted because they are the political expression of the interests of the owners of the means of production, including the means of communication.

At this point the critique of the 'bourgeois' right of freedom of expression splits into the two familiar positions of the reformist and the revolutionary, the former arguing that the negative rights urged by the Mills need to be supplemented by positive rights of access to the means of communication, backed up by the sorts of changes John Stuart Mill hoped to see in human motivation, the latter arguing that the battle for freedom of speech is no more than a historically conditioned expression of the economic power of the bourgeoisie at a certain stage in capitalist development which has no particular significance for the planning and evaluation of life in radically different types of society, such as communism.

The revolutionary's position makes the assumption that the Benthamite justification is the only possible rationale for freedom of speech. This is belied by Marx's assumption that justifying the liberty of the press is quite a different matter from justifying censorship because the

former as a form of liberty needs no justification whereas
the latter as a form of bondage does. Moreover, it is
clear that some elements of the utilitarian's argument
apply to any form of social organisation. Thus the need
for an effective flow of information for the making of
wise choices need not be restricted to market situations.
Cynicism about the possibility of the impartial consideration of competing opinions in a capitalist society does
not destroy the foundations of John Stuart Mill's argument
that the truth emerges from the assertion of the available
competing ideas. And any restriction on freedom of expression is liable to suppress information relevant to the
choices which have to be made in the organisation of equal
need-satisfaction.

There are, however, more fundamental reasons for the
reformist socialist's defence of freedom of expression which
arise from the application of the basic principle of equal
need-satisfaction when the socialist view of the nature of
human needs is taken into account. The ideal of man as an
active, creative subject with an internal need for the
realisation of the wide range of his distinctively human
capacities is inextricably linked to the value of freedom
of expression. To appreciate the force of this contention
we need to look first at the general outline of socialist
justifications of democracy.

SOCIALISM AND FREEDOM OF EXPRESSION

The sort of democracy envisaged by James Mill is not one
which has much appeal to those who look for a society
united by ties of brotherhood and communality which seem
altogether missing from the external contractual relationships of competing individual units of his democratic
society. It is rather the tradition of J. J. Rousseau
and the idea of a participatory democracy in which all come
come together to discover and enact that which is for the
common good that fits naturally into a socialist scheme.
Rousseau is, of course, often seen as a forerunner of
socialism and his emphasis on the need for a certain type
of egalitarian society, based on a distribution of wealth
according to which 'all have something and none to much',
(26) as a precondition of the proper functioning of democratic institutions, is particularly relevant to socialist
views on the priority of economic factors in the determination of political realities.

Rousseau was, of course, concerned with a pre-industrial
society, and we cannot look to his philosophy for a detailed treatment of what might be expected in a socialist

society, but three strands can be taken from Rousseau's thought which have obvious and immediate counterparts in modern socialist theory. The first is that democracy is a value because participation in communal decision-making procedures is an essential part of the development of the individual into a fully social and mature human being. (27)   It is an ingredient in self-realisation. This participatory justification of democracy was part of what John Stuart Mill added to the crude utilitarian theory of his father: to be involved in politics in such a way as to share in the making of decisions is to be required to think, to act and to feel in ways which contribute to the full development of the individual's personality, and is also important for its own sake, quite apart from any further political consequences.   The second strand, and for Rousseau the more fundamental one, is that correct political decisions can be made only by the involvement of all citizens in a process which requires them to regard communal issues from the point of view of the common good, a process which, starting from certain social foundations, brings into being a 'general will' that represents a consensus on what is required to realise the common good, which Rousseau conceives not on the utilitarian individualistic lines of the sum of the goods of all individuals separately considered, but as that which is for the collective good, that is, whatever benefits all citizens as social beings whose interests are not divisible into a multitude of separable units. Such objectives are nowadays called public goods.   On this view democracy as a value lies in the fact that the decisions reached are the correct ones: it realises the common good. (28)

The third aspect to be taken from Rousseau's theory is really a combination of the other two, but it can be separately analysed as the attainment of freedom or self-determination in a social context.   This was, for Rousseau, the primary objective: to find a form of association in which men can live together in society while remaining free.   Where individuals participate in the democratic process as he envisages it, they do not simply develop their capacities, they also make important decisions which affect their own lives and they do so in a way which is effective in that they are able to exercise control over their environment in a manner which other systems did not allow.   This is possible for all citizens because the decisions that are made harmonise around an agreement on their shared objectives and how to attain them: the realisation of the common good is an expression of the general will in which all members of society share and hence which they must obey, and which, since it is their own decision, means that they are in fact obeying themselves. (29)

Each of these elements - self-realisation, discovery of the common good and self-determination - which are to be found in the proto-socialism of J. J. Rousseau have been echoed and developed in socialist theories. In particular we can see that Karl Marx's concept of socialist man as an active, fully developed social being in complete communal control of his historical development, a concept which is egalitarian in so far as it involves all members of communist society, is simply a more economically based version of Rousseau's own ideas. Freedom as control over the most important determinants of human welfare, active participation in a manner which calls on every aspect of human nature, and the attainment of a consensus which has a validity beyond inter-subjective agreement because it manifests a true consciousness or awareness of how the needs of all are best served - all these elements are to be found in Marxian and many other socialist theories, and together they constitute one of the most powerful arguments for, and models of, a democratic society. (30) Socialists' contempt for the 'sham' democracy of bourgeois society in which formal political equality is nullified by economic inequalities, their purely pragmatic attitude towards democratic institutions within capitalism and their stress on the priority of economical or political factors in achieving social change, readily obscure the fact that the most profound Marxist critiques of capitalism are directed at its undemocratic character, in that individuals within the system have no control over their affairs and their products. Alienation is a phenomenon of being rendered impotent, detached from and disillusioned concerning all those things which are necessary to a genuinely human existence - work and its products, other people and even one's self. Its obverse is to be in control of one's own destiny and totally absorbed in a satisfying communal way of life. The fact that this ideal is expressed primarily in economic terms, for to control economic forces is to control everything else, does not mean that this goal is not also political, for the split between the economic and political is not a feature of socialism. Thus the communal control of the means of production for the purposes of directing the resources of society towards the fulfilment of human need inevitably involves corporate decision-making which is binding on the various collectives themselves. For some purposes this will mean control of economic units by their workers, for others the control of public services by those whom they serve, and for some overall, co-ordinating purposes control by the whole body of citizens. It will be suggested, for instance, in the next chapter, that the direction of the economy towards the production of certain types and quantities of goods would naturally be the concern of all consumers and not just of actual and potential producers. This is precisely the sort of control that is lacking in capitalism and which renders that economic system external to, and oppressive for, those involved in it. Considerations of equality, or the beneficial effects of participation in major decision-making, and of sheer efficiency in directing the economy towards the satisfaction of human needs in a society in which false consciousness, and thus the confusion between wants and needs, would have disappeared, all point to the adoption of some form of democratic decision-making procedures. If there are binding corporate decisions to be made, and we have seen that this is the case, then democracy in the sense of the equal share of all in making decisions of this sort could never be otiose in a socialist society. The model of socialist man as having fully developed powers of feeling, intelligence and imagination through the exercise of choices in important matters, makes his participation in the control of all those things which affect him an automatic expectation.

Quite apart from the role of democracy in developing the capacities of the individual, it is clear that the socialist's idea of the social or communal nature of man entails that no isolated individual would be able, by himself, to come to a correct apprehension of the common good, that is, of what will satisfy the needs of all members of a society. Decisions could not, therefore, be left to a few specialists, for this is to assume that they can have knowledge of what is in the common good through procedures which exclude some members of that society whose good is being pursued, whereas it is more in line with the socialist view of man as a communal being that his awareness of his needs and those of others, and how they can best be satisfied, will emerge from a social process and will not be imposed from above by an external authority.

Finally, it would be strange indeed if a society that consisted of active, socially concerned beings, willingly submitting themselves to rules for the ordering of their communal activities without the deployment of threats or sanctions, could be achieved in any way which excluded some of the members of that society from a share in the decision-making processes. The willing acquiescence of rational men and women in non-optional rules is not to be had by decision-making processes which exclude them.

An adequate exposition of this rough sketch of a possible socialist theory of democracy would require the
detailed specification of the methods whereby the idea
of equal participation in the decision-making process is
operationalised. But enough has been said to provide
the basis for a general vindication of the idea that freedom of expression is a fundamental socialist political
right, for free expression in some shape or form is part
of the very definition of the democracy which has been
described. It is inconceivable that effective human
decision-making concerning more than one person should not
involve the exchange of information and opinions, and in a
process which ex hypothesi involves all members of a society, there is at least a prima facie case to be made out
for all sharing in some way in such exchanges. I have
taken Rousseau as providing a model of a socialist democracy and for Rousseau the democratic process is one which
incorporates the decision of all after they have met together to discuss proposed legislation. Discussion is
thus seen as part of a process in which a group comes to a
common realisation of their corporate goals and a common
view of how best to achieve them. The purpose of democratic discussion need not, therefore, be seen as a way of
ensuring that the specific interests of separate individuals are not overlooked, or even as a way of ensuring
that failures by elected representatives (if there are
such) is brought to light, for it can also be seen as a
process whereby information relevant to the determination
of social objectives is pooled and critical reflection
proceeds concerning the adoption and implementation of
these objectives. In so far as the individual's interests are the same as the common interest - and we have
seen that this can be so in a way which goes beyond saying
that the common interest is a sum of particular interests,
for individuals can be concerned about the welfare of
others as well as their own - then the process of discussion is one whereby the individual comes to clarify and
reach his own views on the interests of all, rather than
one to which he comes with certain demands to be added to
those of others. In such a process the individual comes
wishing to hear as much as to speak but since others will
wish to hear his reactions to proposals he will also be
expected to contribute as well as to reflect on what is
said. In particular, opinions would be sought from
representative individuals involving all the different
aspects of life in that particular society. (31)
  Free speech, therefore, comes into this type of
democracy in the first place as an essential contribution
to the processes whereby consensus on the common good

emerges, and thereby also features as an essential element in conferring a share of political decision-making and hence of freedom in the sense of self-determination on those participating in it. For, as decisions are affected by the contributions to discussion, any input from an individual may alter the line of debate and affect the eventual outcome. Of course, one contribution may not coincide with others and an individual may not always wish his stated opinion to be given weight in the final decision since he may in the course of the discussion change his views. But where consensus is reached, the result is not simply to be equated with the prior views held by any of the participants, so there is a sense in which the contribution of all have been incorporated into the outcome. Discussion thus contributes to making a binding decision an expression of individual as well as group determination. For this purpose it is not necessary that all should contribute equally, or at all, since agreement with the outcome is sufficient to make it the case that an individual is sharing in the political control of his life, for he can identify with and even enter into the opinions of others whether or not he expresses them himself. But where his opinions remain different from those of others, his views must be permitted expression and must be accommodated or changed by discussion if unanimity is to be achieved.

Mere agreement with the opinions of others does not, however, seem adequate to satisfy the first reason for endorsing the democratic process, that of participation as a means to the development of the individual's capacities and moral qualities. To follow discussion and come to a decision and register a vote are no doubt important activities which do contribute to the development of the individual, but a fuller development of human capacities would necessarily involve participation in the discussion to some extent. The benefits of participation do not come, however, from a mere ritual contribution which because it is indistinguishable from the opinions of others makes no difference to the eventual decision. Participation brings its advantages in the shape of the self-realisation of the individual only when what is participated in is a significant process. Hence it is doubtful if even this objective would be served by all speaking on every issue, even if this were practicable. But clearly each would have to take a turn, perhaps at expressing the views of those with whom he would normally agree if the participatory element of democracy is to include taking part in discussion at all levels of decision-making with which the individual is concerned.

Would such a situation be correctly described as one in which all members of a democratic political group have the right of free speech? The most important precondition for the existence of such a right or rights certainly pertains. Persons who are part of a society devoted to the development of the social nature of man would have an interest in exercising the faculties of speech and thought as part of the expression of their personalities. No activity could be in itself more human or more social and few communal activities do not have verbal communication as an integral part of them. To be part of such a society is to be interested in communication in general and speech in particular, both as an end in itself - successful communication being a basic form of social relationship - and as a means to operating together in joint projects, political, economical or social. To have such an interest in contributing to social communication is, it should be noted, contrary to the idea that the fundamental purpose of free speech is to defend the interests of the individual. The basic desire of a person to express himself to others need not be regarded as an example of selfishness and, in so far as it is a desire to communicate in order to establish a relationship with another person or to contribute to a communal objective, it may be seen as the very antithesis of selfishness. Nor is the individual's self-expression to be regarded as essentially in conflict with that of others, except in the obvious sense that all cannot speak, although all may write, at once. Speech is not an intrinsically scarce commodity that must be shared around so that what one has another may not have; rather it is an almost indefinitely expandable activity where the fulfilment of one person's interest is not in direct competition with that of another. Moreover, since the purpose of much communication is to engage others in discussion, the object of exercising one's interest in free speech is aided rather than frustrated by the fulfilment of the similar interests of others. Regulations to impose some order on the expression of opinions so that one speaks while others listen and each has their turn, rather than being hostile to the goals which justify free speech, in fact contribute to them. In a large and complex group the right to freedom of speech which involves the equal participation of all in the sort of group decision-making described by Rousseau, would require very extensive regulation and hence the creation of a complex of power-rights to give reality to the ideal of freedom of expression. Moreover, such power-rights would require to be supplemented by extensive positive claim-rights so that the individual would be in a position, as a result of education and material opportunity, to use the facilities afforded to him by his power-rights.

If this is a correct outline of the essence of socialist rights to freedom of expression then it can be granted to the critic of socialist rights that pure formal liberties are unimportant since, if extensive administrative organisations are devoted to ensuring the equal participation of all in discussion, it seems unnecessary to draw attention to the absence of rules limiting freedom of expression. Further, there may well be an increase in the obligations of citizens to refrain from interfering with the freedom of speech of others by exercising their own capacities for expression at particular times and places and this in itself is a diminution of positive claim-rights to freedom of expression, but such limitations, being justified by the general objectives of freedom of expression cannot be held to be inimical to that freedom. The alternative of having relatively few obligations to refrain from interfering with the freedom of expression of others is that effective freedom of expression is limited to a minority. The requirement of the equal satisfaction of needs also limits the distribution of the access to the means of communication which are provided for in the positive claim-rights to freedom of expression. Given that some of these means, which involve the control of modes of communication which enable one individual to communicate with every other member of his society, are in principle limited, such positive claim-rights cannot be of the absolute nature of pure formal liberty-rights which are consistent with the right of everyone to speak co-existing with the absence of obligation on anybody to listen. Nevertheless, occasional access to the means of mass communication is clearly a more valuable form of right than a pure negative liberty. The fact that it is restricted right does not make it less significant for the individual, at least in the political sphere.

Other reasons for limiting political freedom of speech include the defence of moral and political consensus and the protection of state, military and economic secrets. The latter consideration does not arise in a non-militaristic society in which economic competition and its associated industrial secrecy is unknown. The former is an inversion of the socialist argument that freedom of expression, properly regulated, is necessary for the development of a group consensus which is compatible with non-coerced allegiance. In the absence of self-serving opinions and prejudices agreement comes through mutual communication; it is therefore self-contradictory to appeal to the defence of consensus as a reason for limiting freedom of expression in a socialist society. Clearly, this does not dispose of every type of reason which can be given for suppressing opinion and information, but enough has been said to justify the thesis that there will be a very strong prima facie case in a socialist society for a right to freedom of expression in any matter of relevance to political decision-making which is limited only by the requirement of seeing to the equal distribution of genuine opportunities to contribute to the exchange of ideas. The objective of this discussion is not to establish the socialist orthodoxy of any particular theory of freedom of expression or theory of democracy, but to suggest some functions for freedom of expression which are clearly in accordance with central socialist ideals, so that we can establish that it makes sense to talk of socialist rights in this area and say something about their general character. The conclusion reached so far is that we have in the idea of positive claim-rights and power-rights, designed to produce effective and equal inter-personal communication, a socialist right which may justifiably be regarded as a human right, at least in the terms of the modified criteria derived in chapter 6, for the rights in question are the rights of all members of the society (at least all adult members) which are highly important for their interests or concerns as human beings. But, it may be asked, are they fundamental rights in the sense that they would enjoy special protection in a socialist country?

It would seem that there would be no requirement for a Bill of Rights which forbad limitations and freedom of expression if the political organisation of the society is geared to the objective of obtaining positive claim-rights to freedom of expression. The most that might be expected here is a list of possible limitations in prohibitions on interfering with freedom of expression where this conflicts with other human rights. Where there is no danger of the violation of the negative right to freedom of expression there seems little point in insisting on its constitutional protection in fundamental law. There are, however, other ways in which the significance of the rights of freedom of expression can be given a constitutional expression. For instance, a rule of recognition which specifies the criteria which must be met before a putative societal rule is accepted as binding, could make explicit reference to the requirement that decision-making procedures should involve respect for the rights of free expression. If the argument presented above - that free speech and discussion and communication are

necessary elements of a democratic system – is correct,
then the rights of free expression can be an element in
the description of the procedures through which law-making
must pass to create valid law. For instance, the absence
of an opportunity for discussing a measure in an elected
assembly could invalidate any law passed by that assembly,
or elections could be declared void which take place in
situations where the rights of free speech have been
violated. Since such violations need not be intentional
but could result from maladministration it is possible to
see the place of such criteria in the normal workings of a
fully socialist society.

In existing societies such constitutional provisions
are not standard. The right to free speech serves rather
as a background of political norm which has a role in
determining the legitimacy of a regime in the eyes of
democratic theorists. The nearest equivalent to the sort
of constitutional provisions I have in mind are the application of rules of natural justice by courts to the procedures of other bodies and lower courts when the principle that each person should have the opportunity to
respond to any charges against him is used to overturn
the decisions of bodies which violate this principle of
natural justice. (32) Taking this as our model, it could
be argued that in a society where positive claim-rights
and power-rights to freedom of expression were regarded
as central, some similar provisions would be incorporated
into the determination of what is to count as valid law.
This would be sufficient to make the specified rights of
freedom of expression fundamental within that society.
It would not be fundamental in another sense in that it is
a limited right which would be regulated by the rules
affecting its equal distribution and the access to scarce
methods of communication. Nor would it be fundamental in
the sense that it implies that no abridgement of free
speech would ever be justified for if the community were
to decide, after a process involving the respect for the
rights of freedom of expression, that freedom of expression should be limited in certain non-political areas,
perhaps for the protection of other rights, then this also
would not be an abridgement of the fundamental political
right to freedom of expression. Whether or not a socialist society would, after due discussion, decide to have
laws of libel, slander and obscenity, or introduce paternalistic controls to protect the ideas and morals of the
young, must be left an open question. The argument based
on the role of freedom of expression in developing the
capacities of the individual would count against such
restrictions, but this may not always be an overriding

consideration. Even presupposing the lack of any tendency
to deliberately offend and insult others or to use freedom
of expression to slander and deceive others or betray
justified secrets, the possibilities of the rights of
others being unintentionally affected, or harm resulting
from thoughtless and uninformed comment, have to be taken
into account. If such considerations mean that absolute
formal liberty of free expression could not be allowed it
applies, a fortiori, to having access to scarce means of
communication in situations where others are either
obliged to listen or would find it difficult to avoid
being exposed to the views being expressed. This suggests
that, where there is thought to be good reason for inter-
vening in freedom of expression to prevent the violation of
of rights or the infliction of harm, such considerations
will have special force in relation to the positive claim-
rights and power-rights of socialist free expression. It
is possible, therefore, that where the aim is to give each
individual effective equal opportunity to communicate with
his fellows, then particular attention has to be paid to
the possible harm which can be done by the expression of
such injurious opinions.

In this chapter I have explored just some of the com-
plications involved in the transformation of liberties of
expression into positive claim-rights and power-rights.
This has indicated that, far from the right to freedom of
expression being less important in a socialist society, it
is liable to be a constitutive part of its political system. Socialist rights to freedom of expression are bound
to generate a whole host of correlative obligations, particularly on the part of those who administer the political procedures of that society. And, given the justifying purposes of freedom of expression - self-realisation,
the development of consensus and elective self-determination - a whole range of associated rights and duties of an
educational variety would be essential conjuncts to the
narrow political rights of freedom of expression. The
citizen who has a right to address his fellows through a
loudspeaker or over the air, has a right to be provided
with the opportunities to develop his capacities for
articulating his thoughts and making himself well-informed.
Provision of an education which would enable each individual to communicate effectively with others would be an
essential part of a system in which all are assured the
equal opportunity to communicate their views.

The rights of freedom of expression are typical of
socialist rights in that they are not isolable from the
rights and duties which are part of the wider social
organisation. Socialism has no place for the distinction

between the rights of man and the rights of the citizen,
or between political, economic and educational rights.
The comprehensive satisfaction of human needs requires
an integrated system of societal organisation. The
points which have been made regarding the socialist rights
of freedom of expression apply to a wide range of democratic political rights, the right to form political
associations, the right to stand for election, the right
to vote, the right to assemble and to demonstrate, all
these would become more rather than less important in a
socialist community although the reasons for their importance would not be identical with those used to justify
liberal or capitalist democracy. The wide range of matters which fall to communal rather than individual control
under socialism enlarge the significance of politics if
this is seen as including any process whereby communal
decisions are reached over matters of common concern
either in the whole of society or in groups within society.
Moreover, the involvement of the individual in public
rather than private life is seen as a fundamental medium
for the realisation of the personality of socialist man.
Thus all the groups in which a socialist citizen would
be involved, economic, educational, recreational, and
'political' in the narrow sense in which this has to do
with the overall arrangements of a geographica area, will
call upon the participants to share both in the primary
activities of the group (to produce material goods, or to
learn, or to play games, or to make decisions) and in the
organisation of these activities in politics and administration. That this is both for the sake of the individual
participants and for the achievement of group purposes
means that the rights involved will normally also be
duties, although the nature of the duties will be affected
by the idea of the rights of the individual. The conceptual problems of analysing the co-existence of rights and
duties which seem very similar in content will be considered further in the next chapter. For the moment it
can be asserted that political functions can be regarded
as rights because they relate to activities which fulfil
the concerns of individuals and are justifiable by reference to the benefits they bring to the individual as a
social being and not just for their ultimate consequences
to society as a whole.
    At this stage of the argument it may be objected that
the difficulty for socialism and political rights is not
that these rights will be done away with but that they
will become unbearably complex. We seem to have lost the
simple straightforward and relatively inviolable rights
enshrined in the traditional formal and substantive

liberties as a necessary consequence of the attempt to realise the goal of the equal participation of all in decision-making processes. The complexities of the rules that this will generate within socialism spring from the commitment to ensuring that this equality is not merely formal and that the rights lead to an effective equal share in 'ruling'. This complexity may well be a drawback if it leads to a maldistribution of time and effort between the administration of procedures and the purposes those procedures are intended to serve, to the detriment of more primary human intercourse. However, it has to be remembered that the participation in such second order processes involves its own satisfaction for sociable individuals who are concerned for the welfare of others. Be that as it may, it cannot be argued convincingly that the complexities of socialist political rights entail that they are merely aspirational. It may be correct to say that the implementation of such rights must always be a matter of degree, although this is true of negative claim-rights as well as positive ones, but this does not give such rights the status of optional extras to be respected only where favourable circumstances permit. The fact that perfect implementation of such rights must always be a goal to be striven for rather than, for instance, a pre-condition of political obligation, does not mean that they can be put to one side or that the fullest possible realisation of such rights cannot be given the highest priority. Indeed, the analysis presented for the justification of rights of freedom of expression in a socialist society indicates that a society could not be socialist in which democratic political rights were regarded as secondary.

9   Economic rights:
the right to work

This chapter illustrates and develops the conclusions
reached so far about the form and content of socialist
rights in relation to the right to work, one of the new
social and economic rights associated with the emergence
of socialism in the nineteenth and twentieth centuries. (1)
   The right to work is firmly established in modern statements of human rights, some of which afford a degree of
clarification on the nature of this apparently aspirational political objective. Article 23 of the Universal
Declaration states that 'Everyone has the right to work,
to free choice of employment, to just and favourable conditions of work and to protection against unemployment'. (2)
Article 18 of the USSR Constitution (1936) asserts that
'Citizens of the U.S.S.R. have the right to work, that is,
the right to guaranteed employment and payment for their
work in accordance with its quantity and quality', adding
that 'The right to work is ensured by the socialist organization of the national economy, the steady growth of
productive forces of Soviet society, the elimination of
the possibility of economic crises, and the abolition of
unemployment'. (3)   A similar right is established in the
Constitutions of The People's Republic of China (1954), (4)
the Republic of India (1949) (5) and many other recently
established states, particularly socialist ones.
   More traditional statements of the economic Rights of
Man refer instead to the right to own property and the
prohibition on forced labour, except as a punishment,
rights which are retained in contemporary declarations of
rights. (6)   The right not to be enslaved is, however,
often enjoined with affirmations of the duty to work. (7)
This apparent contradiction is resolved by interpreting
the duty to work as excluding the duty to perform specific
work as directed by an official of the state; it therefore
presupposes the right to choose one's employment.

Moreover, it is assumed that the duty is to perform remunerative work; the right to a fair reward for one's labour
is often an explicit element in statements of economic
rights. (8) The right to work, as it features in the Universal Declaration, for instance, combines the idea of the
formal liberty of the absence of legal restraints on working and the negative claim-right to receive just compensation for work done, the right is therefore a right to
perform adequately paid labour. (9)

Something more than this is obviously intended, however,
by the modern right to work. Reference is made in the
Universal Declaration to the right to protection against
unemployment and in the constitutions of 'communist'
states to the abolition of unemployment.

This suggests a positive claim-right to be provided
with remunerated employment, an idea which can be traced
back at least as far as Thomas Paine's 'Rights of Man'
(1972) in which he proposes that government should provide
buildings with 'as many kinds of employemnt as can be con-
trived, so that every person who shall come may find something which he or she can do'. (10) Beyond this, the
slogan 'the right to work' has come to be used for the
notion that persons in employment 'own' their job so that
no one, such as their employer, should be entitled to deprive them of what is rightfully theirs, a job being as
much a possession as a house or a car. (11) It is this
sort of positive right which critics of socialism regard
as a paradigmatic of the unattainable aspirations which
should not be tied together in the same list of fundamental rights with the wholly practicable civil rights,
such as freedom of expression, which form the basis of
political legitimacy.

It is no surprise that socialists should be distinctively concerned with economic rights, or that these
rights are to be received as positive claim-rights. The
right to work seems an appropriate socialist replacement
for the right to own property, where this involves control
over the means of production. Socialists in the Marxist
tradition ascribe sociological priority to economic factors and even those who do not go all the way with
Engels's version of the doctrine of historical materialism
whereby the economic base of society (what is produced and
how it it produced) determines everything else in a
society (all social relationships, politics, religion and
morality), (12) nevertheless ascribe a central place in
the analysis of social reality to the processes whereby
men produce the means of subsistence through their labour
and place enormous importance on the abolition of the private ownership of productive resources.

However, the attitude of socialists is by no means
homogeneous when it comes to the principle of the right to
work as it features in the Universal Declaration. In so
far as this is equated with the right to receive a just
reward for labour performance it is sometimes dismissed as
a relic of capitalism for it presupposes that labour can
be given a monetary value and that there is some objec-
tively determinable measure of its just reward, whereas
the only monetary measure of its worth is its usefulness
to capitalist production. To strive for a fair deal in
wages, is, it is said, to accept the basic premise of
capitalist society that men should be rewarded according
to their merits as viewed by the values of commodity
production. (13)
    This radical line on the idea of just reward for labour
is implicit, for instance, in the maxim 'from each according to his ability, to each according to his needs',
which dissociates the activity of working from the right
to receive consumable necessities. This slogan makes work
a duty on those able to perform it, ascertainable and enforceable without reference to its rewards and the liberal
fear is that such a duty, particularly if it is disconnec-
ted from the right to choose one's employment, is a rever-
sion to slavery, this being the contradiction of the
thesis that the individual is entitled to sell his labour
for whatever it commands in the market place. (14)
    It does appear that the positive right to work is in-
compatible with a market or capitalist system in which, by
definition, production is determined by market forces
rather than directed by a central authority. Capitalist
states can undertake policies designed to encourage entre-
preneurial activity but cannot actually direct production
as a whole without destroying the market system which is
inseparable from the right to enter a market in the attempt to sell competing products in the context of free
consumer choice. Some degree of unemployment is likely to
be a normal feature of capitalism since no one has the
duty to provide employment for every unemployed person.
This explains the conviction that the positive right to
employment is destructive of freedom since in a competitive market society the widespread creation of employment
by a political authority could only be by direct intervention in the productive processes with an overall plan
which would have to curtail the individual's free choice
in respect to employment and employers' freedom to hire
and fire in line with the competitiveness of their enterprise as measured by the effective demand for their
goods. (15)
    Many compromise positions are, of course, canvassed,

including the state acting as a capitalist employer, using
its revenues to set up enterprises which enter into competition with private firms. Alternatively, there is the
standard model of a 'mixed economy' in which non-profit-
making nationalised concerns operate as part of a largely
market economy. Such state operations may provide essential infra-structures, such as roads, which are supportive
of the private economy, and they may be extended into
types of operation which could be carried out profitably
as independent concerns. But they also include the provision of employment in areas for which there is no obvious economic necessity which is designed simply to provide work for those who would be otherwise unemployed.
Clearly, if this latter form of state operation were widespread it would affect, perhaps adversely from the point
of view of the posited benefits of economic competition,
the normal operating of the market which is 'distorted'
where firms can continue to trade without having to make
profits. If this is what is involved in a corporately organised society directly providing work for any and all of
its members who are unemployed, then not only may the alleged benefits of a market economy fail to materialise but
the need to commandeer resources to provide work is liable
to lead to the withdrawal of those economic freedoms which
are fundamental to capitalism, that is, the freedom to
sell and buy labour-time.

To unravel this complex argument adequately would require detailed consideration of the rival economic theories
of socialism and capitalism, particularly in relation to
the ideas of a mixed economy and of market socialism, (16)
a task which is beyond the scope of this book. However,
the crucial issues from the point of view of the analysis
of the idea of socialist rights can be explored by assuming that there is a basic incompatibility in the two systems in that it is a defining feature of socialism that it
allocates to the conscious centre of decision-making power
in a society the duty to determine what is produced, how
much is produced and how this production is to be managed,
whereas liberal capitalism leaves such choices to individuals or groups whose objective is to sell products in
an open market at a price and in such quantaties that enable them to take in more money than it costs to produce
the commodities in question. To be socialist, I will
assume, production must be social, that is primarily based
on units involving large numbers of people working together. Each unit, as well as the system as a whole, must
be consciously directed towards serving what are conceived
to be human needs, an outcome which is not left to the
workings of a 'free' enterprise in which some men hire

others to work for them to produce commodities for sale in a market characterised by formal equality of rights to buy and sell but by actual inequality in purchasing power. The objectives of a socialist economic system is to satisfy human needs both by giving everyone the opportunity to do productive and creative work in congenial physical and social conditions and to produce the abundance of material goods necessary to meet the requirements of all members of a society devoted to the full development of human potential. These objectives are pursued through the public ownership of the means of production and with an emphasis on the provision of public rather than private facilities. It is assumed that in such a system the individual will participate willingly with a view to fulfilling himself through contributing to the general good and that the demands placed on the individual will be compatible with giving everyone the opportunity for satisfying work and the equal enjoyment of the fruits of the productive powers of the community.

The strategy is, once again, to adopt an admittedly extreme and simplistic position in the definition of socialism and consider its implications for the idea of socialist rights.

THE POSITIVE RIGHT TO WORK

The disastrous consequences for the unemployed individual in a capitalist society are primarily economic. Work in most societies is vital as the only means whereby those without inherited wealth or coercive power over the labours of others can legitimately come by the wherewithal to feed, clothe and house themselves and their families without depending on charity. It remains true that even where there is some provision for subsistence welfare benefits for the unemployed the right to work is still essentially a narrow economic demand for the opportunity to earn wages or produce life-supporting material goods. As such, the right to work is squarely based in the self-interest (although not necessarily the selfish interest) of the individual. But in a socialist society in which material sufficiency does not depend for each individual on his particular contribution to production or on his private wealth this purely economic foundation for the right to work collapses. The individual's material needs are met whether or not he works. It would seem then that work would become a duty rather than a right, since the needs of every person could not be met unless at least the majority of those able to participate in productive activity actually do so.

Without denying that there would be such a duty, at least to the point at which each individual's contribution is required for the society to attain material abundance, this does not, however, entail that socialism has no place for the right to work. The right to work is a basic socialist right even in conditions of affluence, and one which is not limited by the extent to which the individuals in question can make a necessary contribution to the communal activities directed towards meeting the needs of others. We have already seen that it is an essential part of the socialist's concept of man that he is a producing and creating individual, a doer rather than a receiver, a maker rather than a getter. It is therefore a fundamental need of socialist man to engage in personally fulfilling creative activity within a social context. This means effort deployed towards the goal of wresting from nature the means to sustain a society that can provide a totally satisfying existence for its members. Such work is important because it calls into play the faculties of mind, body and spirit which are definitive of human activity and hence human life. Work is man's chief need because it is through labour that he expresses himself and fulfils his nature. Work is a need because of the activities intrinsic to it rather than because of its ulterior material benefits. To be work it does not have to be rewarded in any extrinsic way (we cannot therefore define work as remunerative activity since it has no essentail connection with financial reward), but it does have to be effortful and it does have to be productive activity, where production is for the purpose of the satisfaction of human needs. This distinguishes work from leisure activity which may not require the expenditure of energy and is not part of the social means of production.

The right to work is a good example of a socialist right for many reasons. It is a positive right in the sense that it calls, where necessary, for the positive activity of others to provide the effective opportunities for work. Not only is there a tight correlation between the right of the individual to work and the duty of others to see to it that suitable work is available to him, but the fulfilment of that duty requires co-ordinated, that is to say social, activity. It is a right which is intelligible only in particular types of social context in which work opportunities are the outcome of social processes rather than individual ones; that is it assumes a complex and largely industrialised economy. It is a right whose fulfilment depends more on the existence of material conditions (the skills, materials and machinery required to create employment) than on purely legal devices. It is a right which is at once economic and political in that it is a right to participate in economic activity under the direction of a corporately organised system accountable through the political process. Moreover, the right to work clearly relates to the interest of the individual without these interests being antagonistic to those of others. The right to work is not a right of precedence over others, or a purely formal liberty which leaves the matter of who obtains work to be settled by open competition. The exercise of this right is beneficial rather than detrimental to the interests of others, since it is a right to be able to make a contribution to the social product; a right to be given the positive opportunity to fulfil one's duty, a duty which is a burden only in the sense that it involves effortful activity and not because it is disadvantageous, for, given the right sort of work in the right conditions, the fulfilment of the social duty to work benefits the individual through the exercise of his faculties and the actuality of living the life of a social being.

Given that the image of productive man is so basic to socialist philosophy, it makes sense to think of the positive right to work as a fundamental or human right in socialist societies. All human beings need to express and develop their being through labour, so that those who have special handicaps which makes work difficult for them would be entitled to special assistance to enable them to make what they can of their usable abilities. (The fact that there would be no sharp distinction between types of work rewarded by wages and those - like housework and the care of children - which are not usually directly compensated by material benefits, makes the idea of universal work a more realistic goal.) The universality of this right is not affected by the principle that the type of work in question would depend to an extent on the capacities of the individual, although the supposition of socialist egalitarianism would be that those whose capacaties fall below the average level would receive proportionately more educational assistance so that such differences might be minimised. Such differential treatment would be aimed at making it possible for all individuals to develop and engage to the full such capacities and talents as they possess. While this goal has a distinctly aspirational quality since it is always possible to envisage improvements in the quality of work available to any individual, the positive right to work could be established as a human right in the sense of being a right of the highest priority and thus 'fundamental' or absolute in relation to the minimal requirement of the provision of a job or jobs which require for their performance at least some significant human abilities, mental as well as physical. This right is not one which would have to be 'earned', or which is subject to the vicissitudes of political expediency. The social ownership of the means of production is posited on the centrality of labour to human nature. The right to work is therefore constitutive of socialism and could not be made subject to the contingent decisions of social authorities. In a socialist society the right to work is an untouchable right in that the right could not be denied without that society ceasing to be socialist. One technique which such a right would exclude is that of creating or allowing unemployment in order to secure more jobs in the long run. Human rights cannot be traded off against themselves in this way in non-emergency situations. (17)

The right to work is just one example of the sort of economic and social right which evokes the wrath of those liberals who feel that such aspirational rights mischievously dilute the force of the traditional civil and political rights. Even although the virtually unrestricted bourgeois right to own and control property fulfilled an economic function similar to the socialist right to work in that it laid down the basic social framework for economic activity in capitalist society, it is maintained that the former is regarded as a paradigmatic human right while the latter is assigned to the category of a political ideal. (18)

This is an assessment which, we shall see, has important similarities to the revolutionary socialist's claim that certain rights, such as the right to work, are merely empty slogans under capitalist productive relations, but leaving aside for the moment the ambiguous status of socialist rights in non-socialist societies, the socialist must be able to indicate broadly how such a right would be operationalised and hence given the necessary status of a safeguarded and enforceable right. The problems which arise here are common to those positive rights which correlate with duties that cannot be fulfilled by individuals acting alone. A negative right to work could correlate with every individual's duty not to prevent another from working; a duty which falls on citizens and governments alike. On this model the positive right to work seems to require each individual to provide work for every other, a manifest absurdity. Paradoxically, in a capitalist society there are individuals, owners of capital, who are in a position to provide the opportunity for others to work, although the existence of a duty laid on them to do just

that is inconsistent with the economic principles of the
capitalist system according to which when the provision of
work is more than a means to profit-making the individual
employer will soon cease to be able to provide any work.
Individual entrepreneurs can often create employment but
they cannot have the duty to provide work for every citizen, for this they cannot do. However, in a socialist
society, in which there is no private ownership of the means
of production, no one is in a position to provide employment
for others on any scale which could meet the situation.
The critics of such rights maintain therefore that the individual does not have duties correlative with his rights
in this sphere thus rendering the whole notion of a human
right to work incoherent.

   To be caught in such an individualistic straightjacket
is wholly unneccessary when it is considered that many of
the traditional civil rights are similarly unrealisable
through the unco-ordinated efforts of individuals. Any
number of unco-ordinated individuals cannot provide others
with a fair trail, or the right to vote. The notion that
economic but not civic interests cannot be served by social
organisation is no more than a liberal dogma. The duties
which correlate with the right to work are the duties of
men as communal or social beings who exist within an organised framework of practices through which they are
jointly able to protect rights. This is not to say that it
is exclusively the state which has the duty to provide work
except in the sense that the state is the organisational
heart of the communal project which is social existence.
The duties do, in fact, fall on all citizens but they are
duties whose specifics are mediated by the conscious
centres of co-ordinated communal activity. They are there-
for social duties in that they are duties to play a part in
a plan of action involving the co-operation of other members of society. In sum, the socialist right to work does
correlate with the obligation of all to provide that work,
but it is not an obligation which falls on individuals as
such but on them as members of the community, that is, they
have an obligation to play their part in an economic and
political system which is directed to the attainment of
full and humanly satisfying employment. This obligation
may be fulfilled by working productively themselves, hence
helping to produce the wealth which can be used to create
other jobs; perhaps by paying taxes, if that is part of
the system, and certainly by supporting political policies
which are directed towards sustaining an economy in which
everyone can be found an adequate occupation.

   This system of social duties does not entail the suppression of individual initiative directed towards the

total desired objective but it does mean that individual
contributions have to be placed within an overall scheme
which is sufficiently co-ordinated to ensure that good use
is made of available resources. Socialism differs from
laissez-faire liberalism and from individualistic or small
group anarcho-communism in that it assumes that a measure
of large-scale co-ordination is required if modern productive systems are to be adequate for human needs. There is,
therefore, no requirement to say that because individual
obligations are mediated through social organisation that
they cannot underpin human rights. It is not only intel-
legible but practical to think of the obligations of all
being channelled through the organisation of society into
a correlation with the rights of all.

What might be said to be lacking in such a set-up is a
remedy which can be used by an umemployed person to secure
his right to work, for to be wronged by the whole community is not to be wronged by an identifiable individual
who may be sued or charged with an offence. The right to
work would then be like the beggar's right to charity based
on the obligation of other individuals to give to some but
not any specific poor persons. No beggar who remains un-
cared for can make a claim against any particular individual who has not given to him. Hence the alleged incoherence of a duty to be charitable or a right to receive
charity. (19)

All this assumes, however, that it is a prerequisite
for obtaining redress that one is able to identify the
person who is responsible for the injury in question.
This is a normal assumption of private law but one to
which there are many exceptions in existing legal systems
in provisions for strict liability both where the person
who is civilly liable need not be shown to be at fault,
and where his actions may have played no part in the causal
process leading to the injury. (20) Legal responsibility
as answerability for specified circumstances need not always be based on moral fault or proof of causation. It
does, however, require the legal identification of those
whose duty it is to rectify or compensate for the occurrence of specified circumstances. In the case of the right
to work the immediately enforceable legal duties would be
those explicitly laid on officials who are entrusted with
the oversight of the community's capacity to create employment. To fulfil this duty such officials will have
role-based rights to require others to act in accordance
with the scheme devised through the political process,
hence the effect of seeking redress against those officials
whose duty it is to organise full employment is to activate an organisation whose purpose and powers are directed

towards that end. The redress in question is the recti-
fication of a situation in which the individual does not
have that to which he is entitled - a job. The facts in
dispute would relate to the availability of suitable employment for that individual. The issue of 'fault', if it
featured at all, would centre on a pragmatic investigation
of the reasons for the lack of suitable employment. This
would then be used as a basis for improving the processes
of economic management. The finding would be in the form
of a direction to the relevant authority to provide suitable employment for the 'wronged' individual. If this has
the appearance of a procedure and function more characteristic of a tribunal of inquiry than a civil court, this
does not in itself impugn its adjudicative nature.

There is no problem in conceding the feasibility of
such processes. Indeed, they are all realities in the
sphere of welfare legislation. Whether or not they are to
be classified as judicial is a terminological dispute which
is not vital to knowing whether or not an aggrieved person
has a right. If purely administrative procedures are adequate to provide employment to specific persons it is im-
material that this is not the consequence of proceedings
in which evidence is presented and questioned, the interpretation of the rules debated and the decision made by
persons other than those with the obligations to see that
individuals receive that to which they are entitled.
Courts have no monopoly of the concept of a right. What
matters from the point of view of the existence of a right
is that its benefits should not be at the discretion of
officials in any strong sense, that is, in this case, that
the obligation to provide work is unquestionable, although
the precise work that is provided may be left to the decision of the relevant official.

Of course, if the administrative procedure cannot be
challenged by judicial methods in cases where rules and
facts are in dispute then it may well be that rights are
not effectively secured. There is, therefore, scope for a
review of administrative procedures which is judicial in
character, although not necessarily adversarial in procedure. In the conditions posited as characterising a
socialist society such disputes would be rare, thus rendering them of minimal significance in comparison with the
organisation which exists to see to the effective satisfaction of positive claim-rights. Nevertheless, appeals
from administrative to judicial organs are not incompatible
with a system of positive rights and, as we have seen, may
carry no implication of the coerciveness of the judicial
decision.

Given the existence of non-coercive but binding

procedures to determine whether or not a person's 'right'
to work has been met, it would be an act of conceptual dogmatism to argue that it is not a right in the fullest
sense. The situation is less clear if socialism is conceived on a less centralised model in which responsibility
for meeting needs is diffused throughout society, so that
there is only a quasi-legal or social right to work in
that there is a generally recognised societal rule that
everyone should do what they can to generate employment.
It is hard to conceive of this operating successfully outside a small community but provided there is a generally
effective system for identifying the involuntarily unemployed and providing them with the opportunity to work, it
is proper to regard such individuals as having the positive right to work since there is an effective societal
rule directed towards the satisfaction of an individual's
needs.

An alternative view of the right to work which falls
between the administrative-judicial model and the more
spontaneous community model is the political version, according to which the right to work consists in a consensus
political assumption in a society that those who govern
have an obligation to achieve full employment. To distinguish this from a mere aspiration or manifesto right it
has to be the case that, where unemployment does occur,
specific processes would be activated to rectify the situation. Broad policy initiatives to relieve unemployment
can hardly be said to give the individual a right to a job,
particularly if those policies are designed merely to reduce the level of unemployment. If automatic loss of
office were a consequence of miniscule unemployment, or,
less stringently, if in a democratic society those who
fail while in office to secure full employment are for that
reason always rejected at the next election, then it is
appropriate to speak of a political right to work, provided it is the case that a high degree of success in job-
provision is attained. A level of normal unemployment
comparable with the level of normal crime is consistent
with the idea of the existence of a positive right to work
just as the existence of a positive right to security of
person can co-exist with a measure of criminal injury. In
general, for there to be an actual right to work, there
has to be some way in which the failure to provide employment is regarded as an unacceptable failure to comply with
the binding and generally effective societal rules of one
sort or another.

To have a positive right to work, then, is to be able
to make an enforceable claim to be provided with work
without any further justification. Special reasons do not

have to be demonstrated, only the absence of that to which one has the right. To have a right to work excludes, therefore, the acceptance of any argument on the behalf of those entrusted with the task of job-provision that, for reasons of expense, convenience or public policy, the interests in question cannot be met. To have a human right to work is to have a right which takes priority in the case of a clash with other lesser rights. That is, it justifies the imposition of duties on others even where these duties are incompatible with rights which they would otherwise have been able to exercise. It is a 'positive' (as distinct from a 'moral' right) in that its status as a right depends on its explicit recognition in the rules and procedures of binding social regulations, but this does not mean that its existence is dependent upon the decisions of particular socialist states since the right to work is an inextricable part of any socialist society following as it does from the doctrines that are constitutive of socialism, namely the social ownership of the means of production and the deployment of community resources to meet the needs of social man in an egalitarian manner.

It does not follow from this that the right to work is a universal right in the sense of a right which is relevant and attainable in all societies. The need for satisfying productive activity may be regarded as universal but the appropriateness of a right to work depends on the type of economy which exists in any particular society. A hunting or pastoral society is unlikely to have need of rules and procedures directed towards the creation and allocation of jobs, and although large-scale ownership of productive resources, such as the land, makes possible the idea of some providing work for others, this is not an idea which could normally be generalised beyond those families living within the confines of the effective controller of limited areas of territory, and in pre-industrial societies the nature of land ownership was such that the provision of work could not be construed as a right without running counter to the notion of ownership. In capitalist society, where the resources are physically available to provide full employment, it is nevertheless not a realistic capitalist goal since the system of free competition between productive units producing commodities for the open market is posited on the unregulated movements of labour, private control over the means of production, and the need to make profits. In such a system work may be a demand and governments may be able to provide some employment and affect employment levels by general economic management, but full employment, particularly if we are thinking of humanly satisfying work, is not attainable without an end to private ownership of the means of production and the free market.

Critics of the idea of a right to work are correct to argue that the incapacity of governments to bring about full employment dilutes the force of this alleged right to the point where it ceases to be a right. (21) It makes no sense to regard governments as having rule-governed obligations to perform impossible tasks. This criticism applies, however, only when the right to work is introduced into types of economy, such as liberal-capitalism, which are outside the direct control of governments. Certainly, the assertion that in a capitalist society workers could 'own' their jobs is indeed a misguided attempt to use a central capitalist notion - that of ownership - to protect the interests of vulnerable sections of the population in a way which is incompatible with the processes by which employment is created in this type of economic system. In a socialist society the right to work would not be explicated in terms of ownership, nor would it necessarily operate in the context of the unrestricted movement of labour. The socialist right to work could be a right to have a satisfying part to play in a complex and changing pattern of inter-related productive activities. This would not involve either the right to retain the same job throughout one's working life or the right to have the job of one's choosing, since the element of job-selection would have to be subordinated to the requirements of overall economic organisation.

This does not mean that the provision of any productive task satisfies the socialist right to work. A job that does not call into play a wide range of human abilities - mental, physical and volitional - is excluded. In particular unalienated labour is incompatible with the sort of division of labour which allocates dull and monotonous tasks to the majority whilst retaining the more demanding and creative activities for a few especially qualified persons. Any sharp divisions between mental and manual labour, or between management and worker roles, are inimical to the existence of a socialist system of work. (22) The necessary specialisms for modern industrial productive organisations would have to be achieved through the development of machinery to eliminate unfulfilling tasks and the training of individuals to perform more than one type of role during his working day, a further range of satisfying human activities being undertaken in leisure time.

It follows on from the argument of the previous chapter that those involved in a particular work-unit could expect to have a share in making managerial decisions about how it is to operate. Given the need for a society-wide plan

of production and the elimination of the idea that any
group of individuals 'own' the productive forces and may
therefore use them purely for their own interests, un-
limited freedom could not be permitted to any production
group even within its own sphere of operations. The idea
of workers' control in each unit of production is not a
socialist conception since it simply transfers the notion
of the ownership of the means of production from one group
to another. Ownership of productive factors, if by this
is meant the right of control, is ultimately vested in the
public, that is, the democratically established political
organisation, not in a number of economic sub-sets of the
public. This follows from the fact that, within the limits
established by the right to work, the interests of consumers rather than the rights of producers would be the
paramount concern in a society organised to fulfil human
needs. Nevertheless, in so far as control of productive
processes is devolved to those involved in these processes
- and the participatory aspect of democracy dictates that
this should be done when the interests of other groups are
adequately protected - then each employed person could expect to be involved in making such decisions as an integral part of his job. To this extent the right to work
has political as well as economic content just as the individual citizen's political rights have to do very
largely with his share in the control of the economic life
of his society.

THE OBLIGATION TO WORK

The strong Utopian elements which emerge in visualising
the outline of a fully socialist economic system suggests
that, if socialism is to be a practical proposition, it
could only be so in a post-industrial automated society
in which life for most people is dominated by leisure not
work, an eventuality to which Marx gave some credence.
This, however, goes against the idea that man is essentially a productive and creative creature whose fulfilment
is to be found in striving to gain from his interchanges
with nature the material resources for living. (23) Man
needs work not just for its products but to fulfil his
own being, something which is not to be achieved by
hobbies and entertainments which are, by definition, not
labour. No doubt the line between work (which tends to be
regarded as intrinsically burdensome) and leisure (which is
often equated with activity undertaken purely for enjoyment) would require to be redrawn in a society in which
work is satisfying as well as effortful, but it would still

be possible to identify the work process as the co-
operative deployment of human effort and skill to provide
for the approved needs of all members of society. If this
were not the case then there is little left of the conception of man as a producer and maker. Work must be
serious and central in a socialist society. It can only
be so if the contribution of all able persons is required
for that society to meet its objectives. It follows from
this that, under socialism, work must be a duty as well as
a right as the slogan 'from each according to his ability'
suggests.

The moral basis of the socialist obligation to work can
be traced to the utilitarian considerations which, as was
contended in chapter 7, are central to socialist justificatory theory. While it is possible to argue that an
individual's duty to work follows from a principle of re-
ciprocity whereby each person ought to repay as far as he
can the benefits he derives from social co-operation, (24)
the idea that the individual's contribution should reflect
what he is able to do rather than what he has himself obtained from the stock of socially derived benefits, has to
be grounded in the duty to maximise the happiness and
minimise the suffering of others. This general principle
may, as in the case of distributing benefits, be modified
by egalitarian considerations which dictate that no individual should be required to perform more than his share
of socially useful labour, but if this share varies with
the capacities of the potential contributors then the obligation to work is based in something more than recipro-
city, a concept which smacks too much of the sort of commercial transaction which socialists repudiate.

The idea that work is both a duty and a right, a
commonplace in statements of fundamental law, (25) raises
certain conceptual difficulties.

One problem with the idea of a socialist duty to work
is that it appears to conflict with the idea that each
person receives not in accordance with his contribution
but in accordance with his needs. If men do not require
to work to gain entitlement to the full satisfaction of
their approved interests in what sense do they have an
obligation to work? Did socialism not begin in the revolt
of the workers against the idle who live off the fruits of
the labour of others? Would the toleration of 'free-
riders', (26) who take but who do not give, not simply re-
introduce an evil that socialism started out to eliminate?

There is no difficulty here in the case of those unable
to work. In any welfare state it is accepted that those
who are old, sick or incapacitated should have at least
some of their needs met even if they make no contribution

to the social product. But it may seem paradoxical in the
case of the normal individual to require him to work but to
'reward' him whether or not he does so.

What we have here is not really a paradox or even a
puzzle, but a failure of imagination on the part of those
who are unable to think of human beings acting out of a
sense of obligation rather than as a result of self-
interested calculations. We have seen that it is possible
to make sense of the idea of a non-sanctioned obligation.
It is only necessary to add that in a society in which the
average person needs no further reason to act beyond the
existence of a societal rule within a system of rules which
has his approval (including his approval that such rules
are non-optional), then we can conceive of a duty to work
which is not dependent on there being extrinsic rewards for
labour.

Another version of the same alleged paradox is the con-
verse thesis that if, in a socialist society, work is
satisfying and fulfilling, then people will choose to work
without being required to do so. Where work is a right in
that it serves the concerns of working individuals it seems
pointless to think of it as a duty. Have we not under-
mined the initial point made in the analysis of rights,
that they are regarded as advantageous, whereas duties are
regarded as disadvantageous. This is an example of a general difficulty for the notion of socialist rights, namely
that the correlative 'obligations' are not really obligations because they are not burdensome and the 'rights'
themselves are misleadingly described as rights because
they do not advantage the so-called right-bearers over
against other members of society.

In fact, the right to work has the advantage of making
clear the continuing place for the language of rights
alongside that of duty. The argument that in a genuine
community people will be concerned about their duties not
their rights may be sound enough in that where duties are
conscientiously fulfilled, claim-rights will not be violated. But in order to specify the content of many of
these duties it is necessary to indicate the interests towards which they are directed and hence the rights which
they further. It is a case of looking to duties so that
the rights will take care of themselves rather than a dis-
placement of rights by duties, for the duties have an internal reference to rights.

It may be objected that, if the individual has a duty
to work, there is no point in asserting his right to work,
for if he is required to undertake productive activity he
is hardly in a position to complain that he is not able to
work (unless the duty to work is unreasonably construed as

a duty to work even where no employment is available).
This issue arises from a failure to appreciate the different bases of the rights and duties involved. The duty
is grounded in the necessity for the community to produce
sufficient goods to meet the needs of its citizens, but
the right of the individual to work is based on his need
to participate in satisfying labour. This means that the
duty could be fulfilled by undertaking any usefully productive task, however stultifying and unrewarding it might
be to the worker. The right is, on the other hand, a
right to a job which calls on the range of the individual's
human capacities and is carried out under conditions which
make for enjoyable and dignified activity. Such a right,
therefore, limits the type of employment which the individual could be called upon to undertake as part of the
fulfilment of his duty. True, it is a right to participate in socially productive activity; this is a precondition of its worth and therefore part of the satisfactions it affords to the individual. Here the content
of the right and the duty do coincide. But the right
makes more demands on the nature of the task allotted or
acquired by the individual than does the duty. Moreover,
the right to engage in effortful creative activity would
persist even in situations where further work was not required to meet the needs of other members of society.

We can say that work is an obligation in so far as it
involves contributing to the satisfaction of human need
and a right in so far as it enables the individual to develop himself, the latter having more to do with the type
of work done and the former with what the work produces.
But, while this is not entirely misleading, it can be
seen as an attempt to maintain an artifical barrier between the interests of the consumer and the interests of
the producer, for the socialist will wish to assert that
the producer in a socialist society will be interested in
producing for the benefit of others as well as for his own
sake, hence his right is as much based in work qua production as in work qua means of self-development;   moreover, the self-development to be gained from working in a
socialised system, that is, one which involves the co-
operation of many people, is a corporate achievement of
the workers in which each benefits only through benefiting
others, for part of the process of self-fulfilment is the
development of the kind of community relationships which
bring into play man's social propensities and satisfies
his needs for a place in a web of supportive and friendly
human relationships. There is therefore no way in which
the 'benefits' and 'burdens' of work can be rigidly separated and located in specific features of the work process.

Yet, it will be reiterated, if properly organised and satisfying co-operative and socially useful labour is not a burden is it proper to think of it as an obligation? Obviously, it is not if we accept the view that obligations are by definition an unwelcome imposition which those obliged characteristically seek to avoid. But we have seen that this is mere conceptual dogmatism which ignores the fact that people may willingly do what is required of them. The crucial factor in making work in accordance with abilities an obligation is that such work is declared to be non-optional in that it is required of everyone who is able to make a contribution to the social product. Again, some may find it difficult to make sense of this requiredness in the absence of any sanctions or inducements to work but, unless we count as coerced actions undertaken out of a sense of moral duty and insist that any willing fulfilment of a legal obligation means that the willing observer of the law is not really regarding his obligation as a legal obligation, then we will not wish to reduce 'requiredness' or 'bindingness' to 'sanctioned', or 'induced'. The fact that, under socialism, work is required of those able to perform it is sufficient to give point and meaning to speaking of the obligation to work even although work is, on balance, not a burden (it will, of course, have burdensome elements in so far as it involves exertion). And since such obligations are in part to be construed as obligations to provide others with natural benefits it is also proper to regard these others as having the right that such obligations are fulfilled. (It is to the consumer that the obligations are primarily owed, although fellow workers are also the intended beneficiaries and also, therefore, have rights that others work with them.)

By insisting that work is a requirement and hence an obligation in a socialist society we have to allow that the right to work cannot be waived: it is not in the individual's entitlement that he may choose not to exercise his right. This does not mean, of course, that the exercise of the right does not involve the right-bearer in making choices. It is likely to be the case that - given the stress on the development of essentially human faculties, including those of reason and choice - the individual will have many decisions to make about what sort of work to undertake and how to carry it out within the framework of the overall production plan. But in one respect the individual has no choice: he may not choose not to make his contribution to the productive goal of the economy. In this case is there any point in speaking of a right to work?

Certainly, there is no impropriety in doing so. We have
seen that it is not necessary to accept that the power of
waiver is an essential feature of a right in that where
this is taken away the right ceases to exist. Rights,
since they have the function of enabling the right-holder
to pursue or protect his interests, can typically be
passed up or waived according to the individual's judgement as to whether or not the exercise of the right serves
his interests in particular circumstances. But to add an
obligation to X to the right to X cancels only the power
of waiver, not the right itself. Australians have the
right to vote even if they are required to do so by law,
and the right to life is compatible with the obligation
not to commit suicide. This will seem paradoxical only to
those who assume that rights must be for the protection of
self-interest, and that it is never proper to require anyone to act in a self-interested manner. The first is a
less palatable dogma to the socialist than the second, but
neither are part of his philosophical outlook. The absence of the power of waiver will, in fact, be a normal
feature of socialist rights. This accords with the socialist rejection of the power theory of rights which lo-
cates the core of a right in the power it gives the right-
bearer over the actions of others, the assumption being
that this is a power he may choose not to exercise. The
interest theory which, as we have seen, is more in accordance with the broad non-commercial deployment of the concept of rights to cover those who have needs but not necessarily the personal capacity to activate legal proceedings, suggests that the concept of a right is largely
unaffected by the excision of the entitlement to waive
one's rights.

If some conceptual unease remains in speaking concur-
rently of the right and the obligation to work in a socialist society this is, perhaps, because of the cumulative
effect of background assumptions about the social and
psychological situations in which this talk of rights and
obligations would take place. The fact that work is seen
as a need rather than a burden must deeply affect attitudes towards the obligation to work, so much so that we
may say that this is not the sort of obligation with which
we are familiar. In our minds, obligations are associated
with the unpleasantness of unwelcome impositions. But the
fact that it is not conceptually necessary for this association to exist can be illustrated by pointing to those
who find their work on the whole a pleasure and who therefore perform it gladly. Such people are, in existing
societies, as much under an obligation to work as those who
find their jobs distasteful and disagreeable. Nor can we

fall back on saying that if all found their work pleasant
then the idea of an obligation to work would fall away,
for citizens of such a society would still have to be
brought up to appreciate the necessity for work and the
propriety of each contributing according to his or her
abilities, and society would have to consciously organise
production on the basis of the assumption that all will
respond to the request to play their part in the economic
process. What would fall away, therefore, is not the
requirement, the rule prescribing that all those able to
do so must work, but the sanctions to enforce that rule.

It is evident that obligations in this situation would
be regarded quite differently from the way in which they
are received in a society in which they are entirely
burdensome, just as it would certainly be a cultural shock
for someone accustomed to viewing society as a regulated
competition of self-interested beings, to find himself
amongst people who are claiming the right to contribute to
the common good. Attitudes to rights and obligations as
well as the content of these rights and obligations would
be fundamentally different were socialism ever to be
realised, but this is not to say that the essential analytic features of rights and obligations would be radically altered. It is not self-contradictory to speak of
a right to be permitted and enabled to fulfil one's obligations, and where there is a point to such assertions, as
there is when formulating the objectives of socialist
social organisation, such locutions would and should be
retained.

The right to work is not to be taken as exemplifying
all the features of all rights in a socialist society.
There is not reason to doubt that in such societies there
would be large areas of formal liberty which are entirely
unregulated and important prohibitions on interference
with others either by individuals or organised groups, and
hence a role for negative claim-rights. The right to work
as a positive claim-right does, however, focus attention
on a distinctively socialist right which has been subject
to conceptual as well as political objections. The over-
lap between the right and the duty to work, the consequent
absence of the capacity to waive the right to work, the
difficulty of locating the correlative obligation, the lack
of a clear line between violation and non-violation of the
right, the discontinuity between the right to work and the
narrow self-interest of the right-holder, the fact that
such a right can hardly be assured through the deployment
of coercion - all these factors seem to cast doubt on its
conceptual status as a right. I have argued, however,
that once the inessential conceptual assumptions which

have been unearthed and criticised in previous chapters
have been brought into the picture, and an imaginative
effort has been made to enter into the sort of social relationships which would feature in a society of non-
egoists committed to the corporate and mutual realisation
of their common needs, it is apparent that it is conceptually in order to retain the concept of rights within the
socialist vocabulary. The fact that this can be done by
extrapolating from existing uses of the language of rights
and accords with a version of one of the competing
theories of rights as they apply in non-socialist
societies, points to a fruitful continuity of discourse
between the standard political language of existing poli-
ties and the thoughts and aspirations of those who look
for a radical transformation of the human condition.

10   Welfare rights

Up to this point my analysis of the concept of socialist
rights has been posited on highly optimistic but, it is
hoped, not outrageously Utopian assumptions about the
feasibility of a model socialist society. The aim has
been to establish the appropriateness of the language of
rights to describe the normative human relationships within a fully socialist community. Once this has been
achieved, it becomes feasible to begin the formulation of
a set of social and political concepts common to almost
all spectrums of political opinion thus facilitating
fruitful dialogue between theorists of Right and Left on
the problems of existing states, none of which can be said
to have attained anything approaching the socialist vision
of an ideal society. Many of these issues arise in the
area of social policy and some are connected with the con-
tentious 'rights' associated with the twentieth-century
phenomenon of the welfare state. In this chapter the
analysis of rights developed in previous chapters is used
to explore some of the conceptual difficulties and misunderstandings which arise over the contemporary notion of
welfare rights. It is argued that left-wing criticisms of
welfare rights in capitalist and semi-capitalist states,
while they are germane to questions about the adequacy
and long-term desirability of certain welfare policies, do
not affect the coherence of the idea of welfare rights,
some aspects of which can serve as indicators of the sort
of social relationships which would pertain in a genuinely
socialist society.

'Welfare' in the most specific sense in which it is
used in the context of social policy and administration
has to do with the deliberate attempt to reallocate resources according to the criterion of need. It concerns,
therefore, the arrangements made for the public provision
of education, health care, housing and social security.

In particular, it covers the dispensation of monetary and personal assistance to individuals falling within certain categories of need, such as the aged, the unemployed, the disabled, the sick, the young, the very poor and any number of more specific types of person with special difficulties that render it hard for them to attain a tolerable level of material existence. In its wider connotation the idea of the welfare state takes in the endorsement of certain economic and social policies, such as full employment, equality of opportunity and the attainment of social solidarity through a measure of egalitarianism, but I shall be largely concerned in this chapter with the narrower conception of the redistribution of resources with the intention of benefiting directly those who are 'in need' in that they fall below what is considered to be an acceptable standard of living in a modern industrial society. However, this rather limited conception of 'welfare' cannot be sharply distinguished from the over-arching philosophy of the welfare state according to which governments have a general responsibility for the well-being and happiness of all their citizens. (1)

In chapter 6 I dubbed the idea that those in special need have a right to receive appropriate benefit or assistance the 'welfare principle'. This principle states that each individual has the right to receive any requisites that he or she may lack for the satisfaction of basic course-of-life needs. It was argued that such a principle is inadequate to express the full force of the equalitarian aspect of socialist objectives and did not sufficiently take into account the particular functional needs of different individuals or the maximising aspirations of the socialist ideal which incorporate the idea of the full development of the faculties of socialist man which is to be achieved through the active assistance and co-operation of his fellows. However, it would seem that the welfare principle does go some way towards the objectives of socialism, more so, for instance, than the rival principles of meritorian justice or simple utilitarianism. If, in a socialist society, the entire communal effort is directed towards production for the fulfilment of approved human needs, it must surely be a move in the right direction to direct any part of government machinery to the goal of need-satisfaction. If we cannot yet attain 'to each according to his needs', there must be something to be said for the more restricted objective of 'to some according to their needs'. It seems, therefore, that socialists should welcome welfare rights as a step in the right direction and, indeed, this is usually the case. The characteristic socialist view is that the administration of social welfare

operates on lines antithetical to capitalism in that allocation of scarce resources is determined not by market
forces, such as effective demand and profitability, but by
the relatively impartial assessment of the needs of those
involved, and that this represents a significant inroad
into the inhuman and impersonal world of competitive individualism. Consequently, it is argued, this embyronic
socialist organism should be developed to encompass more
and more aspects of the social, cultural and political
life of modern societies. (2)

Further, the sphere of social administration appears to
illustrate a number of the points which I have made about
socialist rights. Welfare rights function primarily as
directives to administrators and only secondarily as legal
instruments in the hands of aggrieved persons. They are
rights whose implementation depends less on their being
activated by the right-bearer than it does on organisation.
Welfare rights serve as the basis for positive action by
government to discover and meet the needs of those requiring assistance. They are rights which relate to the
interests and concerns of individuals which cannot easily
be regarded as self-centred or predatious on the interests
of others; often, as in the case of family support services, welfare rights recognise the claims of fundamentally altruistic concerns. Although welfare rights can
lead to court orders being made against officials who have
failed in or misinterpreted their duties, they do not
characteristically operate as instruments of 'coercion'
against those with the correlative obligations. They are
rights which are necessary for the purposes of the effective social co-ordination of action designed to relieve
poverty and deprivation even when good will and genuine
concern characterise the attitudes of the majority of the
relatively well-off members of society.

Moreover, the significance of speaking in terms of the
'rights' of those in need is clear. (3) It draws attention
to the existence of, or the desirability of creating, rules
directing the actions of those with command over economic
and human resources towards the relief of poverty. It
marks the priority which is normally attached in a modern
society to meeting basic course-of-life needs which in becoming a matter of right are thus given an 'exclusionary'
protection in that the relief of need is removed from the
haphazard exigencies of available resources, official discretion or private initiative. Further, institutionalising
the relief of need, thus making it a matter of entitlement,
gives the poor a dignity lacking in the receipt of charity
through acts of supererogation which, because they go beyond the call of strict duty, endow the giver with special

virtue. Charity goes along with the expectation of gratitude and admiration for the giver and the stigmatising
status of being a beggar, concepts which have no place in
relationships based on correlative rights and duties.
Also, the notion of welfare rights encapsulates the sense
that welfare is an individualising concept in that its objective is to perceive and meet the needs of specific individuals rather than achieve some general social objective which is only indirectly for the good of individuals.
Finally, welfare rights, being based on the degree of need
rather than the instrumental value of benefiting certain
classes of persons, can be a forceful protection of the
most deprived sections of a population against the forces
of selfish majoritarianism. Where constitutional protection or strong political commitments are linked to the
notion of a right to welfare this brings with it some sort
of protection for the poor against the political expression of utilitarianism through the ballot box, a democratic process which inevitably tends to benefit the broad
mass of the population, or those who can manipulate that
mass, to the disadvantage of deprived minorities. (4)

THE SOCIALIST CRITIQUE OF WELFARE RIGHTS

Faced with this battery of favourable considerations, it
might seem unreasonable for socialists to be anything but
enthusiastic about welfare rights and indeed even revolutionary critics of rights rarely concentrate their
attention primarily on welfare as opposed to civil and
political rights. Criticism of welfare rights seems to be
more a prerogative of those on the political Right who see
in the notion the twin dangers of economic inefficiency
and social injustice because of the encouragement it gives
to the idea that it is not necessary to work in order to
be adequately housed, clothed and fed. This is said to
put an unfair burden on those who are in profitable employment, to render recipients unfit for the discipline of
work and to remove the incentives to economic activity
without which the wells of material aid would eventually
dry up. (5) On this view, the language of welfare rights
is counter-productive in that it encourages the growth of
the number of those who are dependent on the state and
undermines the motivational attitudes necessary for the
functioning of the economic system. There is also, for
the critic of the political Right, a moral inappropriate-
ness in the vocal demands of the poor to be given their
'rights' and their acceptance, without gratitude or sub-
missiveness, of benefits which could not be theirs but for

the efforts and skills of others. Such 'rights-mindedness' interferes with the sort of paternalistic relationship between social workers or administrators and their clients or claimants which have sufficient flexibility and authoritativeness to help the specific needs of genuinely helpless individuals while offering suitable guidance and direction to those who could readily manage without cash benefits. (6)

The objections to rights-mindedness depend to some extent on taking for granted the 'will' or 'power' theory of rights, according to which to have a right is to have a legal or institutional power or capacity to pursue a claim by citing established rules and precedents, a power which the right-holder may or may not exercise as he chooses. (7) On this theory, to give the needy rights arms them with the legal power to control administrative action, if necessary through the activation of legal remedies in the courts. A welfare right is therefore primarily a legal or quasi-legal means whereby right-holders can compel those who default in their duties, hence the litigious rights-mindedness of those who demand to know and have their full legal entitlements.

We have seen, however, that this essentially combative theory of rights is no more than a limited expression of one aspect of some rights. (8) On the interest theory of rights, which is more expressive of socialist conceptions of social relationships, no such consequences follow from the notion of a right to welfare. Interestingly, however, it is the 'demanding' aspect of the welfare rights which many socialists see as their prime significance because it encourages a suitably aggressive attitude on the part of the deprived towards their exploiters. For this reason, those who ultimately espouse the revolutionary criticism of the whole notion of rights, are usually keen to make a tactical endorsement of the use of the language of rights to formulate political demands within capitalist states. (9) Thus, although their evaluations of the phenomenon of rights-mindedness differ totally, theorists of both Left and Right seem to agree that it is a central feature of a system of rights. Both groups of theorists take over the background assumption of liberal capitalism that rights are individual possessions or personal property to be wielded by their owners in a competitive struggle for scarce resources, a struggle in which some are bound to get the better of others. Hence the revolutionary's thesis that rights, whatever their usefulness at certain stages in the political development of proletarian consciousness, are at base anti-socialist because they are inextricably linked to social conflict and must inevitably

result in inequality. For this reason, rights including
welfare rights, will have no place in a community of like-
minded and mutually caring persons. Thus the revolutionary critic of rights ultimately shares the right-wing
critics' distaste for rights-mindedness, the main difference between them being that the right-wing rejection
of rights-mindedness does not extend to the same phenomo-
mon when it is manifest in the commercial and other relationships of those who participate in capitalist economic systems.

The reservations of the revolutionary concerning welfare rights as a form of the institutionalisation of competitive individualism can readily be countered by the rejection of the power theory of rights - already justified
on independent grounds - in favour of the 'interest'
theory according to which the crucial thing about a right
is that it marks a legitimate interest which it is the
duty of specified persons to protect or further. The
right to sick pay, a retirement pension, or health care
need not be seen as an entitlement to extract benefits
from an unwilling state, as if it were comparable to rais-
ing an action for damages against the negligent perpe-
tration of injuries by one private citizen against
another. If welfare rights are viewed as part of an essentially administrative procedure in which the initiative
lies with the state and in which no notions of guilt and
injury need feature, then rights-mindedness becomes at
best an ancillary feature of a system of rights to be
fostered only where it is thought necessary for its effective operation. Such an approach leaves as an open
question, to be decided in the light of specific social
circumstances, the extent to which individuals or groups
of needy persons should be encouraged to adopt aggressive
and demanding attitudes towards welfare administrators or
should be required to take positive action themselves in
order to obtain their rights.

A further notable coincidence in the conceptual presuppositions of Left and Right is manifest in their perception of the coercive consequence of instituting rights.
Critics of the political Right reject the view that welfare rights are not coercive simply because they rarely
involve the implementation of sanctions against the officials responsible for their administration. The coercion,
they argue, is directed against the tax-payer who has his
money 'forcibly' removed to pay for services of which he
may not approve, thus depriving him of the justified rewards of his labours to the benefit of the undeserving, an
objective which ought to be left to his voluntary acts of
charity. (10) In a contrary evaluation of the same

phenomenon, many supporters of welfare rights say that this notion is well suited to express the view that need is a justifiable basis for compelling aid. To establish that A has a claim-right to X is to establish that it is right to compel B to meet that claim, this is what it is to have a right. (11)

The alleged connection of rights and coercion provides further grounds for the socialist to qualify his approval of welfare rights as being no more than regrettable and temporary necessities, but, as has been argued in chapter 4, the coercive theory ignores the possibilities raised by the evident fact that many taxpayers do not contribute unwillingly that part of their payments which relate to welfare benefits but wish to share in the communal effort to relieve suffering. Such persons perform their duty uncoerced and, as we have seen, there is no difficulty in regarding their actions as obligation-meeting just because the element of sanction is removed provided that the relevant societal role exists. To argue that when there is no coercion in the procedures of the welfare state what we have is a system of centrally organised charity which cannot be regarded as meeting needs as of right (12) is to miss the crucial distinction between those 'altruistic' or other-benefiting acts which are non-optional and those which are, according to the norms of a society, left to individual choice. Where welfare systems involve more than the provision of a facility for the individual to contribute to the common pool from which distribution in accordance with need is made and assume a requirement that this contribution be made on the grounds that there is a binding obligation arising from the existence of a societal rule to that effect, then it institutes welfare rights. The failure to understand what is meant by a non-optional rule dissociated from coercive sanctions is a common conceptual block which is detrimental to the development of a non-coercive conception of rights according to which the essential obligation-creating feature of a right is the existence of a mandatory rule. That these rules can be established by consent and such consent can be given on the basis of the moral judgment, reasoned self-interest or pure altruism does not undermine their status as positive societal rules properly described as establishing obligations. All that is required for this purpose is the simple notion that these rules are singled out as ones which those affected are not permitted to opt out of. The social functions served by such mandatory rules have been explored in chapter 3.

If the socialist can be weaned from his dependence on the traditional liberal theories of rights and so from the

assumption that a right is a coercive power, does this
then clear the way for his unqualified acceptance of welfare rights, even in capitalist societies? If so, his
energy can then be directed towards ensuring that such
welfare rights as exist are based on a proper assessment
of need and administered in an effective way which minimises the undesirable but mercifully contingent features
of aggressive rights-mindedness and coerced contributions
to welfare funding. Those committed to the socialist
ideology could then whole-heartedly support the development of welfare rights as representing an island of
socialism in a sea of competitive individualism and also
as a tactical way of undermining the capitalist system.
There are, however, further difficulties to be overcome
before socialist endorsement of welfare rights in non-
socialist societies can be expected. These difficulties
relate to the profound scepticism which many socialists
have about the real effects of welfare rights in capitalist societies. The capitalist welfare state, it is
argued, is a sham in that it fails to meet the real needs
of its deprived citizens, and must inevitably do so, because the adequate remedies for such deprivation depends
on the termination of the capitalist system. (13) The
notion of capitalist welfare rights, it can be argued, is
a contradiction in terms since there can be no such rights
in a system based on free market principles. Those welfare rights which appear to benefit the needy are, in
effect, no more than ways of maintaining the stability of
a system which would otherwise collapse under the effects
of its inherent self-destructiveness. (14) The welfare
state is an ideological device for maintaining a peaceful,
healthy and conformist work-force, not a willing accommodation with socialist ideas. (15) There is therefore no
point, it is concluded, in wasting time on campaigns to
implement and extend welfare rights since this is ineffective in relation to the relief of suffering and positively
disadvantageous in the fight to overthrow capitalism except in so far as its promises of welfare benefits raise
expectations which are doomed to disappointment.
     Whatever force these arguments may have as sociological
analyses of the actual workings of capitalist systems, it
would be misleading to present them as attacks on the concept of welfare rights as such. There are, however, important conceptual issues which need to be cleared out of
the way before the more substantive factual assessment of
the operations of actual rights systems can be undertaken.
In fact, there are three rather different lines of argument involved in the above critique which need to be distinguished, all of which raise significant conceptual

points which will occupy our attention for most of this chapter.

This first strand of radical socialist criticism of welfare rights is the moralising basis of rights which was discussed in chapter 2. It is true that those who defend the idea of welfare rights are usually anxious to say that these are not mere positive rights but represent moral claims. (16) Only moral rights, it is argued, can provide an adequate basis for the idea that the justification of state action and political legitimacy depends on the recognition of welfare rights. If it is not possible to criticise a government for failing to respect welfare rights through adequate legislation then, so the thesis goes, the protective and political value of the notion of welfare rights is greatly diminished. Noting this tendency to moralise welfare rights, socialists are alerted to the fact that they may be drawn into a theoretically indefensible position if they put this notion at the centre of their political philosophy. Moral exhortation and metaphysical disputes over the status and content of 'moral' rights are not, it is felt, socialist ways of doing and thinking about politics. Moreover, the attempted incorporation of the idea of welfare rights into the defensive ideology of late capitalism serves to indicate that it may represent yet another ideological device designed to shore up a system which in effect serves the interests of the ruling class.

The general reasons for resisting the notion of moral rights have already been given, (17) but the specific issue which arises over welfare rights relates to the alleged ineffectiveness of purely positive rights in protecting the interests of the needy since such rights are subject to morally arbitrary legislative alterations. As a point of rhetoric, it may well be the case that a general belief in the existence of 'moral' or 'metaphysical' rights which happen to include the right to a minimum standard of living, may have political consequences. It is far from clear, however, that the acknowledgement of this right could have much impact unless it were associated with a relatively specific indication of the correlative positive or affirmative obligations, and such an explicit positive claim-right is not a strong candidate for acceptance as one of those universal 'intuited' rights which follow from rational insight into the nature of man or feature amongst the self-evident commands of 'reason'. Moreover, the thesis that only moral rights can be politically effective against indifferent or evil governments ignores the impact which establishing rules specifying the entitlements of specific categories of person can have on

the effective allocation of assistance to individuals who
would otherwise be ignored by the political process.
Having procedures to identify classes of needy persons,
rather than leaving the dispersion of monetary aid to the
discretion of officials, enables the needs of neglected
minorities to be brought into the welfare system. The
demand that there ought to be welfare rights may therefore
have more tangible effects than the assertion that the
poor have a (moral) right to assistance. If it is argued
that, none the less, the existence of such rules is dependent on the whims of governments and electorates whereas
moral rights are not, then the proper reply is that the
possession of a moral right is in itself no benefit to a
needy person. If special protection is to be given to the
interests of those who are in need, then the way to do
this may be to enact positive welfare rights as part of
fundamental law rather than to endow them with the dubious
status of moral entities. Welfare rights do feature, in
general terms, as constituents of contemporary Declarations and Bills of Rights (18) and there is no reason in
principle why certain of these rights should not be placed
beyond the changes of transient electoral majorities by
the same sort of constitutional devices as are used to
give special exclusionary status to specific civil and
political rights. The danger to the effective existence
of welfare rights which is inherent in regarding them
merely as positive rights is more readily countered by
giving them the priority of fundamental law rather than by
trying to get them accepted as moral rights. Certainly,
this move has obvious advantages for those socialists who
doubt the coherence and political significance of purely
'moral' rights but are uneasy about the vulnerability of
ordinary positive rights to majoritarian encroachments.

The second line of argument against capitalist welfare
rights is that whatever their manifest purpose, their
latent function is to support capitalism. Negatively,
such rights ward off riots and revolution by dealing with
the most severe consequences of individual failure in a
capitalist system. Without unemployment benefit and some
support for those manifestly unable to survive on their
own resources the growth of discontent to the point of
organised resistance would, it is alleged, be inevitable.
Positively, social services, in maintaining the family as
an economic unit, health services, by protecting the health
of the working population, and educational services, in
providing trained manpower, all contribute beneficially to
the maximisation of profit. Capitalist welfare is not, it
is argued, a matter of the relief of need for its own sake
but a means for controlling and moulding the population to

suit the requirements of the free market economy. It
follows that they are not genuine rights at all since they
are not directed towards the concerns of the individuals
alleged to be benefited by the operation of welfare law.

It cannot be doubted that the machinery of the welfare
state is in many ways functional for capitalist economies,
or that the conscious motivation for the introduction of
many welfare measures has been the need to quell or pre-
empt riots and other disruptions of the normal workings of
existing economic systems. Nor is it possible to dismiss
the claim that there is an analytic connection between the
concepts of welfare and need-satisfaction. Without this
connection it would not be possible to distinguish welfare
law from the more traditional legal functions of punishing
wrongdoing, compensating culpably injurious acts and medi-
ating in disputes between contending parties. If there is
no intention directly to alleviate suffering or promote
health and adequate conditions for human development it
cannot be said that there are welfare laws or welfare
rights. It does not follow, however, that where there are
ulterior purposes at work for which the relief of need is
simply a means, this entails that it is not in itself a
case of welfare law. The essential conceptual point in
the definition of welfare rights is that they relate to
rules which make explicit and relatively immediate reference to some category of deprivation so that their
direct purpose is the relief of need. The fact that there
may be further objectives in view, which may include the
extension of personal liberty, the sustenance of community
feeling, or the pursuit of equality, does not affect their
classification as welfare provisions. Certainly, welfare
laws can win elections as well as ameliorate suffering and
the underlying purpose of welfare states may include the
maintenance of social peace and economic prosperity as
well as the simple objective of meeting the needs of deprived persons. But the existence of such instrumental
objectives does not require us to withdraw the 'welfare'
label from those means which do in fact directly benefit
those in need. What it may affect is our moral assessment of the praiseworthiness of those who enact and support such provisions, but this is a criticism of the moral
goodness of their actions and does not settle either the
question of the moral rightness of the welfare rules or
the issue of whether such rules are indeed instances of
welfare rights. To satisfy the interests or concerns of
individuals may often have other, possibly undesirable,
side-effects or further consequences, but this does not
prevent us thinking of such rules as constituting rights.
What it may reveal is that the accepted jusitification for

having such rights is of a utilitarian nature and cannot
be subsumed under the justificatory principle of need-
satisfaction. But even if utility is the reason why such
rights are instituted, this does not affect the conceptual
propriety of regarding them as rights. The assertion that
welfare rights in a capitalist system are not based on the
principle that suffering ought to be relieved for its own
sake does not, therefore, make inroads on the very idea of
welfare rights in a non-socialist society. It may, however, lead us to withhold moral credit from those who rule
in such societies.

The third line of argument against welfare rights is
not entirely consistent with the second. In discussing
the ulterior economic and social purposes of welfare provisions it was assumed that the means adopted do actually
go some way towards meeting the needs of those whose welfare is to the ulterior benefit of the dominant members of
society, but this contention is often presented in a
rather uneasy combination with the assertion that welfare
rights are a sham in the more direct sense that non-
socialist systems in general and capitalist states in particular cannot adequately deal with the problems of deprivation which they create. Formal compatibility between
second and third lines of argument can be achieved by
claiming that capitalism can deal with suffering up to the
point which is necessary for the maintenance of social
order, but that this does not take welfare provision any-
where near the level which would be required to obtain for
every citizen a tolerable standard of living. This, however, omits reference to those instrumental welfare services which are designed, through the promotion of health,
education and housing, to maintain a productive work-
force, and in any case it is not consistent with the more
extreme claims that are made about the inability of capitalist states to do anything significant for those who
cannot contribute to a capitalist economy. Nevertheless,
it is a common and powerful criticism of welfare states
that there is an inescapable tension in any society which
attempts to operate two entirely different types of distributive systems in tandem, one which looks no further
than the needs of potential beneficiaries, and the other
which is based on the capacity to pay for services,
something which is in itself dependent on the possession
of property, capital or labour power which can be used
to produce commodities for which there is effective demand. The effective operation of such an economic system
requires, it is said, that the allocation of resources
should not be affected by such exterior demands as the
needs of non-contributors, and the extended application of

the welfare principle undermines the whole basis of a
system which depends on eliciting valued labour by the
provision of monetary inducements. (19) Again formal consistency between the market and welfare considerations can
be achieved by rigorously distinguishing between their
spheres of operation and limiting the latter to a small
minority of those whose services are in any case superfluous to the demands of the market economy, but it is implausible to attempt such a separation where we are dealing with welfare rights that affect large sections of the
population.

COUNTER-PRODUCTIVE WELFARE LAW (20)

Examples of the alleged incoherence of welfare rights and
capitalist practice can be gleaned from the arguments
which arise concerning the counter-productivity of much
welfare legislation in relation to the assumed objectives
of the welfare state. Interestingly, again, the idea that
welfare rights are counter-productive is part of the
armoury of both extremes of the Left-Right political spectrum, suggesting further conceptual affinities between two
apparently completely opposed ideologies. (21) I will examine this idea of counter-productivity in some detail in
order to exhibit that the very real difficulties to which
it draws our attention are the consequence of the particular circumstances in which welfare rights are effected
and do not reveal any inherent contradiction in the idea
of welfare rights.
    Restricting ourselves to types of counter-productivity
which do not depend on speculations about the superior
efficiency of possible alternative modes of provision, (22)
we can distinguish three main categories of counter-
productivity: (1) legislation which is directly counter-
productive because its immediate effects run counter to
its welfare objectives; (2) legislation which is indirectly counter-productive on account of its long-term
or mediate consequences for the welfare objectives in
question; and (3) legislation which is counter-productive
when its consequences are examined in a wider perspective
which takes in more than its most explicit and manifest
welfare objectives.
    Direct counter-productivity occurs when legislation
which is designed to ameliorate the situation of persons
in one group (G) with respect to some feature (F) has the
relatively immediate consequence of making G worse off
with respect to F, as when the changes in the system of
unemployment benefits introduced by the Unemployment Act

of 1934, which were designed to increase the level of
benefits, in fact did the reverse. (23) Such cases are
readily identifiable and correctable and in themselves
raise no particular theoretical problems or generalise
arguments against welfare legislation.

Of more interest are the charges of counter-productivity
which involve claims about the indirect and hence less obvious consequences of welfare laws. We can distinguish
different versions of this type of charge.

(i) Legislation may become indirectly counter-
productive due to the complacency effect which occurs when
a politically sensitive perceived need is met with ineffective legislation giving the impression that something
has been done to rectify the situation and thus engender-
ing unjustified complacency which leads to a diversion of
attention and so of existing services from that social
problem which, it is erroneously believed, has been adequately dealt with. Thus publicised alleged improvements
in the legal entitlements of G which turn out to be ineffective can lead to general worsening in respect to F because of the weakening of efforts on behalf of G on the
part of non-state organisations. For instance, the introduction of Wage Councils and Wage Inspectorates can make
it appear that something is being done for the low-paid
when the actual result may be to draw trade union and
political attention away from the problem of the low-paid,
thus reducing the pressure on employers to increase wages.
(24) Equal opportunity legislation also provides examples
of the complacency effect by giving the impression that
such problems have been taken care of by the law. Given
that governments tend to respond to pressure group demand
on the behalf of needy persons with measures that are as
inexpensive as possible and have a political interest in
publicising their alleged efficacy, the complacency effect
could well be a recurrent phenomenon in democratic welfare
states.

(ii) A second avenue of indirect counter-productivity
occurs through what might be called the dependency syndrome, in which the immediate benefits to G are counter-
balanced by the long-term effects of encouraging its members to rely on state-administered benefits, thus discouraging them from taking steps they might otherwise have
taken to improve their situation with respect to F, steps
which would have placed them in a more favourable situation than that which they attained through the welfare
provision. This syndrome is most commonly thought to
apply in the case of improvements in unemployment and
social security benefits, but it could be applicable to
any service which can be regarded as doing for people what

they might otherwise have done for themselves.
The dependency syndrome does not rest on positing self-reliance as the objective of the legislation in question but simply takes into the reckoning the effects of a diminution of self-reliance on the over-all situation of G with respect to F (which normally in such cases has to do with having adequate financial means for basic subsistence).

(iii) Related to the dependency syndrome is the stigma effect which is said to arise when there is a shift towards selective means-tested benefits. Welfare assistance, whether in financial or service form, may be regarded as a mark of personal inadequacy and hence as a sign of inferiority. (25) This is counter-productive with respect to F (the provision of more adequate benefits) when it leads to members of G not taking up the offered benefits because of the difficulty they have in reconciling doing so with their personal self-image or the retention of the respect of others. The stigma effect is often cited as a reason for not means-testing retirement pensions.

(iv)   A fourth category of indirect counter-productivity is connected with the effects of bringing legal forms and procedures into the processes of need-satisfaction. The alleged drawbacks of legalism, that is, of the introduction of authoritative, detailed rules enforced ultimately by courts, perhaps with legal sanctions, are many and various.

Some of the drawbacks of legalism which produce indirect counter-productivity arise from the relative inflexibility of legal modes, for while law may be more amenable to change than is custom, it cannot be altered to meet changing circumstances by administrative fiat, or adapted to individual cases by the exercise of official discretion, without losing its character as law. The application of fixed rules after ascertaining the relevant facts by due process without direct reference to the intentions of legislators, using discretionary judgment only where the interpretation of the rules is not clear and even then within the constraints of precedent, may lead to results in particular cases directly contrary to the objectives of the legislation. It is interesting to note that when courts have overruled the exercise of administrative discretion in the interests of formal justice - as in disputes over the level of supplementary benefit - parliament has tended to proceed to legislate in favour of the administrative status quo ante. (26)

This inflexibility of legalism may be reinforced by the attitude of mind to which the existence of legal rights

and duties can give rise. We have already noted that creating legal rights may encourage an attitude of rights-
mindedness which is expressed in demands to be informed
about the rules for the distribution of welfare benefits
and to receive in full that to which the potential beneficiary believes himself to be entitled in accordance
with the rules. We have noted that this is said to destroy
the relationship between the welfare administrator and the
beneficiary so that effective identification and response
to the needs which the legislation was intended to meet is
replaced by distribution in accordance with justiciable
criteria which are of limited relevance to F. Such
rights-mindedness may be counter-productive if it replaces
a less formal administrative machinery backed by personal-
ised services of social workers. (27)

The correlative phenomenon to rights-mindedness is the
obstructionism which is consequent upon the imposition of
legal obligations to protect the welfare of others. For
instance, to make management liable to criminal sanctions
for disregarding safety precautions is said to reduce their
co-operation in the investigation of industrial accidents
and thus to frustrate attempts to reduce the instance of
industrial injuries. More generally, it can be argued
that the threat of legal sanctions is commonly destructive
of the industrial harmony which Industrial Relations Acts
are intended to promote. (28)

(v) A fifth species of indirect counter-productivity
occurs when the effect of a particular piece of welfare
legislation is seen in the context of other enactments,
the combined effect of which is to produce less benefit to
G than would be the case in the absence of one or other of
the contributory provisions. Obvious examples of this
detrimental feed-back effect include the disadvantageous
interplay of welfare payments to members of G under a particular description (e.g. as qualifying for Family Income
Supplement) which has the effect of lifting them out of
the scope of other means-tested benefits thus making their
over-all position worse. Another example is the so-called
'poverty trap' which arises when one welfare benefit is
added to others in such a way that a slight increase of
earned income leads to a loss of eligibility for a range
of benefits which has the combined effect of reducing the
recipient's net income.

Important as these different types of indirect counter-
productivity may be, they are relatively straightforward
in comparison with the third category of counter-
productive legislation. This enters into the picture when
we consider particular examples of welfare law in a perspective wider then its immediately obvious and manifest

objective of benefiting G with respect to F. There are
three sorts of things that fall into this category. The
first two types may be described as side-effects. The
first concerns the multiple effects which a particular law
or cluster of laws may have with respect to G, which gives
rise to the phenomenon of G's situation being improved
with respect of F, but worsened with respect to F1, F2 or
F3, any or all of which may also plausibly be regarded as
objectives of the legislation. Thus tighter immigration
controls may ease the pressure on housing amongst immigrant groups but harm race relations through the resentment to which such restrictions give rise in the immigrant
group. Or policies of positive discrimination may be
counter-productive overall in that while they may improve
the material situation of one favoured group, the implementation of a policy giving special consideration to individuals because of an otherwise irrelevant characteristic such as their sex or race may reinforce attitudes of
negative discrimination which are themselves posited on
the tendency to regard people not as individuals but as
members of a particular (e.g. sexual or racial) group. (29)
Another example is when in an effort to make council house
tenancy more like ownership tenants are made responsible
for their own repairs and maintenance, thus depriving them
of one of the main advantages of non-ownership. (30)

Another type of side-effect occurs when a welfare law
which is designed to help G achieves its objective with
respect to G, but at the expense of G1, G2 or G3. Here we
need not have in mind cases where the expenditure of money
on one group deprives another group of their share of such
scarce resources as are being distributed. There are instances where the other groups deprived as a side-effect
of a welfare law can plausibly be regarded as intended
beneficiaries of the legislation in question. Thus the
1974 Rent Act may have provided security of tenure for one
group - tenants of rented accommodation not living in the
same house as the landlord - but a side-effect has been to
accelerate the continuing decline of the number of furnished properties made available for renting, thus reducing the housing opportunities of those seeking rented
accommodation. If we regard an objective of Rent Acts to
be an improvement of the situation of that class of persons
who need furnished rented accommodation the increased
security of tenure for some may be outweighed by the deprivations suffered by other members of the group. (31)

Examples of this phenomenon are legion. Increasing job
security, pay levels and industrial safety for the employed
may reduce the number of jobs available for those seeking
employment. (32) Wage Councils may set minimum levels of wages

to the benefit of some workers which are then used as
maximum levels for others who might otherwise have been
paid more. Statutory maternity leave may lead to the non-
employment of married women. In general, the costly improvements of occupational welfare rights may be at the
expense of those seeking employment and, since the latter
may legitimately be regarded as part of the wider group
intended to benefit by such welfare provisions, the overall effect of the legislation may be regarded as counter-
productive.

This type of counter-productivity is more pronounced if
we take it to be a general principle of welfare legislation that those in most need ought to receive the greatest benefits, that is, if we assume that there is an
equalitarian element in welfare objectives. Thus policies
designed to meet a particular type of human need would be
assumed to be successful so long as those members of G in
greatest need with respect to F receive the greatest benefit, thus bringing G as a whole closer into line with the
conditions enjoyed by other members of society. But many
programmes, particularly those which involve giving grants
towards the cost of improvements in such areas as housing,
fail most clearly in relation to those who are most deprived in terms of F. Grants for house improvements to
save heating costs or provide basic amenities tend to be
taken up by the more affluent members of G, thus accen-
tuating the relative deprivation of the poorer members of
G. If an objective of such welfare laws is to lessen inequalities with respect to F then such consequences are
seriously counter-productive. This is a third type of
'wider perspective' counter-productivity. (33)

The dominant common factor in these different types of
counter-productivity in welfare legislation is that they
arise at the inter-face of social and economic policy at a
point where the relief of need is affected by the forces
of economic production or free market distribution. This
is particularly evident in the attempts to regulate the
housing and employment resources in favour of groups which
are at risk when purely market considerations dominate,
but it is also present to a greater or lesser extent in the
other examples of indirect and wider perspective counter-
productivity. The important feature here, from the point
of view of the concept of welfare rights, is the implication that capitalism is simply unable to deliver the
welfare goods which - at any rate in its more developed
forms - it promises. The implication drawn from this
failure is that there can be no capitalist welfare rights
since it is not possible for a capitalist state to fulfil
the correlative obligations and it makes no sense to say

that those who are unable to perform an act ought to do so.
The weakness of this argument is that it suggests that the
satisfaction of basic course-of-life needs is an all-or-
nothing achievement when in fact it is very much a matter
of degree, as may be seen from the difficulty of determining what is to count as a tolerable minimum level of
material existence. It is not plausible to assert that
capitalist systems cannot take measures which go some of
the way towards meeting the needs of at least some of their
relatively deprived citizens. The material benefits dispensed by social security systems adequately demonstates
the falsehood of such a contention. What counter-
productivity may well indicate is that there are strict
limits to what capitalist systems can do in the extension of welfare provision without undermining the operations
of the productive and distributive processes on which their
welfare provisions ultimately depend. But this does not
empty talk of welfare rights of all content since this is
not the same as saying that capitalist societies can do nothing for those in need. The actual extent to which the
welfare principle can be applied without worsening the
overall situation of the poor in a capitalist system is a
topic for empirical investigation but the intelligibility
of the idea of capitalist welfare rights does not rest on
the outcome of this investigation.

In fact, many of the alleged examples of counter-
productivity depend on the existence of attitudes and practices which are part of the capitalist ethic and whose removal or reduction does not affect the importance of the
rights in question. Thus the stigma effect occurs because
according to the accepted work ethic of capitalism,
material benefits should depend on some form of contribution to the productive process. It is this which makes
it appropriate to despise those who cannot support themselves and so reduces the self-image of those dependent on
state aid. If the capitalist ethos declines, the stigma
effect will fade and the provision of welfare benefits
through bureaucratic methods could proceed more effici-
ently. Similarly, the dependency syndrome is a feature of
an economy in which work is inherently unattractive and
burdensome; it will therefore be less of a problem if the
socialist conception of satisfying productive labour is
put into effect. Again, the unpleasant aspects of rights-
mindedness is a natural development only where individuals
have to adopt a legalistic and aggressive stance in order
to receive their entitlements (the dignified acceptance of
a welfare entitlement is another matter, but it is not
argued that this is counter-productive). Even more
clearly, the economic examples of wider perspective

counter-productivity arise only because the welfare legislation in question is being applied in situations where
those with the correlative duties are motivated by considerations of profit and loss and therefore act in such a
way as to negate the benefits which would otherwise flow
from the relevant legislation. Thus increasing job
security through regulations affecting dismissals reduces
the number of jobs available only because of the behaviour
of employers in a market economy. There is always the
prospect, therefore, of further regulations and incentives
being used to manipulate the behaviour of those whose
actions render nugatory the effects of welfare laws. The
multiplication of rules which constant reform in welfare
policy required to counteract the counter-productiveness
caused by the countervailing forces of capitalist economics obviously creates administrative problems which provide ammunition for those who wish to retract existing
welfare benefits and protections, particularly in the
economic spheres such as employment and private house let-
ting, but the intervention of law to curb the worst
effects of capitalist competition is very far from totally
ineffective, as it would have to be to justify the thesis
that there can be no substance to the idea of welfare
rights in capitalist economies. Conversely, while the introduction of a socialist economic system outside market
forces would render much of this sort of legislation unnecessary, right-conferring rules would still be required
to guide the economic decisions in the new system.

The transition from capitalism to socialism would certainly involve radical changes in the substance of welfare
rights and in the attitude of citizens towards such rights,
but this does not create a hiatus in the continuity of the
concept of welfare rights. What would follow from the transition to socialism - and this point may lie behind some
of the revolutionary critics' argument - is that the clear
distinction between social and economic policy and thus
between social welfare and the general objectives of the
economic activity would dissolve. In a society in which
all social arrangements are directed towards the satisfaction of human need the classification of a special
narrow class of needs on the grounds that they generate
obligations of a sort which do not feature in the normal
processes of social interaction has little relevance. In
a socialist society the concept of welfare rights as the
rights based on the needs of minorities requiring special
assistance will have no role to play. At present the distinction between welfare and other rights is already
blurred in the universalisation of some welfare rights to
cover the needs of all citizens regardless of their means

(as in the UK Health services) and even more so in the
development of the welfare protection which feature as
fringe-benefits for the average wage-earner. While the
latter development is antithetical to socialism in so far
as it leads to further inequalities between the employed
and the unemployed, occupational welfare rights serve to
indicate the way in which a socialist society could gradually extend the welfare principle from the basic course-
of-life needs of the needy few to take in the ordinary
course-of-life needs of the average citizen. This is,
however, essentially a matter of the extension of welfare
rights rather than their negation.

CONCLUSION

Socialist rights are more positive, less dependent on the
activation of the right-holder, more directed towards the
protection and furtherance of those concerns which express
the needs of active and creatively productive social
beings than is the case with capitalist rights. Socialist
rights are more organisational than political in that they
inform the co-operative social effort rather than represent demands to be disputed and traded-off against each
other. They are devices to secure the benefits which can
be derived from harmonious communal living, not protections for the individual against the predations of others.
Socialist rights are highly dependent on others fulfilling
their correlative obligations, but are not conditional on
the right-holders fulfilling their own obligations, although in practice socialist rights and socialist duties
tend to coalesce, as in the case of the right and duty to
work. They are tangible social phenomena which actually
describe the standard relationships within a socialist
society. Socialist rights relate to mandatory rules but
not to a supporting set of coercive sanctions. They may
involve institutional machinery to monitor and correct un-
intentional deviations from right-conferring rules and to
decide issues in which the facts or particular situations
or the rules which apply to these situations are unclear,
but this machinery would have none of the aura or the
techniques of a penal system.
    In total, these characterisations describe a system of
rights which is far from the norm in contemporary societies
but individually they do not mark a radical break with
features of existing rights systems and in total they do
not amount to an abandonment of the concept of rights, unless this concept is unwarrantably restricted to a narrow
version of the power theory of rights taken in conjunction

with the sanctions theory of positive obligations. The contrast between the typical rights of the welfare state and those of Utopian socialism is a matter of degree and attitude, not of categories.

To demonstrate the conceptual continuity between socialist and other rights does not solve very many of the problems which I have touched on in this final chapter. It leaves unsettled, for instance, whether a socialist who looks for the radical transformation of society should support existing welfare rights on the grounds that they approximate to socialist rights or ought to denounce them either because they offer far more than they can deliver or because they in effect retard the breakdown of the capitalist system and hence the emergence of a better way of life. But we have reached the point at which it can be made clear that the latter tactic is not just a matter of putting to one side an unimportant and unsocialist set of considerations in favour of an obviously overriding political goal. At least some of the welfare (and, indeed, the political) rights which may have to be temporarily suspended embody the very type of social objective to which socialism is committed. This must rule out a callous disregard of any existing rights which in any way serve to succour the fulfilment of basic human needs. The socialist can therefore be expected to treat the concept of rights with respect and where actual rights do connect with human welfare activity support their enforcement unless there are overwhelming overriding circumstances which stand in the way. Moreover, if the argument of chapter 6 is correct and the need principle is antithetical to utilitarianism, then the socialist will not indulge in any crude arithmetical balancing of present (justifiable) rights of individuals against the prospects of benefiting future generations. He may have no absolutely universal concept of human rights to preclude any such calculations, for in terms of human rights socialism is committed to no more than the desirability of giving all members of a society some rights which enjoy special political or constitutional protection, but we have seen that it is incompatible with socialist justificatory principles to underplay the enormity of sacrificing the concerns of existing persons on the ground that only the interests of future generations of socialists have moral significance. This is in itself an important reason for socialists to take seriously the language of rights in which the social and political issues of contemporary societies are so frequently debated.

The concepts of rights, I conclude, is not inherently biased against socialist ideals and aspirations. This

does not, in itself, decide the feasibility or desirability of socialism, but it may serve to keep open the
lines of communication between theorists of Right and Left
and enable socialist philosophers to make a clearer distinction between the capitalist conception of rights and the
concept of rights itself. Socialists may be reasonably
ambivalent about the former, but they have no grounds for
hostility to the latter.

Notes

1 REFORMISTS AND REVOLUTIONARIES

1 For the constitutions of the USSR (1936) and the People's Republic of China (1954) see Ian Brownlee (ed.), 'Basic Documents on Human Rights', Oxford, Clarendon Press, 1971, pp. 25-8 and 48-9.

2 Thus Raymond Williams, analysing his reaction to Stalinism, writes of 'the sense that this had gone wrong not only because of historical accidents and historical circumstances but that there was something within the degeneration itself related to a political system and a political theory, not just to a man', in B. Parekh (ed.), 'The Concept of Socialism', New York, Homes & Meier, 1975, p. 232.

3 Historically, we may consider Babeuf, Proudhon, Lassalle, the Fabian and Guild socialists and modern social democrats like C.A.R. Crosland, R.H. Tawney and Richard Titmuss as reformists, and Marxists, notably E.B. Pashukanis, as revolutionaries. Amongst recent works, we may contrast the reformism of Adam Schaff, 'Marxism and the Human Individual', New York, McGraw Hill, 1970; Mihailo Markovic, 'The Contemporary Marx', Nottingham, Spokesman Books, 1974; and J. Halasz, (ed.), 'The Socialist Concept of Human Rights', Budapest, Akadémiai Kiado, 1966, with the more revolutional positions outlined in Ruth Anna Putnam, Rights of Persons and the Liberal Tradition, in Ted Honderich (ed.), 'Social Ends and Political Means', London, Routledge & Kegan Paul, 1976, pp. 90-110; Bertell Ollman, Marx's vision of communism in S. Bider (ed.), 'Radical Visions of the Future', Colorado, Westview Press, 1977, pp. 55-73; and Paul Hirst, Law, Socialism and Rights, in Pat Carlen and Mike Collison (eds), 'Radical Issues in Criminology',

Oxford, Martin Robinson, 1980, pp. 58-104.

4   See, for instance, D.D. Raphael (ed.), 'Political Theory and the Rights of Man', London, Macmillan, 1967.

5   John Lewis, 'Marxism and the Open Mind', Connecticut, Greenwood Press, 1973, p. 53.

6   Lewis, op.cit., p. 59.

7   Putnam, op.cit., p. 106.

8   See Maurice Cranston, 'What are Human Rights?', London, Bodley Head, 1973, p. 43.

9   Putnam, loc.cit.

10   Richard Flathman, 'The Practice of Rights', Cambridge University Press, 1976, pp. 1-2.

11   Flatham, op.cit., p. 80.

12   Ibid., p. 190.

13   See Friedrich Engels, 'Socialism: Utopian and Scientific' (1880) in Lewis S. Feur. 'Marx and Engels: Basic Writings on Politics and Philosophy', Glasgow, Fontana, 1969, pp. 109-52.

14   See R.C. Tucker, 'The Marxian Revolutionary Idea', London, Allen & Unwin, 1970, pp. 37-48.

15   Karl Marx, 'Critique of the Gotha Programme' (1875), in Feuer, op.cit., p. 160: 'This equal right [of the producers proportional to their labour] is an unequal right for unequal labour. It recognises no class differences because everyone is a worker like everyone else, but it tacitly recognises unequal individual endowments and thus productive capacity as natural privileges. It is, therefore, a right of inequality, in its content, like every right.'

16   For instance: 'It has been shown that the recognition of the rights of man by modern State has only the same significance as the recognition of slavery by the State in antiquity', 'The Holy Family' (1844) in T.B. Bottomore and M. Rubel, 'Karl Marx: Selected Writings in Sociology and Social Philosophy', Harmondsworth, Penguin, 1963, p. 223.

17   Engels, op.cit., p. 141: 'When at last it [the State] becomes the real representative of the whole society, it renders itself unnecessary....State interference in social relations becomes, in one domain after another, superfluous, and then dies out of itself; the government of persons is replaced by the administration of things, and by the conduct of the processes of production.'

18   A convincing case has been made out for Marx having rejected the moral but not the juridical concept of rights, the content of the latter being assessed by its correspondence with the operative mode of

production; see Allen W. Wood, The Marxian Critique of
Justice, 'Philosophy and Public Affairs', vol I, 3,
1972, pp. 244-82. But for a contrary view, see Derek
P.H. Allen, Is Marxism a Philosophy?, 'Journal of
Philosophy', 71, 1974, pp. 601-12.

19 For a recent attempt to define socialism, see R.N.
Berki, 'Socialism', London, Dent, 1975, ch. 1.

20 I use the term social policy to cover prescriptions
about state activity in relation to the distribution
of resources in accordance with need; see Noel Timms
(ed.), 'Social Welfare: Why and How?', London,
Routledge & Kegan Paul, 1980, Introduction; and
R. Titmuss, The subject of social administration, in
'Commitment to Welfare', London, Allen & Unwin, 1968.
It will be apparent that in a socialist society there
could be no sharp distinction between social and
economic policy.

2 THE MORALISM OF RIGHTS

1 Compare, for instance, (1) 'The modern era, presumably
replacing the arbitrary rule of men with the objective
impartial rule of law, has not brought any fundamental
change in the facts of unequal wealth and unequal
power' (Howard Zinn, The Conspiracy of Law, in R.P.
Wolff (ed.), 'The Rule of Law', New York, Simon &
Schuster, 1971, p. 17), and (2) 'The ethics of love,
of service, of aesthetic enhancement, no less than
those of instinct and of "supermanship", can only meet
justice as an inferior attribute and an unworthy end'
(Judith N. Shklar, 'Legalism', Cambridge, Mas.,
Harvard University Press, 1969, p. 113).

2 See Otto Kahn-Freund, 'Selected Writings', London,
Stevens, 1978, ch. 7, also Peter Stein and John Shand,
'Legal Values in Western Society', Edinburgh University Press, 1974, pp. 21f: 'Where any social relationship has the character of a true fellowship the law
should keep away. If the law attempts to define the
relations of its members in terms of rights and duties
- and they are effectively the only terms that it can
define them in - the members of the true fellowship
will ignore what the law says.'

3 See Richard Quinney, 'Critique of Legal Order',
Boston, Little, Brown & Co., 1974. ch. 4; Michael E.
Tiger, Socialist Law and Legal Institutions, in
R. Lefcourt (ed.) 'Law Against the People', New York,
Random House, pp. 327-47; and I. Taylor, P. Walton and
J. Young, 'The New Criminology', London, Routledge &

Kegan Paul, 1973.

4 The classical expression of this model is contained in
T. Hobbes, 'Leviathan' (1651). It is arguable that
approximately the same model underlies all social contract views which are predicated on egoistic theories
of human nature, even when impartiality is super-
imposed through the background conditions of the social
contract. See my review of John Rawls, 'A Theory of
Justice', in 'Political Quarterly', vol. 43, No, 4,
1972, pp. 510-12.

5 See F. Engels, 'Socialism, Utopian and Scientific'
(1892), in 'The Essential Left', London, Unwin Books,
1960, p. 117: 'To all these [Utopians] socialism is
the expression of absolute truth, reason, and justice,
and has only to be discovered to conquer all the world
by virtue of its own power.'

6 The label 'ideal rights' is sometimes used for the
rights which people have independently of law and custom; see David Miller, 'Social Justice', Oxford,
Clarendon Press, 1976, p. 66: 'An ideal right...is
constituted by its content. A person has an ideal
right because of that to which he had the right,
whether or not that right is socially recognised.'
The more common label is 'moral right' but, as we shall
see, this term his highly ambiguous.

7 See H.D. Aitken, Rights, Human and Otherwise, 'Monist',
vol. 52, 1968, pp. 502-15; at p. 504: 'To assert a
right...is to make a demand which purports to be lawful or proper or right.'

8 See R. Wasserstrom, Rights, Human Rights and Racial
Discrimination, 'Journal of Philosophy', vol. 61,
1964; at p. 630: 'To have a right is...to have a very
strong moral or legal claim upon it. It is the
strongest kind of claim that there is.'

9 See Istrán Kovács: 'Formerly even the most democratic
capitalist state had remained content with the formal
protection of rights as laid down in statutes, and
with redressing their infringements. However, as
soon as the means of production, and the cultural,
social and public health institutions have passed
into public ownership, it became a duty incumbent upon
the community, society and the state as their representative to regulate and organize the constant building up of material wealth and its general distribution
which is necessary to make these rights a living
reality' (General Problems of Rights, in Joseph
Halasz (ed.), 'The Socialist Concept of Human Rights',
Budapest, Akadémai Kiado, 1966, p. 7).

10 For defences of this view, see T.D. Campbell, Rights

without justice, 'Mind', vol. 83, 1974, pp. 445-8, and
Humanity before Justice, 'British Journal of Political
Science', vol. 4, 1974, pp. 1-16; also Robert Young,
Dispensing with moral rights, 'Political Theory',
vol. 6.1, 1978, pp. 63-74; and R.G. Frey, 'Interests
and Rights', Oxford, Clarendon Press, 1980, ch. 1.

11   The phrase 'manifesto rights' was coined by Joel
Feinberg. See his Nature and Value of Rights,
'Journal of Value Enquiry', vol. 4, 1970, pp. 243-57.
It is an apt term in that it is usually in the context
of political debate that the existence of moral rights
is asserted. Feinberg himself warns us against taking
this type of talk too literally: ibid., p. 255: 'When
manifesto writers speak of them [claims based on need
alone] as if already actual rights, they are easily
forgiven, for this is a powerful way of expressing the
conviction that they ought to be recognized by states
here and now as potential rights and consequently as
determinant of *present* aspirations and guides to
present policies. That usage, I think, is a valid
exercise of rhetorical license.' Similarly, Miller
argues that to speak of 'ideal rights' is 'derivative
and strictly from the analytical point of view, misleading', op.cit., p. 82.

12   Consider the contrast in moral philosophy between
'objectivists', such as G.E. Moore ('Principia
Ethica', Cambridge University Press, 1903), who accept
that moral judgements are propositions, and 'subjec-
tivists', such as C.L. Stevenson, 'Facts and Values',
(New Haven, Conn., Yale University Press, 1963), who
interpret them as expressions of feeling or attitudes.

13   Peter Jones, Rights, Welfare and Stigma, in Noel Timms
(ed.), 'Social Welfare: Why and How', London, Routledge & Kegan Paul, 1980, p. 126, commenting on T.D.
Campbell, Humanity before Justice, 'British Journal of
Political Science', vol. 4, 1974, pp. 1-12.

14   Frey, op.cit., p. 17. A similar mistake appears to be
made by Feinberg when he alleges that a world without
rights would be a world in which no one could justifiably complain. This assumes that the only basis
for making complaints is the violation of one's
rights. There is no reason to think that without
rights we would all be supplicants rather than com-
plainants. See W. Nelson, On the Alleged Importance
of Moral Rights, 'Ratio', vol. 18, 1975, p. 145-55.

15   See Wasserstrom, loc.cit., and Timms, op.cit., p. 136f.

16   Feinberg notes a similar ambiguity in the use of
'claim' as a synonym for 'right', 'Social Philiosphy',
Englewood Cliffs, New Jersey, Prentice-Hall, 1973,
p. 64.

17 For sympathetic treatments of natural law theory see
    A.P.d'Entrèves, 'Natural Law', 2nd edn, London,
    Hutchinson, 1970; and John Finnis, 'Natural Law and
    Natural Rights', Oxford, Clarendon Press, 1980.

18 Paul Hirst, Law, Socialism and Rights, in Pat Carlen
    and Mike Collison (eds), 'Radical Issues in Crimi-
    nology', Oxford, Martin Robertson, 1980, ch. 4, p. 58.

19 Op.cit. p. 95.

20 R.M. Hare, Abortion and the Golden Rule, 'Philosophy
    and Public Affairs', vol. 4, 1974, p. 20f. See T.D.
    Campbell and A.J.M. McKay, Antenatal Injury and the
    Rights of the Foetus, 'Philosophical Quarterly',
    vol. 28, 1974, pp. 17-30.

21 It is interesting to note that Hirst's rejection of
    all rights is based on essentially the same grounds as
    Young's rejection of moral rights. See Young, op.cit.,
    p. 68: Talk about moral rights, Young suggests, is
    based on the false hope that there are 'secure and
    objective criteria beyond the whims of human will and
    the contingencies of particular historical situations
    in virtue of which we can be sure what we ought to
    do'.

22 This is equivalent to John Austin's concept 'positive
    morality' 'The Province of Jurisprudence Determined'
    (1832), ed. H.L.A. Hart, Lecture I, London, Weidenfeld
    & Nicolson, 1953. See H.L.A. Hart, 'Concept of Law',
    Oxford, Clarendon Press, 1961, pp. 54-60.

23 See T.D. Campbell, Rights without Justice, 'Mind',
    vol. 83, 1974, p. 445-8.

24 See Derek P.H. Allen, Is Marxism a Philosophy,,
    'Journal of Philosophy', vol. 71, 1974, pp. 601-12.

25 See Wesley N. Hohfeld, 'Fundamental Legal Con-
    ceptions', New Haven, Conn., Yale University Press,
    1919. Helpful expositions with minor developments are
    to be found in 'Salmond on Jurisprudence', 12th ed,
    London, Sweet & Maxwell, 1966, pp. 224-33; G. Williams,
    The Concept of Legal Liberty, in R.S. Summers (ed.),
    'Essays in Legal Philosophy', Oxford, Blackwell, 1970,
    pp. 121-45; and Thomas D. Parry, A Paradigm of
    Philosophy: Hohfeld on Rights, 'American Philosophical
    Quarterly', vol. 14, 1977, pp. 41-50.

26 'Leviathan', ch. 14.

27 See p. 143

28 This last example illustrates that power-rights may be
    shared with others. In this case they may be called
    participant powers (see Lawrence C. Becker, 'Property
    Rights', London, Routledge & Kegan Paul, 1977, p. 14).

29 For the notion of 'exclusion' in connection with
    social norms see J. Raz, 'Practical Reason and Norms',

London, Hutchinson, 1975, pp. 35–45 and 73–6.

3 THE LEGALISM OF RIGHTS

1 For a discussion of legalism and ideology see Judith N. Shklar, 'Legalism', Cambridge, Mass., Harvard University Press, 1964. Shklar defines legalism as 'the ethical outlook that holds moral conduct to be a matter of rule-following, and moral relationships to consist of duties and rights determined by rules' (p. 1). She argues that the legalistic policy of justice is 'to resolve as many conflicts by judicial means as possible' (p. 117). For the idea of 'legal fetishism', see E.B. Pashukanis, 'Law and Marxism', ed. Chris Arthur, London, Ink Links, 1978, p. 117.

2 For a persuasive argument that morality is not, in general, a matter of adhering to rules, see G.J. Warnock, 'The Object of Morality', London, Methuen, 1971, chs 4 and 5.

3 A sympathetic analysis of the principles of legalism is to be found in Lon Fuller, 'The Morality of Law', revised edition, New Haven, Conn., Yale University Press, 1969. Fuller argues that the requirements that rules be general, promulgated, prospective, clear, non-contradictory, constant, congruent with each other and demand only conduct within the powers of the affected party, follow from the undertaking of 'subjecting human conduct to the governance of rules' (p. 96f).

4 See Shklar, op.cit., p. 13f: 'The more the bar concentrates on formal perfection of established rules and procedures, the more removed it may become from the social ends that law serves.'

5 See Ch. Perelman, 'The Idea of Justice and the Problem of Argument', London, Routledge & Kegan Paul, 1963, essays 1 and 3, and the criticism of Perelman's position in D.D. Raphael, 'Problems of Political Philosophy', London, Pall Mall, 1970, p. 175f.

6 See R.M. Hare, 'Freedom and Reason', Oxford University Press, 1963, pp. 7–50.

7 Aristotle, 'Politics', III and XVI, 1287a: 'it is more proper that law should govern than any one of the citizens'.

8 See Peter P. Nicholson, The Internal Morality of Law: Fuller and his Critics, 'Ethics', vol. 84, 1973–4, pp. 307–26.

9 For a socialist's defence of the importance of the role of law in pre-socialist societies, see

E.P. Thompson, 'Whigs and Hunters', London, Allen Lane, 1975, especially pp. 258-69: 'The inhibitions upon power imposed by law seem to me a legacy as substantial as any handed down from the struggles of the seventeenth century' (p. 265).

10 See Perelman, op.cit., essay 1. For a similar distinction between the concept of justice and conceptions of justice see John Rawls, 'A Theory of Justice', Oxford, Clarendon Press, 1979, p. 5f.

11 See Alf Ross, 'On Law and Justice', London, Stevens, p. 272 'applied to characterize a general rule or order the words "just" or "unjust" are entirely devoid of meaning....A person who maintains that a certain rule or order...is unjust does not indicate any discernible quality in the order...but merely gives to it an emotional expression'.

12 See 'Politics', III, 12, 1282b.

13 For an account of the interpretation and scope of these principles, see Paul Jackson, 'Natural Justice', London, Sweet & Maxwell, 2nd edn, 1979.

14 See J.R. Lucas, 'On Justice', Oxford, Clarendon Press, 1980, p. 97: 'These rules of procedure do not guarantee that decisions will be just. Rather they constitute necessary, or near necessary, conditions of the decision making process with which a man could be expected to identify.'

15 See Kenneth Davis, 'Discretionary Justice', Louisiana State University Press, 1969; T.D. Campbell, Discretionary 'Rights', in Noel Timms and David Watson (eds), 'Philosophy in Social Work', London, Routledge & Kegan Paul, 1978, pp. 50-77; and T.D. Campbell, Discretion and Rights within the Children's Hearing System, 'Philosophical Journal', vol. 14, 1977, pp. 1-21.

16 See T.D. Campbell, Formal Justice and Rule-change, 'Analysis', vol. 33, 1973, pp. 113-18.

17 See R.C. Tucker, 'Philosophy and Myth in Karl Marx', Cambridge University Press, 1961, pp. 18-20.

18 See Allen W. Wood, The Marxian Critique of Justice, 'Philosophy and Public Affairs', vol. 1, 1971-2, pp. 244-82; at p. 257 'For Marx, the justice or injustice of an action or institution does not consist in its exemplification of a juridical form or its conformity to a universal principle. Justice is not determined by the universal compatibility of human acts and interests, but by the concrete requirements of a historically conditioned mode of production.' In support of this thesis Wood quotes the following passage from 'Capital': 'The justice of transactions

which go on between agents of production tests on the
fact that these transactions arise as natural consequences from the relations of production. The juristic forms in which these economic transactions appear
as voluntary actions of the participants, as expressions of their common will and as contracts that
may be enforced by the state against a single party,
cannot, being mere forms, determine this content.
They purely express it. This content is just whenever
it corresponds to the mode of production, is adequate
to it. It is unjust whenever it contradicts that
mode' ('Werke', 25: 351f).

19   See Ziyad I. Husami, Marx on Distributive Justice,
     'Philosophy and Public Affairs', vol. 8, 1978, pp. 27-
     64, especially p. 30 and p. 36.

20   For general treatments of the instrumental functions
     of rules see R. Summers and C. Howard, 'Law, Its
     Nature, Function and Limits, Englewood Cliffs, New
     Jersey, Prentice-Hall, 2nd edn, 1972, and J. Raz, On
     the Functions of Law, in A.W.B. Simpson, 'Oxford
     Essays in Jurisprudence', 2nd Series, Oxford, Claren-
     don Press, 1973, pp. 278-304.

21   See D.N. MacCormick, Rights in Legislation, in P.M.S.
     Hacker and J. Raz (eds), 'Law, Morality and Society',
     Oxford, Clarendon Press, 1977, pp. 189-209.

22   For a discussion of this 'left-idealism', see Jock
     Young, Left Idealism, reformism and beyond: from the
     new criminology to Marxism, in Bob Fine et al. (eds),
     'Capitalism and the Rule of Law', London, Hutchinson,
     1979.

23   For the variety of types of property right see A.M.
     Honoré, Ownership, in A.G. Guest (ed.), 'Oxford Essays
     in Jurisprudence', 1st Series, Oxford, Clarendon
     Press, 1961, pp. 107-47.

24   It is interesting that Putnam's example of non-
     regulated co-operation is that of helping to push a
     stalled car. See p. 5. Anarchists in general have
     tended to oppose large bureaucratic organisations and
     advocate a society of small, face-to-face groupings.
     See April Carter, 'The Political Theory of Anarchism',
     London, Routledge & Kegan Paul, 1971, ch. 3.

25   The general convenience of the institution of promis-
     ing is lucidly demonstrated in David Hume, 'A Treatise
     of Human Nature', (1739), ed. L.A. Selby-Bigge, Oxford,
     Clarendon Press, 1888, III.ii.5, pp. 516-25.

26   See Marx, 'Capital', vol. I, ch. 13, Harmondsworth,
     Penguin, 1976, p. 448f: 'All directly social or com-
     munal labour on a large scale requires, to a greater
     or lesser degree, a directing authority, in order to

secure the harmonious co-operation of activities of
individuals, and to perform the general functions that
have their origin in the motion of the total productive organism, as distinguished from the motion of its
separate organs. A single violin player is his own
conductor, an orchestra requires a separate one.'
This idea is developed in E.P. Pashukanis's notion of
technical as distinct from legal regulation. See his
'Law and Marxism', London, Ink Links, 1978, ch. 2.
See pp. 90-92.

27 Thus F.A. Hayek ('Law, Legislation and Liberty', vol.
2, London, Routledge & Kegan Paul, 1976), having dismissed the use of the notion of social or distributive
justice as confused and dishonest, nevertheless regards his idea of 'catallaxy' - 'the special kind of
spontaneous order provided by the market through
people acting within the rules of property, tort and
contract' (p. 109) - as bringing about a distribution
which reflects the knowledge and skill of individuals
as well as their good fortune. For the idea that one
purpose of equality of opportunity is to bring about
a distribution which is in accordance with merit, see
T.D. Campbell, Equality of Opportunity, 'Proceedings
of the Aristotelian Society', vol. 75, 1974, pp. 51-
68.

28 To interpret Marx in this way requires us to view his
endorsement of the distribution principle 'to each
according to his needs' as applying only in a transitional state of socialism before genuine communism
emerges and all distributive rules are transcended.
See Tucker, 'Philosophy and Myth in Karl Marx',
Cambridge University Press, 1961, Introduction and
ch. X.

29 See F.A. Hayek, op.cit., p. 85, and Robert Nozick,
'Anarchy, State and Utopia', New York, Basic Books,
1974, pp. 160-4.

4 THE COERCIVENESS OF RIGHTS

1 The Scandinavian Realist, K. Olivecrona, expresses
the standard positivist view thus: 'Law consists
chiefly of rules about force, rules which contain patterns of conduct for the exercise of force' ('Law as
Fact', London, Steven & Sons, 2nd edn, 1971, p. 134).
This positivist view is adopted by radical socialist
critics of criminal law such as Richard Quinney, 'The
Legal system provides the mechanism for the forceful
control of the rest of the population' ('Critique of

Legal Order', Boston, Little, Brown, 1974, p. 52). It follows that in a communist society, which has no need of coercion, there would be no law, see Bertell Ollman, Marx's Vision of Communism, in S. Bider (ed.), 'Radical Visions of the Future', Boulder, Colorado, Westview Press, 1977.

2 'Leviathan', ch. XXVI, Everyman Edition, London, Dent, 1914, p. 140, 'Civill Law, is to every subject, those rules, which the commonwealth hath commended him.'

3 'Principles of Morals and Legislation', in 'Collected Works of Jeremy Bentham', London, University of London, Athlone Press, 1920, p. 207f.2. Bentham gives a variety of definitions of obligation, some of them in terms of predicted sanctions, some in terms of commanded ones. See P.M.S. Hacker, Sanction Theories of Duty, in A.W.B. Simpson, 'Oxford Essays in Jurisprudence', Clarendon Press, Oxford, 1973, at pp. 135-48.

4 For an exposition of the command theory of law based on Austin, see H.L.A. Hart, 'The Concept of Law', Clarendon Press, Oxford, 1961, ch. 2.

5 'Province of Jurisprudence Determined' (1832), Lecture I, ed. H.L.A. Hart, London, Weidenfeld & Nicolson, 1954, p. 10.

6 'Fragment on Government', 'Collected Works', p. 107n.

7 'Principles of Morals and Legislation', 'Collected Works', pp. 35f.

8 'Utilitarianism', (1863), ed. A.D. Lindsay, London, Dent, 1957, p. 26: cf. 'Its [moral obligation's] binding force...consists in a mass of feeling which must be broken through in order to do what violates our standard of right, and which, if we do nevertheless violate that standard, will probably have to be encountered afterwards in the form of remorse'.

9 Op.cit., p. 45.

10 Op.cit., p.6.

11 I am arguing that there must be a sense of moral obligation which is logically prior to statements about the acts for which a person ought to be punished because we have to be able to decide that an act is morally wrong before we can judge that it ought to be punished. This involves the use of the term 'obligation' in a way which runs counter to my earlier decision to use 'obligation' only for circumstances in which statements about rightness and wrongness were based on the existence of a legal or societal rule, for in the case of critical morality there need be no such rule. It may be said that the rule is a personal one adopted by the individual to guide his conduct,

his personal morality consisting of just such private
rules. And it is indeed part of an individual's moral
life that he decides to act in accordance with certain
rules and that his conscience comes to serve as a
guide to him, monitoring his conformity to his private
rules. But this cannot be all that is meant by critical morality, for the individual still has to make
moral decisions about what rules he is going to adopt.
Here he cannot ultimately fall back on any rules since
all rules must be assessed if they are to form part of
a genuine autonomous morality. Such judgments are ill
described as being about what his moral obligations
are, for they are in effect non-rule-based judgments
about what his moral obligations are going to be. But
even supposing that Mill was speaking only of moral
obligations, that is, the individual's judgments about
what he ought to do which are based on his own private
rules, it is implausible to analyse the individual's
decision to make conformity to such and such a rule a
moral obligation for himself as a decision to punish
himself by the pangs of conscience if he violates that
rule.

12 'The Pure Theory of Law', trans. Max Knight, Berkeley
University of California Press, 1967, p. 54: 'If
social orders designated as law *did* contain significant
numbers of sanctionless norms, then the definition of
law as a coercive order could be questioned; and if
from the existing social orders designated as law the
element of coercion were to disappear - as predicted
by Marx's socialism - then these social orders would
indeed fundamentally change their character. They
would - from the point of view of the offered definition of law - lose their legal character, and the
social orders constituted by them would lose their
character as states.'

13 The Pure Theory of Law and Analytical Jurisprudence,
'Harvard Law Review', LV, 1941-2, p. 58. See
'General Theory of Law and State', New York, Russell
& Russell, 1945, pp. 45f.

14 See 'Pure Theory of Law', pp. 15f.

15 The Pure Theory of Law and Analytical Jurisprudence,
pp. 58f.

16 'What is Justice?', 'Collected Essays', Berkeley, University of California Press, 1957, p. 289.

17 Loc.cit. See 'General Theory of Law and State', pp.
19, 26 and 28.

18 The Pure Theory of Law and Analytical Jurisprudence,
p. 50.

19 Op.cit., p. 58.

20 See The Pure Theory of Law, pp. 10 and 46; 'The
    General Theory of Law and State', p. 42.
21 'General Theory of Law and State', p. 30.
22 Op.cit., p. 39.
23 See J. Raz, 'The Concept of a Legal System', Oxford
    University Press, 1970, ch. 8.
24 For the distinction between 'internal' and 'external'
    points of view, see H.L.A. Hart, 'The Concept of Law',
    Oxford, Clarendon Press, 1961, pp. 86ff.
25 The principle of desuetude illustrates this. See J.W.
    Harris, 'Law and Legal Science', Oxford, Clarendon
    Press, 1979, pp. 122-7.
26 Kelsen agrees that if the robber's commands are part
    of a system or order which is generally obeyed it is
    like a legal order.
27 Hart, op. cit., pp. 79-88.
28 Op. cit., p. 213f.
29 Op. cit., chs 3 and 4.
30 Op. cit., ch. 10.
31 Op. cit., p. 92: 'Thus they [secondary rules] may all
    be said to be on a different level from the primary
    rules, for they are all *about* such rules.'
32 For an argument along similar lines see J. Raz,
    'Practical Reason and Norms', London, Hutchinson, 1975,
    pp. 157-61.
33 See Adam Podgorécki, 'Law and Society', London, Rout-
    ledge & Kegan Paul, 1974, pp. 192f: 'Historical ex-
    perience reveals, above all if we analyze the devel-
    opment that has taken place in some fields of social
    life and of economic conduct, state coercion is no
    longer devisive and is gradually being replaced by
    social pressure.'

5   THE INDIVIDUALISM OF RIGHTS

1   The possible exception being pure negative liberties,
    see p. 28f. The different types of correlativity are
    discussed in David Lyons, The Correlativity of Rights
    and Duties, 'Nous', vol. 4, 1970, pp. 45-55.
2   Thus socialist theorists always stress the need to in-
    corporate duties as well as rights in constitutional
    provisions; see J. Halasz (ed.) 'The Socialist Concept
    of Rights', Budapest, Akadémai Kiado, 1966, p. 49:
    'Citizens' duties being devoid of any outstanding sig-
    nificance within bourgeois philosophy, the thinkers of
    the age of Enlightenment and bourgeois legal philoso-
    phers were at a loss as to how to deal with them.'
    See also Kruschev's address at the XX Congress of the
    Communist Party of the Soviet Union: 'We must develop

among Soviet people Communist morality, at the foundation of which lie loyalty to Communism and uncom-
promising enmity to its foes, the consciousness of
social duty, active participation in labour, the
voluntary observance of the fundamental rules of human
communal life, comradely help, honesty, truthfulness
and intolerance of the disturbance of social order'
(quoted in E. Kamenka, 'Ethical Foundations of
Marxism', London, Routledge & Kegan Paul, 2nd edn,
1972, p. 184).

3 See C.B. Macpherson, 'The Political Theory of Posses-
sive Individualism', Oxford, Clarendon Press, 1962,
for this interpretation of Hobbes and Locke in terms
of market relationships. Similar assumptions underlie
later utilitarian theory of democracy; see James Mill,
'Essay on Government' (1819), Cambridge University
Press, 1937.

4 See R. Flathman, 'The Practice of Rights', Cambridge
University Press, 1976, p. 70: 'A striking feature of
such discourse has been the often unabashedly self-
assertive and insistent character of the speech and
other actions of those who hold rights. It is not
only common but generally thought unexceptional for
us to claim, maintain, assert, demand and insist upon
our rights.'

5 Flathman argues that the language of rights presupposes that right-bearers have the capacity to be
self-directing and assertive (op.cit. pp. 71f).

6 If we discount Hobbes's natural rights as not being
genuine rights since they do not correlate with any
obligations, the Hobbesian version of the social contract exemplifies the contract theory of rights in its
purest form. More commonly, it is a theory applied to
conventional or positive rights as opposed to natural
or moral rights.

7 This is roughly the stance adopted in R. Nozick,
'Anarchy, State and Utopia', New York, Basic Books,
1974, although, with Locke, Nozick allows that there
are moral side-constraints on how individuals may use
their natural liberty.

8 See Stephen Lukes, 'Individualism', Oxford, Blackwell,
1973, especially chs 11 and 12.

9 For the idea of a right as a 'legally respected individual choice', see H.L.A. Hart, Bentham on Legal
Rights, in A.W.B. Simpson (ed.), 'Oxford Essays in
Jurisprudence', 2nd series, Oxford, Clarendon Press,
1973, pp. 171-201.

10 See Flathman, op.cit., p. 79: 'There cannot be a right
to an X unless having or doing X is in general, and in

A's judgement, advantageous for A.'

11 See A.I. Melden, 'Rights and Persons', Oxford, Black-
    well, 1977, pp. 72f: 'The infant son surely has no
    obligation to his father, but he does have a right to
    the care and protection the father is able to give
    him; and this right exists as no mere augury of the
    future but as a right that he has then and there as
    an infant. Granted that certain conceptual linkages
    of this right are missing – for it makes no sense to
    speak of infants claiming or asserting their rights
    or forgiving those who violate them – the talk of the
    rights of infants is no mere *façon de parler* which
    could be put in a more straightforward and literal
    manner by speaking of what they need or ought to have
    in order that they may develop into beings who in a
    literal sense of the terms have rights.'

12 Paul Hirst, Law, Socialism and Rights, in Pat Carlen
    and Mike Collison (eds), 'Radical Issues in Crimi-
    nology', Oxford, Martin Robertson, 1980, p. 100:
    '"Rights" in law establish a capacity for a person to
    advance in the courts a claim for relief or for an
    agent acting as a legal subject for that person to
    make the claim.'

13 'General Theory of Law and State', p.136.

14 See Karl Marx, 'Capital', Book I, Part II, ch. 6,
    Harmondsworth, Penguin, 1976, p. 280 'The sphere of
    circulation or commodity exchange, within whose
    boundaries the sale and purchase of labour-power goes
    on, is in fact a very Eden of the innate rights of
    man. It is the exclusive realm of Freedom, Equality,
    Property and Bentham. Freedom, because both buyer
    and seller of a commodity, let us say of labour-
    power are determined only by their own free will.
    They contract as free persons, who are equal before
    the law. Their contract is the final result in which
    their joint will finds a common legal expression.
    Equality, because each enters into relation with the
    other, as with a simple owner of commodities, and
    they exchange equivalent for equivalent. Property,
    because each disposes only of what is his own. And
    Bentham, because each looks only to his own advantage.
    The only force bringing them together, and putting
    them into relation with each other, is the selfish-
    ness, the gain and the private interest of each. Each
    pays heed to himself only, and no one worries about
    the others. And precisely for that reason, either in
    accordance with the pre-established harmony of things,
    or under the auspices of an omniscient providence,
    they all work together to their mutual advantage, for

the common weal, and in the common interest.'
15 See particularly 'Law and Marxism, A General Theory',
London, Ink Links, 1978, trans. Barbara Einhorn from
a German edition of 1929 which followed two previous
editions in Russian. For discussions of Pashukanis's
work, see C.J. Arthur, Towards a Materialist Theory
of Law, 'Critique', vol. 7, 1976-7, pp. 31-46, and
Richard Kinsey, Marxism and the Law, 'British Journal
of Law and Society', vol. 5, 1978, pp. 202-27.
16 See 'Law and Marxism', ch. 2.
17 op.cit., pp. 100f.
18 See op.cit., p. 81: 'A basic prerequisite for legal
regulation is therefore the conflict of private
interests...the juridical factor in this regulation
arises at the point when differentiation and opposition of interests begin.'
19 See op.cit., pp. 117ff.
20 See op.cit., p. 103: 'If all economic life is to be
built on the principle of agreement between autonomous
wills, every social function, in reflecting this,
assumes a legal character.'
21 See op.cit., p. 71f 'Law not as an appendage of human
society in the abstract, but as an historical category corresponding to a particular social environment
based on the conflict of private interests.'
22 See Hans Kelsen, 'The Communist Theory of Law',
London, Stevens & Sons, 1955, p. 93: '"Ownership" in
an "extra-judicial sense" is a contradiction in terms.
Pashukanis must inevitably fall into this contradiction because he describes the legal relationship of
ownership without recurring to the legal norms constituting this relationship.'
23 See 'Law and Marxism', ch. 7.
24 Thus, 'the prerequisite for technical regulation is
unity of prupose. For this reason the legal norms
governing the railways' liability are predicated on
private claims, private differentiated interests,
while the technical norms of rail traffic presuppose
the common aims of, say, maximum efficiency of the
enterprise' ('Law and Marxism', p. 81).
25 For an able defence of the interest theory of rights,
see D.N. MacCormick, Rights in Legislation, in
P.M.S. Hacker and J. Raz (eds), 'Law, Morality and
Society', Oxford, Clarendon Press, 1977, pp. 189-209.
26 This encapsules Hume's idea of justice as an artificial virtue or social contrivance useful in view of
man's limited altruism in situations of scarcity.
See 'A Treatise of Human Nature', London, 1739,
Book III, Part II. Bertell Ollman expresses the

communist corrolary of this view: 'What happens...to
the notion of private property in a society where no
one ever claims a right to things he is using, wear-
ing, eating or living in, where instead of refusing to
share with others he is only too happy to give them
what they want, where - if you like - all claims to
use are equally legitimate? This is the situation of
communism: the clash of competing interests has disappeared and with it the need to claim rights of any
sort' (Marx's vision of communism, p. 63).

27 For a discussion of this distinction, see R.G. Frey,
'Interests and Rights', Oxford, Clarendon Press,
1980, ch. 7.

28 See, for instance, Christopher D. Stone, 'Should Trees
have Standing? Toward Legal Rights for Natural
Objects', New York, Avon Books, 1975.

29 Some of the points which follow are argued at greater
lengths in T.D. Campbell and A.J.M. McKay, Antenatal
Injury and the Rights of the Foetus, 'Philisophical
Quarterly', vol. 24, 1974, pp. 17-30.

6 SOCIALISM AND HUMAN RIGHTS

1 See Alice Erh-Soon Tay, Marxism, Socialism and Human
Rights, in Eugene Kamenka and Alice Erh-Soon Tay (eds),
'Human Rights', London, Edward Arnold, 1978, ch. 8,
p. 105: 'In the thought of Marx and socialism
generally...there is a certain fundamental ambivalence, direct and implied, on the question of human
rights.'

2 See M. Cranston, Human Rights, Real and Supposed, in
D.D. Raphael (ed.), 'Political Theory and the Rights
of Man', London, Macmillan, 1967, pp. 43-53.

3 Thus, for instance, Galvano Della Volpe, The Legal
Philosophy of Socialism, in Ehrich Fromm (ed.),
'Socialism and Humanism', London, Allen Lane, 1967,
p. 402; and Istvan Mészáros, Marxism and Human
Rights, in Alan D. Falconer (ed.), 'Understanding
Human Rights', Dublin, Irish School of Ecumenics,
1980, p. 50: 'The human rights of "Liberty" "Fraternity" and "Equality" are therefore problematical,
according to Marx, not in and by themselves, but in
the context in which they originate as abstract and
unrealisable ideal postulates, set against the dis-
concerting reality of the society of self-seeking
individuals. A society ruled by the inhuman forces
of antagonistic competition and ruthless acquisition
coupled with the concentration of wealth and power in

fewer and fewer hands. There can be no a prioristic
opposition between Marxism and human rights. Quite
the contrary. In point of fact, Marx never ceases to
advocate "the free development of individualities" in
a society of associated, and not antagonistically opposed, individuals (the necessary condition of both
"Liberty" and "Fraternity") simultaneously anticipat-
ing "the artistic, scientific, etc. development of
individuals in the time set free, and with the means
created, for all of them" (the necessary condition of
a true equality). The object of Marx's criticism is
not human rights as such but the use of the alleged
"rights of man" as prefabricated rationalisations of
the prevailing structures of inequality and domination.' But see p. 7f. Also Maurice Cornford, 'The
Open Philosophy and the Open Society', London,
Lawrence & Wishart, 1968, Part III.

4   See Paul Hirst, Law, Socialism and Rights, in Pat
Carlen and Mike Collison (eds), 'Radical Issues in
Criminology', Oxford, Martin Robertson, 1980, p. 103:
'The danger of the discourse of absolute "rights" is
that rights are conceived as inherent in the subject,
expression of its nature...a problem with such onto-
logizing of "rights" is that they privilege a certain
specific category of agents.'

5   Thus Karl Marx, 'The Communist Manifesto': 'The selfish misconception that induces you to transform into
eternal laws of nature and of reason the social forms
springing from your present mode of production and
form of property - historical relations that rise and
disappear in the progress of production - this misconception you share with every ruling class that has
preceded you' (Marx and Engels, 'Basic Writings on
Politics and Philosophy' ed. Lewis S. Feuer, London,
Fontana, 1969, pp. 65f).

6   Engels, Socialism Utopian and Scientific, in 'The
Essential Left', London, Unwin Books, 1960, p. 106:
'We know this kingdom of reason was nothing more than
the idealized kingdom of the bourgeoisie; that this
eternal right found its realization in bourgeois
justice; that this equality reduced itself to
bourgeois equality before the law; that bourgeois
property was declared as one of the essential rights
of man.'

7   This standard device of seventeenth and eighteenth
century political philosophy (see T. Hobbes,
'Leviathan' (1651); J. Locke, 'Two Treatises of
Government'; J. J. Rousseau, 'The Social Contract'
(1762)) has recently been revised and reviewed in

modern dress (see John Rawls, 'A Theory of Justice', Oxford, Clarendon Press, 1972; and Robert Nozick, 'Anarchy, State and Utopia', New York, Basic Books, 1974).

8 See p. 28. This is probably Hobbes's position. See T.D. Campbell, 'Seven Theories of Human Society', Oxford University Press, 1981, ch. 4.

9 Even Locke appeals to 'Reason' as well as to history (second Treatise of Government', ch. 9, section 104) and modern quasi-contractual theories which reject the historicity of the contract are explicitly justicatory rather than analytical in that they do not depend on the meaning of rights being explicated in terms of a hypothetical state of nature (see Rawls, op.cit., pp. 11-21).

10 For instance, The Universal Declaration of Human Rights, in Ian Brownlee (ed.), 'Basic Documents on Human Rights', Oxford, Clarendon Press, 1971, pp. 106-12. Cranston uses the historical relativity of social and economic rights to exclude them from the class of human rights (op.cit., pp. 49-51). See also A.I. Melden, 'Rights and Reasons', Oxford, Blackwell, 1979, ch. 6. But this argument applies with equal force to many of the standard civil liberties (see David Watson, Welfare Rights and Human Rights, 'Journal of Social Policy', vol. 6, pp. 39-46, at p. 39.)

11 Such as J.D. Mabbott, 'The State and the Citizen', London, Hutchinson, 1948, ch. 7.

12 See H.L.A. Hart, Are there any Natural Rights?, 'Philosophical Review', vol. 64, 1955, pp. 175-91.

13 Thus H.D. Aitken, Rights, Human and Otherwise, 'Monist', vol. 50, 1968, pp. 502-20; at p. 513: 'I submit that claims about so-called universal rights, at least, are intelligibly made, in historical contexts where there is a personal sense, whether individual or communal, that a right should be extended beyond the limits of some class which has come to appear "arbitrary". All assertions of "universal" rights, in this dimension, are best understood, first as efforts to extend the range of acceptable assertions of rights beyond some acknowledged specificity.

14 For a (basically unsuccessful) attempt to display the idea of equal consideration of 'treatment as an equal' in order to justify substantive human rights, see Ronald Dworkin, 'Taking Rights Seriously', London, Duckworth, 1977, ch. 9, Reverse Discrimination.

15 See p. 31f.

16 As, for instance, in the United States of America and in the German Federal Republic, Brownlee, op.cit.,

pp. 11 and 18.   See Louis Henkin, 'The Rights of Man Today', London, Stevens, 1979, ch. 2.

17 Thus the European Convention on Human Rights, whose machinery for supervision and enforcement includes the European Court of Human Rights.   See Brownlee, op.cit., pp. 338-65, also Louis B. Sohn and Thomas Buergenthall, 'The International Protection of Human Rights', New York, Bobbs Merrill, 1973

18 See D. Lloyd, Do we need a Bill of Rights?, 'Modern Law Review', vol. 39, 1976, p. 121.

19 On this topic, see Stanley I. Benn, Human rights - for whom and for what?, in Kamenda and Tay, op.cit., pp. 59-73.

20 For modern discussions of political obligation in the context of democratic theory, see John Rawls, op.cit., pp. 363-91; Ronald Dworkin, op.cit., pp. 206-22; and Peter Singer, 'Democracy and Disobedience', Oxford, Clarendon Press, 1973, pp. 63-4.

21 See, for instance, Milton Friedman, 'Capitalism and Freedom', Chicago University Press, 1962, pp. 19ff.

22 Brownlee, op.cit., p. 112.   Modern commentators tend to take it for granted that human rights are not absolute in the sense that they can never be abridged. See Louis Henkin, op.cit., p.3.

23 These points are briefly but effectively discussed in Joel Feinberg, 'Social Philosophy', Englewood Cliffs, New Jersey, Prentice-hall, 1973, pp. 94-7.

24 This is essentially Putnam's point.   See p. 5

25 Brownlee, op.cit., p. 57.

26 A problem with which J.S. Mill wrestles in his essay 'On Liberty' (1859).

27 Reformist socialists tend to note with regret that sometimes political liberties must be curtailed to achieve socialist objectives.   See Adam Schaff, 'Marxism and the Human Individual', New York, McGraw Hill, 1970, p. 214: 'Granted that bourgeois democracy is only formal, this is no reason for pleasure over the fact that some of these "formal" liberties are, for one reason or another, constrained in our part of the world [Poland].   This is not a virtue but a necessity imposed by the struggle.'

28 The most obvious example of this is in the use by the Supreme Court of the United States of the 'due process' of right to property clauses of the Constitution to prevent the implementation of Franklin Roosevelt's 'Need Deal' measures, such as the imposition of a minimum usage rate in the 1930s.   (Schechter Poultry Corporation v. U.S., 295 U.S. 495 (1935) and U.S. v. Butler, both of which are discussed in W. Friedmann,

'Legal Theory', New York, Columbia University Press,
5th edn, 1967, pp. 141f.

29 See Friedrich Engels and Karl Kautsky, Juridical
Socialism (1887), trans. Piers Beirne, 'Politics and
Society', vol. 7, 1977, pp. 203-20, at p. 204: 'Con-
vinced that dealing with this problem on the basis of
legal rights could never abolish the miserable circumstances occasioned by the production methods of modern
bourgeois-capitalism and large-scale industry, the
best minds among early socialists - St. Simon,
Fourier, Owen - abandoned the legal-political arena,
declaring all political struggles to be worthless.'

30 Ibid., p. 219: having admitted that the appeal to
basic rights changes nothing, the authors go on: 'This
is not say, of course, that socialists will fail to
present certain legalistic demands. An active socialist party is inconceivable without such demands',
but: 'The demands carrying from the common interests
of a class can only be realized when that class gains
political power and can give its demands universal
validity in the form of legislation.'

31 Mészáros, op.cit., p. 59f/

7   JUSTIFICATORY PRINCIPLES

1   This point is elaborated in T.D. Campbell, Rights
without Justice, 'Mind', vol 83, 1974, pp. 445-58.

2   R. Dworkin is, therefore, correct to hold that rights
are properly respected only when matters of policy
are excluded from the adjudicative process, but his
thesis that at least some utilitarian arguments are
intrinsically hostile to the right to equal concern
and respect is much more questionable and does not,
in any case, apply to rights in general; see 'Taking
Rights Seriously', London, Duckworth, 1977, especially ch. 9 and pp. 274-8.

3   For a helpful historical treatment of this theme
which comes to a different conclusion, see D.D.
Raphael, 'Justice and Liberty', London, Athlone Press,
1980, chs 10 and 11.

4   See James M. Ratcliffe (ed.), 'The Good Samaritan and
the Law', New York, Doubleday, 1966, particularly
Anthony M. Honoré, Law, Morals and Rescue.

5   The connection between justice and desert is considered at greater length in T.D. Campbell, Humanity
before Justice, 'British Journal of Political Science',
vol. 4, 1974, pp. 1-16.

6   See 'Utilitarianism', London, Fontana, 1962, p. 299:

'It is universally considered that each person should
obtain that (whether good or evil) which he deserves;
and unjust that he should obtain a good, or be made to
undergo an evil, which he does not deserve. This is,
perhaps, the clearest and most emphatic form in which
the idea of justice is conceived by the general mind.'

7 See 'Methods of Ethics', 7th edn, London, Macmillan,
1963, p. 283: 'It is the Requital of Desert that constitutes the chief element of Ideal Justice, in so far
as this imports something more than mere Equality and
Impartiability.'

8 M. Ginsberg, The Concept of Justice, 'Philosophy',
vol. 38, 1963, pp. 99-116, p. 109. For a contrary
view see Roger Hancock, Meritorian and Equalitarian
Justice, 'Ethics', vol. 80, 1969-70, pp. 165-9.

9 See, for instance, John Rawls, 'A Theory of Justice',
p. 3.

10 See ibid., pp. 310-15. For a contrary view, see Joel
Feinberg, Justice and Personal Desert, 'Nomos VI:
Justice', ed. C.J. Friedrich and J.W. Chapman, New
York, Atherton Press, 1963, pp. 63-97.

11 See, for instance, A. Kenny, 'Will, Freedom and
Power', Oxford, Blackwell, 1975, ch. 8, Michael Ayers,
'The Refutation of Determinism', London, Methuen,
1968; T. Honderich (ed.), 'Essays on Freedom of
Action', London, Routledge & Kegan Paul, 1973.

12 Thus, 'The German Ideology', ed. C.J. Arthur, London,
Lawrence & Wishart, 1970, pp. 104f: 'The communists
do not preach *morality* at all...they do not put to
people the moral demand: love one another, do not be
egoists, etc; on the contrary, they are very well
aware that egoism, just as much as self-sacrifice, *is*
in definite circumstances a necessary form of the
self-assertion of individuals.' See Eugene Kamenka,
'Marxism and Ethics', New York, Macmillan, 1968,
ch. 2.

13 See S. Hampshire, 'Freedom of the Individual', London,
Chatto & Windus, 1965.

14 See F. Engels, Socialism, Utopian and Scientific, in
'The Essential Left', London, Unwin, 1960, p. 144:
'The law of his own social action, hitherto standing
face to face with man as laws of Nature foreign to,
and dominating, him, will then be used with full
understanding, and so mastered by him. Man's own
social organization, hitherto confronting him as a
necessity imposed by Nature and history, now becomes
the result of his own free action.'

15 'Critique of the Gotha Programme', in Karl Marx,
'Selected Writings', ed. David McLellan, Oxford

University Press, 1977, p. 569: 'In a higher phase of communisty society, after the enslaving subordination of the individual to the division of labour, and therewith also the antithesis between mental and physical labour, has vanished; after labour has become not only a means of life but life's prime want; after the productive forces have also increased with the all-found development of the individual, and all the springs of co-operative wealth flow more abundantly – only then can the narrow horizon of bourgeois right be crossed in its entirety and society inscribe on its banners: from each according to his ability, to each according to his needs!'

16 This is discussed in T.D. Campbell, Humanity before Justice, pp. 7ff.

17 See David Braybrooke, Let Needs Diminish that Preferences may Prosper, in N. Rescher (ed.), 'Studies in Moral philosophy', Oxford, Blackwell, 1968, p. 90.

18 The concept of 'need' is subjected to careful analysis in the context of social policy issues in Raymond Plant, Harry Lesser and Peter Taylor-Gooby, 'Political Philosophy and Social Welfare', London, Routledge & Kegan Paul, 1980, especially Part One.

19 See Karl Marx, 'Grundisse', London, Allen Lane, 1973, p. 321 and p. 528 and Harry Lesser, True and False Needs, in Plant, Lesser and Taylor-Gooby, op.cit., ch. 7.

20 'Critique of the Gotha Programme', in 'Selected Writings', p. 568f: 'Right by its very nature can consist only in the application of an equal standard, but unequal individuals (and they would not be different individuals if they were not unequal) are measurable only by an equal standard in so far as they are brought under an equal point of view, are taken from one definite side only, for instance, in the present case are regarded only as workers...to avoid all these defeats, right instead of being equal would have to be unequal.' See also D.D. Raphael, 'Justice and Liberty', London, Athlone Press, 1980, pp. 49ff.

21 See F.A. Hayek, 'Law, Legislation and Liberty', London, Routledge & Kegan Paul, 1976, ch. 10.

22 Some of these problems are explored in Agnes Heller, 'The Theory of Need in Marx', London, Allison & Busby, 1974.

23 'German Ideology', p. 48.

24 See John Stuart Mill, 'Utilitariansim', ch. 2. Since the evaluative problems under discussion concern the justification of societal rules, it is rule-utilitarianism rather than act-utilitarianism with

which we are concerned, that is, we are not here de-
bating the principle of private morality that each
individual should act so as to maximise human happiness. For discussion of the various types of utilitarianism, see D. Lyons, 'Forms and Limits of Utilitarianism', Oxford, Clarendon Press, 1965.
25 Derek P.H. Allen, The Utilitarianism of Marx and
Engels, 'American Philosophical Quarterly', vol. 10,
1973, pp. 189-99.
26 See Dworkin, op.cit., pp. 234-9.
27 For a brief but lucid treatment of the various ways of
determining what is to count as the general happiness,
see Philip Pettit, 'Judging Justice', London, Routledge & Kegan Paul, 1980.
28 See ibid., ch. 13.
29 See Allen W. Wood, The Marxian Critique of Justice,
'Philosophy and Public Affairs', vol. 1, 1971-2,
pp. 244-82.
30 Rawls, 'A Theory of Justice', p. 157: Rights and
duties should be so distributed so as to 'maximise...
the long-term prospects of the least advantaged'.
For criticism, see Brian Barry, 'The Liberal Theory of
Justice', Oxford, Clarendon Press, 1973, ch. 10.
31 See Henry W. Ehrmann, 'Comparative Legal Cultures',
Englewood Cliffs, New Jersey, Prentice-Hall, 1976,
ch. 5.

8   POLITICAL RIGHTS: FREEDOM OF EXPRESSION

1   See Karl Popper, 'The Open Society and its Enemies',
London, Routledge & Kegan Paul, 4th edn, 1962, vol. 2,
especially ch. 19.
2   For general discussions of freedom of expression, see
H.J. McCloskey, Liberty of Expression, its Grounds
and Limits, 'Inquiry', vol. 13, 1970, pp. 219-37, and
Thomas Scanlon, A Theory of Freedom of Expression,
'Philosophy and Public Affairs', vol. 1, 1972,
pp. 204-26.
3   H.L.A. Hart, 'Concept of Law', Oxford, Clarendon
Press, 1961, pp. 89-91.
4   Op.cit., pp. 92-107.
5   Thus, Galvano Della Volpe, noting that the post-Stalin
constitution of the Soviet Union includes rights to
liberty of conscience, of speech, of the Press, of
assembly, of organising labour and habeus corpus, adds
'the specific and basic reasons of these liberties,
however, cannot be the same as those which obtain in
a liberal or democratic bourgeois state, if for no

other reason than that those liberties and subjective
rights, those technical constitutional norms, are incorporated into the social and political philosophy
of the first socialist state - and that state has
foundations which are original and proper to itself'
(in E. Fromm (ed.), 'Socialism and Humanism', London,
Allen Lane, 1967, p. 399).

6   Ian Brownlee (ed.), 'Basic Documents on Human Rights',
Oxford, Clarendon Press, 1971, p. 110.

7   Thus Article I of The United States Bill of Rights
(1791) declares that 'Congress shall make no law...
abridging freedom of speech, or the press', Article
125 of the USSR Constitution (1936) guarantees all
citizens freedom of speech and freedom of the press,
rights which are also provided for in Article 87 of
the Constitution of the People's Republic of China
(1954) (Brownlee, op.cit., pp. 11, 27 and 32).

8   Ibid., p. 9.

9   For a summary of the law of the UK in this area see
Harry Street, 'Freedom, the Individual and the Law',
Harmondsworth, Penguin, 4th edn, 1977.

10 Brownlee, op.cit. p. 9.

11 Ibid., p. 19.

12 Ibid., p. 27.

13 References will be to the Everyman edition, ed. A.J.
Lindsay, London, Dent, 1910. For detailed discussion
of J.S. Mill's social and political ideas see A. Ryan,
'The Philosophy of John Stuart Mill', London, Mac-
millan, 1971; and R.J. Halliday, 'John Stuart Mill',
London, Allen & Unwin, 1976.

14 What follows is a summary of the argument in James
Mill, 'Essay on Government' (1819), New York, Bobbs
Merrill, 1955.

15 Thus, James Mill, Liberty of the Press, 'Encyclo-
pedia Britannica', 5th edn, 1821, pp. 258-72; at
p. 265 'It is perfectly clear that all chance of advantage to the people from having the choice of their
rulers, depends on their making a good choice. If
they make a bad choice - if they elect people either
incapable, or disinclined, to use well the power entrusted to them, they incur the same evils to which
they are doomed when they are deprived of the due
control over those by whom their affairs are administered. We may then ask, if there are any possible
means by which the people can make a good choice,
but by the liberty of the press? The very foundation
of a good choice is knowledge. The fuller and more
perfect the knowledge, the better the chance, where
all sinister interests are absent, of a good choice.

How can the people receive the most perfect knowledge
relative to the characters of those who present themselves to their choice, but by information conveyed
freely, and without reserve, from one to another?

16   See Joseph Schumpeter, 'Socialism, Capitalism and
Democracy', 3rd edn, London, Allen & Unwin, 1950;
Antony Downs, 'An Economic Theory of Democracy', New
York, Harper & Brothers, 1957; and B.M. Barry,
'Sociologists, Economists and Democracy', London,
Collier-Macmillan, 1970.

17   James Mill, op.cit., p. 265: 'The end which is sought
to be obtained by allowing any thing to be said in
censure of government, is to ensure the goodness of
the government, the most important of all objects, to
the attainment of which the wisdom of man can be
applied. If the goodness of government could be obtained by any preferable means, it is evident that all
censure of government ought to be prohibited.'

18   Ibid., p. 261: 'There can be no doubt that the feelings of the individual can be as painful, where the
actions of a disreputable nature are truly, as where
they are falsely imputed to him. It is equally certain that no painful feeling ought to be wilfully
excited in any man, where no good, sufficient to over-
balance that evil, is its natural consequence'.
Also p. 262: 'We have now ascertained the cases in
which it would not be good that men should be protected
from the declaration of the truth by the press, and
also the cases in which it would be good that they
should be so protected....It would be desirable that,
in the one set of cases, the declaration should be
allowed, in the other case it should not be allowed.'

19   Ibid., pp. 74ff.

20   See Halliday, op.cit., ch. 4.

21   James Mill, Liberty of the Press, p. 267.

22   'Representative Government' (1861), London, Dent,
1910, p. 255.

23   Op.cit., p. 107.

24   Ibid., p. 217.

25   For a fuller discussion of relationships between 'On
Liberty' and 'Representative Government', see T.D.
Campbell, John Stuart Mill and Freedom of Speech,
'Il Pensiero Politico', vol 4, 1971, pp. 443-50.

26   J. J. Rousseau, 'The Social Contract' (1762), Book I,
ch. ix, p. 19, n.1. See also II, xi. References are
to the translation by G.D.H. Cole, London, Dent, 1913.
For Rousseau as a forerunner of socialism, see Albert
Fried and Ronald Saunders, 'A Documentary History of
Socialist Thought', Edinburgh University Press, 1964,

ch. 2; E. Durkheim, 'Socialism', trans. Charlotte
Sattler, New York, Collier Books, 1962, ch. 3; and
R.N. Berki, 'Socialism', London, Dent, 1973, ch. 3.

27 It is only in a democratic policy that the advantages
Rousseau attributes to the civil state are realised
and 'His [man's] faculties are so stimulated and de-
veloped, his ideas so extended, his feeling so en-
nobled, and his whole soul so uplifted' ('The Social
Contract', I, viii, p. 16). See Carole Pateman,
'Participation and Democratic Theory', Cambridge
University Press, 1970, pp. 22-36.

28 Thus 'The Social Contract', II, i, p. 20: 'The general
will alone can direct the State according to the object for which it was instituted, i.e. the common
good: for if the clashing of particular interests made
the establishment of societies necessary, the agreement of these interests made it possible. The common
element in these different interests is what forms the
social tie; and, were there no point of agreement
between them all, no society could exist. It is
solely on the basis of common interest that every
society should be governed.' Rousseau's attempt to
connect the general will with the common good is well
discussed in John C. Hall, 'Rousseau: An Introduction
to his Political Philosophy', London, Macmillan, 1973.

29 Thus 'The essence of the body politic lies in the re-
conciliation of obedience and liberty, and the words
subject and Sovereign are identical correlatives, the
idea of which meet in the single word "citizen"'
('The Social Contract', III, xiii, p. 75). See ibid.,
IV, ii.

30 See, for instance, Michael Harrington, 'Socialism',
New York, Saturday Review Press, 1972.

31 For a modern statement of the connection between free-
dom of expression and democracy, see Alexander
Meiklejohn, 'Free Speech and its Relation to Self-
Government', New York, Harper, 1948.

32 See Paul Jackson, 'Natural Justice', London, Sweet &
Maxwell, 2nd edn, 1979, ch. 8.

9 ECONOMIC RIGHTS: THE RIGHT TO WORK

1 See G.D.H. Cole, 'Socialist Thought: The Forerunners,
1989-1850', London, Macmillan, 1967, ch. 2.

2 Brownlee, 'Basic Documents on Human Rights', Oxford,
Clarendon Press, 1971, p. 111.

3 Ibid., p. 25.

4 Ibid., p. 47, article 9.

5　Ibid., p. 49, article 43.
6　See United States, Bill of Rights, 1791, Article XIII
　　1. - 'Neither slavery nor involuntary servitude, ex-
　　cept as a punishment for crime whereof the party shall
　　have been duly convicted, shall exist within the
　　United States, or any place subject to its juris-
　　diction'. (Brownlee op.cit., p. 13). Also the Consti-
　　tutions of Nigeria (1963), article 20 (ibid., p. 57),
　　India (1949), article 23 (ibid., p. 35), and article 4
　　of The Universal Declaration of Human Rights (1949)
　　(ibid., p. 108).
7　See article 21 of the Constitution of the United Arab
　　Republic (1964): 'Work in the United Arab Republic is
　　a right, a duty and an honour for every able citizen.'
8　For instance, the Constitution of the USSR article 18
　　(Brownlee, op.cit., p. 25).
9　The Universal Declaration, article 23 (in ibid.,
　　p. 111).
10　'Rights of Man' (1792), Harmondsworth, Penguin, 1969,
　　p. 268.
11　See Charles A. Reich, The New Property, 'Yale Law Re-
　　view', vol 73, 1964, pp. 733-87.
12　See Socialism, Utopian and Scientific (1892), in Marx,
　　Engels, Lenin, 'The Essential Left', London, Unwin
　　Books, 1960, pp. 103-46.
13　This is the force of Marx's criticism of Lassalle in
　　'Critique of the Gotha Programme'. The relevant
　　excerpt is in Lewis S. Feuer, 'Marx and Engels, Basic
　　Writings on Politics and Philosophy', Glasgow,
　　Fontana, 1969, pp. 153-73. The idea that labour is
　　the source of wealth which is derived from Locke and
　　Adam Smith is used by Marx as a tool for the analysis
　　of capitalism, not as the moral standard it has be-
　　come in democratic socialism and in 'communist' coun-
　　tries such as the USSR.
14　See Robert Nozick, 'Anarchy, State and Utopia', New
　　York, Basic Books, 1974.
15　See William E. Connolly, A Note on Freedom Under
　　Socialism, 'Political Theory', vol. 5., 1977, pp. 181-
　　9.
16　See, for instance, Radoslav Selucky, 'Marxism, Soci-
　　alism, Freedom', London, Macmillan, 1978.
17　See pp. 111-19.
18　See pp. 116f.
19　See T.D. Campbell, Perfect and Imperfect Obligations,
　　'Modern Schoolman', vol. 52, 1975, pp. 285-94.
20　See W. Friedmann, 'Legal Theory', New York, Columbia
　　University Press, 5th edn, 1967, ch. 5.
21　See H.B. Acton, 'The Morals of Markets', London, Allen
　　& Unwin, 1971.

22 See T.B. Bottomore, Industry, Work and Socialism, in
    E. Fromm, 'Socialism and Humanism', London, Allen
    Lane, 1967, pp. 365-7.
23 See Agnes Heller, 'The Theory of Need in Marx',
    London, Allison & Busby, 1974, pp. 29-39.
24 This is the position adopted in Lawrence C. Becker,
    The Obligation to Work, 'Ethics', vol 91, 1980,
    pp. 35-49.
25 A typical example is article 12 of the Constitution of
    the USSR (1936): 'Work in the U.S.S.R is a duty and a
    matter of honour for every able-bodied citizen in ac-
    cordance with the principle: "he who does not work,
    neither shall he eat."' Article 14 states that 'the
    Labour of Soviet people, free from exploitation, is
    the source of the growth of public wealth and of the
    well-being of the people and of every soviet citizen.
    ...In accordance with the principle of socialism:
    "From each according to his abilities, to each accor-
    ding to his work."' In this chapter it is assumed
    that this is not a fully socialist principle since it
    makes contribution, not need, the basis of
    distribution.
26 This is a common theme of, for instance, Utopian
    socialists, such as Saint-Simon, Fourier and Robert
    Owen; see Albert Fried and Ronald Saunders, 'A Docu-
    mentary History of Socialist Thought', Edinburgh
    University Press, 1964, ch. 3.

10 WELFARE RIGHTS

1 For the concept of welfare see Noel Timms (ed.),
   'Social Welfare: Why and How', London, Routledge &
   Kegan Paul, 1980, Introduction; Raymond Plant, Harry
   Lesser and Paul Taylor-Gooby, 'Political Philosophy
   and Social Welfare', London, Routledge & Kegan Paul,
   1980, ch. 1, and T.H. Marshall, 'The Right to Welfare', London, Hutchesons Educational Books, 1981.
2 See Vic George and Paul Wilding, 'Ideology and
   Social Welfare', London, Routledge & Kegan Paul, 1976,
   p. ix 'The central element in this failure is the
   nature of capitalism as a set of values and as an
   economic system, for the ethic of welfare and the
   ethic of capitalism are in basic opposition'; and
   Richard Titmuss, 'Commitment to Welfare', London,
   Allen & Unwin, 1968.
3 Most of the subsequent points are made at greater
   length by Peter Jones in Timms, op.cit., ch. 7.
4 This process can be seen in the growth of occupation-

related benefits for the average worker as distinct
from the benefits available to the unemployed and
the sick. See David Donnison, Social Policy since
Titmuss, 'Journal of Social Policy', vol. 8, 1979,
pp. 145-56.

5 See Robert A. Pinker, 'Social Work and Social Policy',
London, Chelsea College, 1978, p. 16: 'The idea of a
welfare right defined exclusively in terms of social
justice could only properly fit into a body of professional knowledge and practice which visualized
social services as defences against an essentially
predatory economic system. Carried to extremes, that
philosophy of welfare would end by converting social
services into predators on the economic system,
undermining the will to produce and thereby preju-
dicing still further our chances of social survival.'

6 See Paul Halmos, 'The Faith of Counsellors', London,
Constable, 1965, pp. 28ff.

7 See pp. 87f.

8 See pp. 88-92.

9 See F. Engels and Karl Kautsky, Juridical Socialism,
(1887) in 'Politics and Society', vol. 7, 1977,
pp. 203-20.

10 This is argued in Robert Nozick, 'Anarchy, State and
Utopia', New York, Basic Books, 1974, pp. 167-74.
See also J.R. Kearl, Do Entitlements imply that Taxation is Theft?, 'Philosophy and Public Affairs',
vol. 7, 1977, pp. 74-81.

11 This is the standard analysis discussed in chapter 4,
for which the authority of J.S. Mill's theory of
justice as having to do with 'what a person may
rightfully be compelled to fulfil' ('Utilitarianism',
ch. 2) is often cited. See Peter Jones in Timms,
op.cit., p. 124, and R. Plant et al., op.cit.,
pp. 55ff.

12 The problems for the idea of welfare rights in the
conception of social welfare as organised charity
have been much debated in connection with R. Titmuss,
'The Gift Relationship'. Titmuss's awkward notion of
an ultra-obligation fails to combine the concept of
giving and that of fulfilling an obligation. See
Plant et at., op.cit., p. 24, pp. 56-8, pp. 146-58
and pp. 239-46.

13 See R. Miliband, 'The State in Capitalist Society',
London, Quartet Books, 1973, Weidenfeld & Nicolson,
1969.

14 See H. Laski, 'The State in Theory and Practice',
London, Allen & Unwin, 1934, p. 270: 'Social legislation is not the outcome of a rational and objective

willing of the common good by all members of the community alike; it is the price paid for those legal
principles which secure the predominance of the owners
of property. It is a body of concessions offered to
avert a decisive challenge to the principles by which
their authority is maintained'.

15 See Ian Gough, 'The Political Economy of the Welfare
State', London, Macmillan, 1979, p. 137: '[The
function of the welfare state is] to secure the effective reproduction of capitalist social relationships
and the accumulation of capital.'

16 See P. Jones in Timms, op.cit., pp. 126ff.

17 See pp. 18-26.

18 See The Universal Declaration of Human Rights, Article
22: 'Everyone as a member of a society has a right to
social security, and is entitled to realisation
through national effort and international co-operation
and in accordance with the organisation and resources
of each state of the economic, social and cultural
rights indispensible for his dignity and the free development of his personality.' See also Article 24,
in Brownlee, op.cit., p. 111.

19 See George and Wilding, op.cit., p. 129: 'We see the
conflict between the values of capitalism and the
ethic of welfare as the underlying reason for the
failure of social policies to achieve agreed aims.'

20 This section is based on T.D. Campbell, Counter-
Productive Welfare Law, 'British Journal of Political
Science', vol. 11, 1981, pp. 331-50.

21 Examples of right-wing charges of counter-productivity
abound in current attacks on Employment Protection and
Rent Acts. Thus the 'Daily Telegraph', 26 September
1979, welcomed the affirmation by Mr James Prior, the
Employment Secretary, that 'the Government believes
some aspects of the legislation [Employment protection
Act] are actually working against the interests of
working people', while Mr D.A. Trippier, MP, speaking
on the Employment Bill, said in the House of Commons:
'That law is counter-productive because it has never
really helped people for whom it was originally designed' ('Hansard', House of Commons Debates, 17
December 1979, vol. 976, col. 125).

22 See Ralph Harris and Arthur Seldon, 'Over-ruled on
Welfare', London, Institute of Economic Affairs, 1979,
p. 179: 'when tax costs are brought into the reckoning
we might also say that the Welfare State impoverishes
even the poorer of its intended beneficiaries'.
Harris and Seldon go on to argue that the money saved
by the state's withdrawal of universal welfare

services in health and education would enable the
genuine poor to be better cared for, perhaps through
negative taxation.

23 See Gilbert, 'British Social Policy', 1914-39, London,
Batsford, 1970, p. 180.

24 See Steve Winyard, 'Policing Low Wages', London, Low
Pay Unit, 1976. While such window-dressing legislation may be counter-productive from the point of
view of G, it may be politically effective in distrac-
ting attention from a social problem and hence highly
productive from the point of view of governments seeking to avoid criticism.

25 The empirical evidence for the widespread occurrence
of this effect is by no means conclusive; see Theodore
Marmor, On Comparing Income Maintenance Alternatives,
'American Political Science Review', vol. 65, 1971,
pp. 83-96, p. 87.

26 See Tony Prosser, Politics and Judicial Review: The
Atkinson Case and its Aftermath, 'Public Law', Spring
1979, pp. 59-80. Atkinson, a student, succeeded in
the Court of Appeal in overturning the decision of the
Supplementary Benefits Tribunal to uphold the use of
the discretionary powers under Schedule 1, para 4 (1)
of the Social Security Act (1976) to take unpaid paren-
tal contribution into account in calculating the amount
of supplementary benefit: R. v. Barnsley Supplementary
Benefits Tribunal, ex parte Atkinson (1976) 2 All E.R.
686, D.C. (1973) 3 All E.R. 1031, C.A. This was immediately countered by the provisions of the Social
Security (Miscellaneous Provisions) Act, 1978.

27 For a fuller discussion of the tension between legal-
istic and pastoral approaches to social work see T.D.
Campbell, Discretionary 'Rights', in Noel Timms and
David Watson (eds), 'Philosophy in Social Work',
London, Routledge & Kegan Paul, 1978, pp. 50-77.

28 Otto Kahn-Freund, 'Labour and the Law', London,
Stevens, 1977, p. 1, points to 'the inherent contradiction between the requirements of the public welfare
and the spirit and the possibilities of the common
law'. Industrial peace depends on 'a balance of collective forces of which our common law knows nothing'.
Statute law was not conspicuously more successful in
the case of the Industrial Relations Act, 1971. For a
discussion of the ineffectiveness of the law in preventing industrial accidents, see R.M. Titmuss, 'Social
Policy', London, Allen & Unwin, 1974, p. 82. The
harmful effects of imposing strict liability on employers who default in terms of the Factory Act 1971
are mitigated by the use of discretion by inspectors;

see W.G. Carson, Some Sociological Aspects of Strict
Liability and the Enforcement of Factory Legislation,
'Modern Law Review', vol 33, 1970, pp. 396-412. A
somewhat similar phenomenon is claimed to arise when
legal requirements limiting the introduction of drugs
on grounds of safety reduce the range of medicines
available to the public, the preservation of whose
health is the objective of the legislation. See
Harvey Teff and Colin R. Munro, 'Thalidomide: The
Legal Aftermath', London, Saxon House, 1976, pp. 124ff.
This contention is disputed by Teff and Munro, p. 147.

29   See Virginia Black, The Erosion of Legal Principles in
the Creation of Legal Policies, 'Ethics', vol 84,
1973-4, pp. 93-115; at p. 93: 'certain special edicts
that impose discriminating restrictions on the
formerly undiscriminated against, so that the disad-
vantaged may be raised to a par, create new inequities
themselves and hurt those they are meant to help'.
This is a version of Titmuss's thesis that stereo-
typing 'paradoxically widens rather than narrows class
relationships' (On the Social Division Welfare, in
'Essays on the Welfare State', 3rd edn. London, Allen
& Unwin, 1976, p. 45).

30   See Valerie Karn, How Can We Liberate Council Tenants?,
'New Society', 29 March 1979, pp. 738-40; at p. 739:
'Unthinking moves to make renting more like owning
could deprive council tenants of one of their few remaining advantages.'

31   M. Partington, 'Landlord and Tenant', London, Weidenfeld & Nicolson, 1975, p. xxviff. See F.G. Pennance
(ed.), 'Verdict on Rent Control', London, Institute of
Economic Affairs, 1978. This is a constantly reiterated comment on the history of rent restrictions in
the private sector. See Gilbert, op.cit., p. 139:
'The effect of the [Rent and Mortgage Restriction Act
of 1915] was to make subsidised building of working-
class houses virtually impossible.' There seems
little doubt that the effects of the 1974 Rent Act in
giving security of tenure to the majority of those
living in rented accommodation has been to accelerate
the decline in private rented accommodation and to
discriminate against newly married couples or co-
habitees, students, divorced or separated persons
starting out on a career, e.g. nursing, for whom
owner-occupancy or council house renting is not an
open option. See Lyn Reynolds, 'Some Effects of the
1974 Rent Act in London', London, Middlesex Polytech-
nic, 1978. A similar phenomenon is the plan to sell
off council hoses to their existing tenants, thus

reducing the stock of housing available to housing
authorities.

32 See the 'Daily Telegraph' leader, 26 September 1979:
'Among the many valid criticisms levelled against so-
called employment protection provisions imposed by
successive governments, particularly the last, is that
they destroy far more employment than they create or
protect.' The Employment Bill then before Parliament
was intended 'to have the purpose of reducing the
burden placed on employers, especially small employers. This burden, perceived and real, has been a
deterrent to the employment of more people'
('Hansard', 17 December 1979, vol. 976, col. 123).

33 Thus fair rents policy has been said to bring about
social polarisation by leading to high rents in 'desirable' areas thus driving out poorer tenants. See
A. Nevitt, 'Housing and Taxation Subsidies', London,
Nelson, 1960. In general, housing policy appears to
provide most subsidy for the better-off council
tenants and owner-occupiers.

Index

Routledge Social Science Series

Routledge & Kegan Paul   London, Henley and Boston

39 Store Street,
London WC1E 7DD
Broadway House,
Newtown Road,
Henley-on-Thames,
Oxon RG9 1EN
9 Park Street,
Boston, Mass. 02108

Contents

*Authors wishing to submit manuscripts for any series
in this catalogue should send them to the Social Science Editor,
Routledge & Kegan Paul Ltd, 39 Store Street,
London WC1E 7DD.*
● *Books so marked are available in paperback.*
○ *Books so marked are available in paperback only.*
*All books are in metric Demy 8vo format (216 × 138mm approx.)
unless otherwise stated.*

International Library of Sociology
General Editor   John Rex

GENERAL SOCIOLOGY

Barnsley, J. H. The Social Reality of Ethics. *464 pp.*
Brown, Robert. Explanation in Social Science. *208 pp.*
● Rules and Laws in Sociology. *192 pp.*
Bruford, W. H. Chekhov and His Russia. *A Sociological Study. 244 pp.*
Burton, F. and **Carlen, P.** Official Discourse. *On Discourse Analysis, Government Publications, Ideology. About 140 pp.*
Cain, Maureen E. Society and the Policeman's Role. *326 pp.*
● **Fletcher, Colin.** Beneath the Surface. *An Account of Three Styles of Sociological Research. 221 pp.*
Gibson, Quentin. The Logic of Social Enquiry. *240 pp.*
Glassner, B. Essential Interactionism. *208 pp.*
Glucksmann, M. Structuralist Analysis in Contemporary Social Thought. *212 pp.*
Gurvitch, Georges. Sociology of Law. *Foreword by Roscoe Pound. 264 pp.*
Hinkle, R. Founding Theory of American Sociology 1881–1913. *About 350 pp.*
Homans, George C. Sentiments and Activities. *336 pp.*
Johnson, Harry M. Sociology: *A Systematic Introduction. Foreword by Robert K. Merton. 710 pp.*
● **Keat, Russell** and **Urry, John.** Social Theory as Science. *278 pp.*
Mannheim, Karl. Essays on Sociology and Social Psychology. *Edited by Paul Kecskemeti. With Editorial Note by Adolph Lowe. 344 pp.*
Martindale, Don. The Nature and Types of Sociological Theory. *292 pp.*
● **Maus, Heinz.** A Short History of Sociology. *234 pp.*
Myrdal, Gunnar. Value in Social Theory: *A Collection of Essays on Methodology. Edited by Paul Streeten. 332 pp.*
Ogburn, William F. and **Nimkoff, Meyer F.** A Handbook of Sociology. *Preface by Karl Mannheim. 656 pp. 46 figures. 35 tables.*
Parsons, Talcott and **Smelser, Neil J.** Economy and Society: *A Study in the Integration of Economic and Social Theory. 362 pp.*
Payne, G., Dingwall, R., Payne, J. and **Carter, M.** Sociology and Social Research. *About 250 pp.*
Podgórecki, A. Practical Social Sciences. *About 200 pp.*
Podgórecki, A. and **Łos, M.** Multidimensional Sociology. *268 pp.*
Raffel, S. Matters of Fact. *A Sociological Inquiry. 152 pp.*
● **Rex, John.** Key Problems of Sociological Theory. *220 pp.*
Sociology and the Demystification of the Modern World. *282 pp.*
● **Rex, John.** (Ed.) Approaches to Sociology. *Contributions by Peter Abell, Frank Bechhofer, Basil Bernstein, Ronald Fletcher, David Frisby, Miriam Glucksmann, Peter Lassman, Herminio Martins, John Rex, Roland Robertson, John Westergaard and Jock Young. 302 pp.*
Rigby, A. Alternative Realities. *352 pp.*
Roche, M. Phenomenology, Language and the Social Sciences. *374 pp.*
Sahay, A. Sociological Analysis. *220 pp.*
Strasser, Hermann. The Normative Structure of Sociology. *Conservative and Emancipatory Themes in Social Thought. About 340 pp.*
Strong, P. Ceremonial Order of the Clinic. *267 pp.*
Urry, John. Reference Groups and the Theory of Revolution. *244 pp.*
Weinberg, E. Development of Sociology in the Soviet Union. *173 pp.*

FOREIGN CLASSICS OF SOCIOLOGY

● **Gerth, H. H.** and **Mills, C. Wright.** From Max Weber: *Essays in Sociology. 502 pp.*

● **Tönnies, Ferdinand.** Community and Association *(Gemeinschaft und Gesell-schaft).\Translated and Supplemented by Charles P. Loomis. Foreword by Pitirim A. Sorokin. 334 pp.*

SOCIAL STRUCTURE

Andreski, Stanislav. Military Organization and Society. *Foreword by Professor A. R. Radcliffe-Brown. 226 pp. 1 folder.*

Broom, L., Lancaster Jones, F., McDonnell, P. and **Williams, T.** The Inheritance of Inequality. *About 180 pp.*

Carlton, Eric. Ideology and Social Order. *Foreword by Professor Philip Abrahams. About 320 pp.*

Clegg, S. and **Dunkerley, D.** Organization, Class and Control. *614 pp.*

Coontz, Sydney H. Population Theories and the Economic Interpretation. *202 pp.*

Coser, Lewis. The Functions of Social Conflict. *204 pp.*

Crook, I. and **D.** The First Years of the Yangyi Commune. *304 pp., illustrated.*

Dickie-Clark, H. F. Marginal Situation: *A Sociological Study of a Coloured Group. 240 pp. 11 tables.*

Giner, S. and **Archer, M. S.** (Eds) Contemporary Europe: *Social Structures and Cultural Patterns, 336 pp.*

● **Glaser, Barney** and **Strauss, Anselm L.** Status Passage: *A Formal Theory. 212 pp.*

Glass, D. V. (Ed.) Social Mobility in Britain. *Contributions by J. Berent, T. Bottomore, R. C. Chambers, J. Floud, D. V. Glass, J. R. Hall, H. T. Himmelweit, R. K. Kelsall, F. M. Martin, C. A. Moser, R. Mukherjee and W. Ziegel. 420 pp.*

Kelsall, R. K. Higher Civil Servants in Britain: *From 1870 to the Present Day. 268 pp. 31 tables.*

● **Lawton, Denis.** Social Class, Language and Education. *192 pp.*

McLeish, John. The Theory of Social Change: *Four Views Considered. 128 pp.*

● **Marsh, David C.** The Changing Social Structure of England and Wales, 1871–1961. *Revised edition. 288 pp.*

Menzies, Ken. Talcott Parsons and the Social Image of Man. *About 208 pp.*

● **Mouzelis, Nicos.** Organization and Bureaucracy. *An Analysis of Modern Theories. 240 pp.*

● **Ossowski, Stanislaw.** Class Structure in the Social Consciousness. *210 pp.*

● **Podgórecki, Adam.** Law and Society. *302 pp.*

Renner, Karl. Institutions of Private Law and Their Social Functions. *Edited, with an Introduction and Notes, by O. Kahn-Freud. Translated by Agnes Schwarzschild. 316 pp.*

Rex, J. and **Tomlinson, S.** Colonial Immigrants in a British City. *A Class Analysis. 368 pp.*

Smooha, S. Israel: Pluralism and Conflict. *472 pp.*

Wesolowski, W. Class, Strata and Power. *Trans. and with Introduction by G. Kolankiewicz. 160 pp.*

Zureik, E. Palestinians in Israel. *A Study in Internal Colonialism. 264 pp.*

SOCIOLOGY AND POLITICS

Acton, T. A. Gypsy Politics and Social Change. *316 pp.*

Burton, F. Politics of Legitimacy. *Struggles in a Belfast Community. 250 pp.*

Crook, I. and **D.** Revolution in a Chinese Village. *Ten Mile Inn. 216 pp., illustrated.*

Etzioni-Halevy, E. Political Manipulation and Administrative Power. *A Comparative Study. About 200 pp.*

Fielding, N. The National Front. *About 250 pp.*

● **Hechter, Michael.** Internal Colonialism. *The Celtic Fringe in British National Development, 1536–1966. 380 pp.*

Kornhauser, William. The Politics of Mass Society. *272 pp. 20 tables.*

Korpi, W. The Working Class in Welfare Capitalism. *Work, Unions and Politics in Sweden. 472 pp.*
Kroes, R. Soldiers and Students. *A Study of Right- and Left-wing Students. 174 pp.*
Martin, Roderick. Sociology of Power. *About 272 pp.*
Merquior, J. G. Rousseau and Weber. *A Study in the Theory of Legitimacy. About 288 pp.*
Myrdal, Gunnar. The Political Element in the Development of Economic Theory. *Translated from the German by Paul Streeten. 282 pp.*
Varma, B. N. The Sociology and Politics of Development. *A Theoretical Study. 236 pp.*
Wong, S.-L. Sociology and Socialism in Contemporary China. *160 pp.*
Wootton, Graham. Workers, Unions and the State. *188 pp.*

CRIMINOLOGY

Ancel, Marc. Social Defence: *A Modern Approach to Criminal Problems. Foreword by Leon Radzinowicz. 240 pp.*
Athens, L. Violent Criminal Acts and Actors. *104 pp.*
Cain, Maureen E. Society and the Policeman's Role. *326 pp.*
Cloward, Richard A. and **Ohlin, Lloyd E.** Delinquency and Opportunity: *A Theory of Delinquent Gangs. 248 pp.*
Downes, David M. The Delinquent Solution. *A Study in Subcultural Theory. 296 pp.*
Friedlander, Kate. The Psycho-Analytical Approach to Juvenile Delinquency: *Theory, Case Studies, Treatment. 320 pp.*
Gleuck, Sheldon and **Eleanor.** Family Environment and Delinquency. *With the statistical assistance of Rose W. Kneznek. 340 pp.*
Lopez-Rey, Manuel. Crime. *An Analytical Appraisal. 288 pp.*
Mannheim, Hermann. Comparative Criminology: *A Text Book. Two volumes. 442 pp. and 380 pp.*
Morris, Terence. The Criminal Area: *A Study in Social Ecology. Foreword by Hermann Mannheim. 232 pp. 25 tables. 4 maps.*
Rock, Paul. Making People Pay. *338 pp.*
● **Taylor, Ian, Walton, Paul** and **Young, Jock.** The New Criminology. *For a Social Theory of Deviance. 325 pp.*
● **Taylor, Ian, Walton, Paul** and **Young, Jock.** (Eds) Critical Criminology. *268 pp.*

SOCIAL PSYCHOLOGY

Bagley, Christopher. The Social Psychology of the Epileptic Child. *320 pp.*
Brittan, Arthur. Meanings and Situations. *224 pp.*
Carroll, J. Break-Out from the Crystal Palace. *200 pp.*
● **Fleming, C. M.** Adolescence: Its Social Psychology. *With an Introduction to recent findings from the fields of Anthropology, Physiology, Medicine, Psychometrics and Sociometry. 288 pp.*
● The Social Psychology of Education: *An Introduction and Guide to Its Study. 136 pp.*
Linton, Ralph. The Cultural Background of Personality. *132 pp.*
● **Mayo, Elton.** The Social Problems of an Industrial Civilization. *With an Appendix on the Political Problem. 180 pp.*
Ottaway, A. K. C. Learning Through Group Experience. *176 pp.*
Plummer, Ken. Sexual Stigma. *An Interactionist Account. 254 pp.*
● **Rose, Arnold M.** (Ed.) Human Behaviour and Social Processes: *an Interactionist Approach. Contributions by Arnold M. Rose, Ralph H. Turner, Anselm Strauss, Everett C. Hughes, E. Franklin Frazier, Howard S. Becker et al. 696 pp.*
Smelser, Neil J. Theory of Collective Behaviour. *448 pp.*
Stephenson, Geoffrey M. The Development of Conscience. *128 pp.*
Young, Kimball. Handbook of Social Psychology. *658 pp. 16 figures. 10 tables.*

SOCIOLOGY OF THE FAMILY

Bell, Colin R. Middle Class Families: *Social and Geographical Mobility. 224 pp.*
Burton, Lindy. Vulnerable Children. *272 pp.*
Gavron, Hannah. The Captive Wife: *Conflicts of Household Mothers. 190 pp.*
George, Victor and **Wilding, Paul.** Motherless Families. *248 pp.*
Klein, Josephine. Samples from English Cultures.
  1. Three Preliminary Studies and Aspects of Adult Life in England. *447 pp.*
  2. Child-Rearing Practices and Index. *247 pp.*
Klein, Viola. The Feminine Character. *History of an Ideology. 244 pp.*
McWhinnie, Alexina M. Adopted Children. *How They Grow Up. 304 pp.*
● **Morgan, D. H. J.** Social Theory and the Family. *About 320 pp.*
● **Myrdal, Alva** and **Klein, Viola.** Women's Two Roles: *Home and Work. 238 pp. 27 tables.*
Parsons, Talcott and **Bales, Robert F.** Family: Socialization and Interaction Process. *In collaboration with James Olds, Morris Zelditch and Philip E. Slater. 456 pp. 50 figures and tables.*

SOCIAL SERVICES

Bastide, Roger. The Sociology of Mental Disorder. *Translated from the French by Jean McNeil. 260 pp.*
Carlebach, Julius. Caring For Children in Trouble. *266 pp.*
George, Victor. Foster Care. *Theory and Practice. 234 pp.*
  Social Security: *Beveridge and After. 258 pp.*
George, V. and **Wilding, P.** Motherless Families. *248 pp.*
● **Goetschius, George W.** Working with Community Groups. *256 pp.*
Goetschius, George W. and **Tash, Joan.** Working with Unattached Youth. *416 pp.*
Heywood, Jean S. Children in Care. *The Development of the Service for the Deprived Child. Third revised edition. 284 pp.*
King, Roy D., Ranes, Norma V. and **Tizard, Jack.** Patterns of Residential Care. *356 pp.*
Leigh, John. Young People and Leisure. *256 pp.*
● **Mays, John.** (Ed.) Penelope Hall's Social Services of England and Wales. *368 pp.*
Morris, Mary. Voluntary Work and the Welfare State. *300 pp.*
Nokes, P. L. The Professional Task in Welfare Practice. *152 pp.*
Timms, Noel. Psychiatric Social Work in Great Britain (1939–1962). *280 pp.*
● Social Casework: *Principles and Practice. 256 pp.*

SOCIOLOGY OF EDUCATION

Banks, Olive. Parity and Prestige in English Secondary Education: a Study in Educational Sociology. *272 pp.*
● **Blyth, W. A. L.** English Primary Education. *A Sociological Description.*
  2. Background. *168 pp.*
Collier, K. G. The Social Purposes of Education: *Personal and Social Values in Education. 268 pp.*
Evans, K. M. Sociometry and Education. *158 pp.*
● **Ford, Julienne.** Social Class and the Comprehensive School. *192 pp.*
Foster, P. J. Education and Social Change in Ghana. *336 pp. 3 maps.*
Fraser, W. R. Education and Society in Modern France. *150 pp.*
Grace, Gerald R. Role Conflict and the Teacher. *150 pp.*
Hans, Nicholas. New Trends in Education in the Eighteenth Century. *278 pp. 19 tables.*
● Comparative Education: *A Study of Educational Factors and Traditions. 360 pp.*
● **Hargreaves, David.** Interpersonal Relations and Education. *432 pp.*
● Social Relations in a Secondary School. *240 pp.*
  School Organization and Pupil Involvement. *A Study of Secondary Schools.*

● **Mannheim, Karl** and **Stewart, W. A. C.** An Introduction to the Sociology of Education. *206 pp.*
● **Musgrove, F.** Youth and the Social Order. *176 pp.*
● **Ottaway, A. K. C.** Education and Society: An Introduction to the Sociology of Education. *With an Introduction by W. O. Lester Smith. 212 pp.*
Peers, Robert. Adult Education: *A Comparative Study. Revised edition. 398 pp.*
Stratta, Erica. The Education of Borstal Boys. *A Study of their Educational Experiences prior to, and during, Borstal Training. 256 pp.*
● **Taylor, P. H., Reid, W. A.** and **Holley, B. J.** The English Sixth Form. *A Case Study in Curriculum Research. 198 pp.*

SOCIOLOGY OF CULTURE

Eppel, E. M. and **M.** Adolescents and Morality: *A Study of some Moral Values and Dilemmas of Working Adolescents in the Context of a changing Climate of Opinion. Foreword by W. J. H. Sprott. 268 pp. 39 tables.*
● **Fromm, Erich.** The Fear of Freedom. *286 pp.*
● The Sane Society. *400 pp.*
Johnson, L. The Cultural Critics. *From Matthew Arnold to Raymond Williams. 233 pp.*
Mannheim, Karl. Essays on the Sociology of Culture. *Edited by Ernst Mannheim in co-operation with Paul Kecskemeti. Editorial Note by Adolph Lowe. 280 pp.*
Merquior, J. G. The Veil and the Mask. *Essays on Culture and Ideology. Foreword by Ernest Gellner. 140 pp.*
Zijderfeld, A. C. On Clichés. *The Supersedure of Meaning by Function in Modernity. 150 pp.*

SOCIOLOGY OF RELIGION

Argyle, Michael and **Beit-Hallahmi, Benjamin.** The Social Psychology of Religion. *256 pp.*
Glasner, Peter E. The Sociology of Secularisation. *A Critique of a Concept. 146 pp.*
Hall, J. R. The Ways Out. *Utopian Communal Groups in an Age of Babylon. 280 pp.*
Ranson, S., Hinings, B. and **Bryman, A.** Clergy, Ministers and Priests. *216 pp.*
Stark, Werner. The Sociology of Religion. *A Study of Christendom.*
　　Volume II. *Sectarian Religion. 368 pp.*
　　Volume III. *The Universal Church. 464 pp.*
　　Volume IV. *Types of Religious Man. 352 pp.*
　　Volume V. *Types of Religious Culture. 464 pp.*
Turner, B. S. Weber and Islam. *216 pp.*
Watt, W. Montgomery. Islam and the Integration of Society. *320 pp.*

SOCIOLOGY OF ART AND LITERATURE

Jarvie, Ian C. Towards a Sociology of the Cinema. *A Comparative Essay on the Structure and Functioning of a Major Entertainment Industry. 405 pp.*
Rust, Frances S. Dance in Society. *An Analysis of the Relationships between the Social Dance and Society in England from the Middle Ages to the Present Day. 256 pp. 8 pp. of plates.*
Schücking, L. L. The Sociology of Literary Taste. *112 pp.*
Wolff, Janet. Hermeneutic Philosophy and the Sociology of Art. *150 pp.*

SOCIOLOGY OF KNOWLEDGE

Diesing, P. Patterns of Discovery in the Social Sciences. *262 pp.*

● **Douglas, J. D.** (Ed.) Understanding Everyday Life. *370 pp.*
● **Hamilton, P.** Knowledge and Social Structure. *174 pp.*
Jarvie, I. C. Concepts and Society. *232 pp.*
Mannheim, Karl. Essays on the Sociology of Knowledge. *Edited by Paul Kecskemeti. Editorial Note by Adolph Lowe. 353 pp.*
Remmling, Gunter W. The Sociology of Karl Mannheim. *With a Bibliographical Guide to the Sociology of Knowledge, Ideological Analysis, and Social Planning. 255 pp.*
Remmling, Gunter W. (Ed.) Towards the Sociology of Knowledge. *Origin and Development of a Sociological Thought Style. 463 pp.*
Scheler, M. Problems of a Sociology of Knowledge. *Trans. by M. S. Frings. Edited and with an Introduction by K. Stikkers. 232 pp.*

URBAN SOCIOLOGY

Aldridge, M. The British New Towns. *A Programme Without a Policy. 232 pp.*
Ashworth, William. The Genesis of Modern British Town Planning: *A Study in Economic and Social History of the Nineteenth and Twentieth Centuries. 288 pp.*
Brittan, A. The Privatised World. *196 pp.*
Cullingworth, J. B. Housing Needs and Planning Policy: *A Restatement of the Problems of Housing Need and 'Overspill' in England and Wales. 232 pp. 44 tables. 8 maps.*
Dickinson, Robert E. City and Region: *A Geographical Interpretation. 608 pp. 125 figures.*
    The West European City: *A Geographical Interpretation. 600 pp. 129 maps. 29 plates.*
Humphreys, Alexander J. New Dubliners: *Urbanization and the Irish Family. Foreword by George C. Homans. 304 pp.*
Jackson, Brian. Working Class Community: *Some General Notions raised by a Series of Studies in Northern England. 192 pp.*
● **Mann, P. H.** An Approach to Urban Sociology. *240 pp.*
Mellor, J. R. Urban Sociology in an Urbanized Society. *326 pp.*
Morris, R. N. and **Mogey, J.** The Sociology of Housing. *Studies at Berinsfield. 232 pp. 4 pp. plates.*
Mullan, R. Stevenage Ltd. *About 250 pp.*
Rex, J. and **Tomlinson, S.** Colonial Immigrants in a British City. *A Class Analysis. 368 pp.*
Rosser, C. and **Harris, C.** The Family and Social Change. *A Study of Family and Kinship in a South Wales Town. 352 pp. 8 maps.*
● **Stacey, Margaret, Batsone, Eric, Bell, Colin** and **Thurcott, Anne.** Power, Persistence and Change. *A Second Study of Banbury. 196 pp.*

RURAL SOCIOLOGY

Mayer, Adrian C. Peasants in the Pacific. *A Study of Fiji Indian Rural Society. 248 pp. 20 plates.*
Williams, W. M. The Sociology of an English Village: *Gosforth. 272 pp. 12 figures. 13 tables.*

SOCIOLOGY OF INDUSTRY AND DISTRIBUTION

Dunkerley, David. The Foreman. *Aspects of Task and Structure. 192 pp.*
Eldridge, J. E. T. Industrial Disputes. *Essays in the Sociology of Industrial Relations. 288 pp.*
Hollowell, Peter G. The Lorry Driver. *272 pp.*
● **Oxaal, I., Barnett, T.** and **Booth, D.** (Eds) Beyond the Sociology of Development.

8

Economy and Society in Latin America and Africa. 295 pp.
Smelser, Neil J. Social Change in the Industrial Revolution: *An Application of Theory to the Lancashire Cotton Industry, 1770–1840. 468 pp. 12 figures. 14 tables.*
Watson, T. J. The Personnel Managers. *A Study in the Sociology of Work and Employment, 262 pp.*

ANTHROPOLOGY

Brandel-Syrier, Mia. Reeftown Elite. *A Study of Social Mobility in a Modern African Community on the Reef. 376 pp.*
Dickie-Clark, H. F. The Marginal Situation. *A Sociological Study of a Coloured Group. 236 pp.*
Dube, S. C. Indian Village. *Foreword by Morris Edward Opler. 276 pp. 4 plates.*
India's Changing Villages: *Human Factors in Community Development. 260 pp. 8 plates. 1 map.*
Fei, H.-T. Peasant Life in China. *A Field Study of Country Life in the Yangtze Valley. With a foreword by Bronislaw Malinowski. 328 pp. 16 pp. plates.*
Firth, Raymond. Malay Fishermen. *Their Peasant Economy. 420 pp. 17 pp. plates.*
Gulliver, P. H. Social Control in an African Society: a Study of the Arusha, Agricultural Masai of Northern Tanganyika. *320 pp. 8 plates. 10 figures.*
Family Herds. *288 pp.*
Jarvie, Ian C. The Revolution in Anthropology. *268 pp.*
Little, Kenneth L. Mende of Sierra Leone. *308 pp. and folder.*
Negroes in Britain. *With a New Introduction and Contemporary Study by Leonard Bloom. 320 pp.*
Tambs-Lyche, H. London Patidars. *About 180 pp.*
Madan, G. R. Western Sociologists on Indian Society. *Marx, Spencer, Weber, Durkheim, Pareto. 384 pp.*
Mayer, A. C. Peasants in the Pacific. *A Study of Fiji Indian Rural Society. 248 pp.*
Meer, Fatima. Race and Suicide in South Africa. *325 pp.*
Smith, Raymond T. The Negro Family in British Guiana: *Family Structure and Social Status in the Villages. With a Foreword by Meyer Fortes. 314 pp. 8 plates. 1 figure. 4 maps.*

SOCIOLOGY AND PHILOSOPHY

Adriaansens, H. Talcott Parsons and the Conceptual Dilemma. *About 224 pp.*
Barnsley, John H. The Social Reality of Ethics. *A Comparative Analysis of Moral Codes. 448 pp.*
Diesing, Paul. Patterns of Discovery in the Social Sciences. *362 pp.*
● **Douglas, Jack D.** (Ed.) Understanding Everyday Life. *Toward the Reconstruction of Sociological Knowledge. Contributions by Alan F. Blum, Aaron W. Cicourel, Norman K. Denzin, Jack D. Douglas, John Heeren, Peter McHugh, Peter K. Manning, Melvin Power, Matthew Speier, Roy Turner, D. Lawrence Wieder, Thomas P. Wilson and Don H. Zimmerman. 370 pp.*
Gorman, Robert A. The Dual Vision. *Alfred Schutz and the Myth of Phenomenological Social Science. 240 pp.*
Jarvie, Ian C. Concepts and Society. *216 pp.*
Kilminster, R. Praxis and Method. *A Sociological Dialogue with Lukács, Gramsci and the Early Frankfurt School. 334 pp.*
● **Pelz, Werner.** The Scope of Understanding in Sociology. *Towards a More Radical Reorientation in the Social Humanistic Sciences. 283 pp.*
Roche, Maurice. Phenomenology, Language and the Social Sciences. *371 pp.*
Sahay, Arun. Sociological Analysis. *212 pp.*
● **Slater, P.** Origin and Significance of the Frankfurt School. *A Marxist Perspective. 185 pp.*

Spurling, L. Phenomenology and the Social World. *The Philosophy of Merleau-Ponty and its Relation to the Social Sciences. 222 pp.*
Wilson, H. T. The American Ideology. *Science, Technology and Organization as Modes of Rationality. 368 pp.*

International Library of Anthropology
General Editor Adam Kuper

● **Ahmed, A. S.** Millennium and Charisma Among Pathans. *A Critical Essay in Social Anthropology. 192 pp.*
Pukhtun Economy and Society. *Traditional Structure and Economic Development. About 360 pp.*
Barth, F. Selected Essays. *Volume I. About 250 pp.* Selected Essays. *Volume II. About 250 pp.*
Brown, Paula. The Chimbu. *A Study of Change in the New Guinea Highlands. 151 pp.*
Foner, N. Jamaica Farewell. *200 pp.*
Gudeman, Stephen. Relationships, Residence and the Individual. *A Rural Panamanian Community. 288 pp. 11 plates, 5 figures, 2 maps, 10 tables.*
The Demise of a Rural Economy. *From Subsistence to Capitalism in a Latin American Village. 160 pp.*
Hamnett, Ian. Chieftainship and Legitimacy. *An Anthropological Study of Executive Law in Lesotho. 163 pp.*
Hanson, F. Allan. Meaning in Culture. *127 pp.*
Hazan, H. The Limbo People. *A Study of the Constitution of the Time Universe Among the Aged. About 192 pp.*
Humphreys, S. C. Anthropology and the Greeks. *288 pp.*
Karp, I. Fields of Change Among the Iteso of Kenya. *140 pp.*
Lloyd, P. C. Power and Independence. *Urban Africans' Perception of Social Inequality. 264 pp.*
Parry, J. P. Caste and Kinship in Kangra. *352 pp. Illustrated.*
Pettigrew, Joyce. Robber Noblemen. *A Study of the Political System of the Sikh Jats. 284 pp.*
Street, Brian V. The Savage in Literature. *Representations of 'Primitive' Society in English Fiction, 1858–1920. 207 pp.*
Van Den Berghe, Pierre L. Power and Privilege at an African University. *278 pp.*

International Library of Phenomenology and Moral Sciences
General Editor John O'Neill

Apel, K.-O. Towards a Transformation of Philosophy. *308 pp.*
Bologh, R. W. Dialectical Phenomenology. *Marx's Method. 287 pp.*
Fekete, J. The Critical Twilight. *Explorations in the Ideology of Anglo-American Literary Theory from Eliot to McLuhan. 300 pp.*
Medina, A. Reflection, Time and the Novel. *Towards a Communicative Theory of Literature. 143 pp.*

International Library of Social Policy
General Editor Kathleen Jones

Bayley, M. Mental Handicap and Community Care. *426 pp.*
Bottoms, A. E. and **McClean, J. D.** Defendants in the Criminal Process. *284 pp.*
Bradshaw, J. The Family Fund. *An Initiative in Social Policy. About 224 pp.*

Butler, J. R. Family Doctors and Public Policy. *208 pp.*
Davies, Martin. Prisoners of Society. *Attitudes and Aftercare. 204 pp.*
Gittus, Elizabeth. Flats, Families and the Under-Fives. *285 pp.*
Holman, Robert. Trading in Children. *A Study of Private Fostering. 355 pp.*
Jeffs, A. Young People and the Youth Service. *160 pp.*
Jones, Howard and Cornes, Paul. Open Prisons. *288 pp.*
Jones, Kathleen. History of the Mental Health Service. *428 pp.*
Jones, Kathleen with **Brown, John, Cunningham, W. J., Roberts, Julian** and **Williams, Peter.** Opening the Door. *A Study of New Policies for the Mentally Handicapped. 278 pp.*
Karn, Valerie. Retiring to the Seaside. *400 pp. 2 maps. Numerous tables.*
King, R. D. and **Elliot, K. W.** Albany: Birth of a Prison—End of an Era. *394 pp.*
Thomas, J. E. The English Prison Officer since 1850: *A Study in Conflict. 258 pp.*
Walton, R. G. Women in Social Work. *303 pp.*
● **Woodward, J.** To Do the Sick No Harm. *A Study of the British Voluntary Hospital System to 1875. 234 pp.*

International Library of Welfare and Philosophy
General Editors Noel Timms and David Watson

● **McDermott, F. E.** (Ed.) Self-Determination in Social Work. *A Collection of Essays on Self-determination and Related Concepts by Philosophers and Social Work Theorists. Contributors: F. P. Biestek, S. Bernstein, A. Keith-Lucas, D. Sayer, H. H. Perelman, C. Whittington, R. F. Stalley, F. E. McDermott, I. Berlin, H. J. McCloskey, H. L. A. Hart, J. Wilson, A. I. Melden, S. I. Benn. 254 pp.*
● **Plant, Raymond.** Community and Ideology. *104 pp.*
Ragg, Nicholas M. People Not Cases. *A Philosophical Approach to Social Work. 168 pp.*
● **Timms, Noel** and **Watson, David.** (Eds) Talking About Welfare. *Readings in Philosophy and Social Policy. Contributors: T. H. Marshall, R. B. Brandt, G. H. von Wright, K. Nielsen, M. Cranston, R. M. Titmuss, R. S. Downie, E. Telfer, D. Donnison, J. Benson, P. Leonard, A. Keith-Lucas, D. Walsh, I. T. Ramsey. 320 pp.*
● Philosophy in Social Work. *250 pp.*
● **Weale, A.** Equality and Social Policy. *164 pp.*

Library of Social Work
General Editor Noel Timms

● **Baldock, Peter.** Community Work and Social Work. *140 pp.*
○ **Beedell, Christopher.** Residential Life with Children. *210 pp. Crown 8vo.*
● **Berry, Juliet.** Daily Experience in Residential Life. *A Study of Children and their Care-givers. 202 pp.*
○ Social Work with Children. *190 pp. Crown 8vo.*
● **Brearley, C. Paul.** Residential Work with the Elderly. *116 pp.*
● Social Work, Ageing and Society. *126 pp.*
● **Cheetham, Juliet.** Social Work with Immigrants. *240 pp. Crown 8vo.*
● **Cross, Crispin P.** (Ed.) Interviewing and Communication in Social Work. *Contributions by C. P. Cross, D. Laurenson, B. Strutt, S. Raven. 192 pp. Crown 8vo.*

● **Curnock, Kathleen** and **Hardiker, Pauline.** Towards Practice Theory. *Skills and Methods in Social Assessments. 208 pp.*

● **Davies, Bernard.** The Use of Groups in Social Work Practice. *158 pp.*

● **Davies, Martin.** Support Systems in Social Work. *144 pp.*

Ellis, June. (Ed.) West African Families in Britain. *A Meeting of Two Cultures. Contributions by Pat Stapleton, Vivien Biggs. 150 pp. 1 Map.*

● **Hart, John.** Social Work and Sexual Conduct. *230 pp.*

● **Hutten, Joan M.** Short-Term Contracts in Social Work. *Contributions by Stella M. Hall, Elsie Osborne, Mannie Sher, Eva Sternberg, Elizabeth Tuters. 134 pp.*

Jackson, Michael P. and **Valencia, B. Michael.** Financial Aid Through Social Work. *140 pp.*

● **Jones, Howard.** The Residential Community. *A Setting for Social Work. 150 pp.*

● (Ed.) Towards a New Social Work. *Contributions by Howard Jones, D. A. Fowler, J. R. Cypher, R. G. Walton, Geoffrey Mungham, Philip Priestley, Ian Shaw, M. Bartley, R. Deacon, Irwin Epstein, Geoffrey Pearson. 184 pp.*

Jones, Ray and **Pritchard, Colin.** (Eds) Social Work With Adolescents. *Contributions by Ray Jones, Colin Pritchard, Jack Dunham, Florence Rossetti, Andrew Kerslake, John Burns, William Gregory, Graham Templeman, Kenneth E. Reid, Audrey Taylor. About 170 pp.*

○ **Jordon, William.** The Social Worker in Family Situations. *160 pp. Crown 8vo.*

● **Laycock, A. L.** Adolescents and Social Work. *128 pp. Crown 8vo.*

● **Lees, Ray.** Politics and Social Work. *128 pp. Crown 8vo.*

● Research Strategies for Social Welfare. *112 pp. Tables.*

○ **McCullough, M. K.** and **Ely, Peter J.** Social Work with Groups. *127 pp. Crown 8vo.*

● **Moffett, Jonathan.** Concepts in Casework Treatment. *128 pp. Crown 8vo.*

Parsloe, Phyllida. Juvenile Justice in Britain and the United States. *The Balance of Needs and Rights. 336 pp.*

● **Plant, Raymond.** Social and Moral Theory in Casework. *112 pp. Crown 8vo.*

Priestley, Philip, Fears, Denise and **Fuller, Roger.** Justice for Juveniles. *The 1969 Children and Young Persons Act: A Case for Reform? 128 pp.*

● **Pritchard, Colin** and **Taylor, Richard.** Social Work: Reform or Revolution? *170 pp.*

○ **Pugh, Elisabeth.** Social Work in Child Care. *128 pp. Crown 8vo.*

● **Robinson, Margaret.** Schools and Social Work. *282 pp.*

○ **Ruddock, Ralph.** Roles and Relationships. *128 pp. Crown 8vo.*

● **Sainsbury, Eric.** Social Diagnosis in Casework. *118 pp. Crown 8vo.*

● Social Work with Families. *Perceptions of Social Casework among Clients of a Family Service. 188 pp.*

Seed, Philip. The Expansion of Social Work in Britain. *128 pp. Crown 8vo.*

● **Shaw, John.** The Self in Social Work. *124 pp.*

Smale, Gerald G. Prophecy, Behaviour and Change. *An Examination of Self-fulfilling Prophecies in Helping Relationships. 116 pp. Crown 8vo.*

Smith, Gilbert. Social Need. *Policy, Practice and Research. 155 pp.*

● Social Work and the Sociology of Organisations. *124 pp. Revised edition.*

● **Sutton, Carole.** Psychology for Social Workers and Counsellors. *An Introduction. 248 pp.*

● **Timms, Noel.** Language of Social Casework. *122 pp. Crown 8vo.*

● Recording in Social Work. *124 pp. Crown 8vo.*

● **Todd, F. Joan.** Social Work with the Mentally Subnormal. *96 pp. Crown 8vo.*

● **Walrond-Skinner, Sue.** Family Therapy. *The Treatment of Natural Systems. 172 pp.*

● **Warham, Joyce.** An Introduction to Administration for Social Workers. *Revised edition. 112 pp.*

◗ An Open Case. *The Organisational Context of Social Work. 172 pp.*

○ **Wittenberg, Isca Salzberger.** Psycho-Analytic Insight and Relationships. *A Kleinian Approach. 196 pp. Crown 8vo.*

Primary Socialization, Language and Education
General Editor   Basil Bernstein

Adlam, Diana S., *with the assistance of Geoffrey Turner and Lesley Lineker.* Code in *Context. 272 pp.*

Bernstein, Basil. Class, Codes and Control. *3 volumes.*
- 1. *Theoretical Studies Towards a Sociology of Language. 254 pp.*
- 2. *Applied Studies Towards a Sociology of Language. 377 pp.*
- 3. *Towards a Theory of Educational Transmission. 167 pp.*

Brandis, W. and **Bernstein, B.** Selection and Control. *176 pp.*

Brandis, Walter and **Henderson, Dorothy.** Social Class, Language and Communication. *288 pp.*

Cook-Gumperz, Jenny. Social Control and Socialization. *A Study of Class Differences in the Language of Maternal Control. 290 pp.*

● **Gahagan, D. M.** and **G. A.** Talk Reform. *Exploration in Language for Infant School Children. 160 pp.*

Hawkins, P. R. Social Class, the Nominal Group and Verbal Strategies. *About 220 pp.*

Robinson, W. P. and **Rackstraw, Susan D. A.** A Question of Answers. *2 volumes. 192 pp. and 180 pp.*

Turner, Geoffrey J. and **Mohan, Bernard A.** A Linguistic Description and Computer Programme for Children's Speech. *208 pp.*

Reports of the Institute of Community Studies

Baker, J. The Neighbourhood Advice Centre. A Community Project in Camden. *320 pp.*

● **Cartwright, Ann.** Patients and their Doctors. *A Study of General Practice. 304 pp.*

Dench, Geoff. Maltese in London. *A Case-study in the Erosion of Ethnic Consciousness. 302 pp.*

Jackson, Brian and **Marsden, Dennis.** Education and the Working Class: *Some General Themes Raised by a Study of 88 Working-class Children in a Northern Industrial City. 268 pp. 2 folders.*

Marris, Peter. The Experience of Higher Education. *232 pp. 27 tables.*

● Loss and Change. *192 pp.*

Marris, Peter and **Rein, Martin.** Dilemmas of Social Reform. *Poverty and Community Action in the United States. 256 pp.*

Marris, Peter and **Somerset, Anthony.** African Businessmen. *A Study of Entrepreneurship and Development in Kenya. 256 pp.*

Mills, Richard. Young Outsiders: *a Study in Alternative Communities. 216 pp.*

Runciman, W. G. Relative Deprivation and Social Justice. *A Study of Attitudes to Social Inequality in Twentieth-Century England. 352 pp.*

Willmott, Peter. Adolescent Boys in East London. *230 pp.*

Willmott, Peter and **Young, Michael.** Family and Class in a London Suburb. *202 pp. 47 tables.*

Young, Michael and **McGeeney, Patrick.** Learning Begins at Home. *A Study of a Junior School and its Parents. 128 pp.*

Young, Michael and **Willmott, Peter.** Family and Kinship in East London. *Foreword by Richard M. Titmuss. 252 pp. 39 tables.*

The Symmetrical Family. *410 pp.*

Reports of the Institute for Social Studies in Medical Care

Cartwright, Ann, Hockey, Lisbeth and **Anderson, John J.** Life Before Death. *310 pp.*
Dunnell, Karen and **Cartwright, Ann.** Medicine Takers, Prescribers and Hoarders. *190 pp.*
Farrell, C. My Mother Said. . . *A Study of the Way Young People Learned About Sex and Birth Control. 288 pp.*

Medicine, Illness and Society
General Editor W. M. Williams

Hall, David J. Social Relations & Innovation. *Changing the State of Play in Hospitals. 232 pp.*
Hall, David J. and **Stacey, M.** (Eds) Beyond Separation. *234 pp.*
Robinson, David. The Process of Becoming Ill. *142 pp.*
Stacey, Margaret *et al.* Hospitals, Children and Their Families. *The Report of a Pilot Study. 202 pp.*
Stimson, G. V. and **Webb, B.** Going to See the Doctor. *The Consultation Process in General Practice. 155 pp.*

Monographs in Social Theory
General Editor Arthur Brittan

● **Barnes, B.** Scientific Knowledge and Sociological Theory. *192 pp.*
Bauman, Zygmunt. Culture as Praxis. *204 pp.*
● **Dixon, Keith.** Sociological Theory. *Pretence and Possibility. 142 pp.*
   The Sociology of Belief. *Fallacy and Foundation. About 160 pp.*
Goff, T. W. Marx and Mead. *Contributions to a Sociology of Knowledge. 176 pp.*
Meltzer, B. N., Petras, J. W. and **Reynolds, L. T.** Symbolic Interactionism. *Genesis, Varieties and Criticisms. 144 pp.*
● **Smith, Anthony D.** The Concept of Social Change. *A Critique of the Functionalist Theory of Social Change. 208 pp.*

Routledge Social Science Journals

The British Journal of Sociology. *Editor – Angus Stewart; Associate Editor – Leslie Sklair. Vol. 1, No. 1 – March 1950 and Quarterly. Roy. 8vo. All back issues available. An international journal publishing original papers in the field of sociology and related areas.*
Community Work. *Edited by David Jones and Marjorie Mayo. 1973. Published annually.*
Economy and Society. *Vol. 1, No. 1. February 1972 and Quarterly. Metric Roy. 8vo. A journal for all social scientists covering sociology, philosophy, anthropology, economics and history. All back numbers available.*

Ethnic and Racial Studies. *Editor – John Stone. Vol. 1 – 1978. Published quarterly.*
Religion. Journal of Religion and Religions. *Chairman of Editorial Board, Ninian Smart. Vol. 1, No. 1, Spring 1971. A journal with an inter-disciplinary approach to the study of the phenomena of religion. All back numbers available.*
Sociology of Health and Illness. *A Journal of Medical Sociology. Editor – Alan Davies; Associate Editor – Ray Jobling. Vol. 1, Spring 1979. Published 3 times per annum.*
Year Book of Social Policy in Britain. *Edited by Kathleen Jones. 1971. Published annually.*

Social and Psychological Aspects of Medical Practice
Editor Trevor Silverstone

Lader, Malcolm. Psychophysiology of Mental Illness. *280 pp.*
● **Silverstone, Trevor** and **Turner, Paul.** Drug Treatment in Psychiatry. *Revised edition. 256 pp.*
Whiteley, J. S. and **Gordon, J.** Group Approaches in Psychiatry. *240 pp.*